RENÉ ANGÉLIL

THE UNAUTHORIZED BIOGRAPHY

RENÉ ANGÉLIL
THE MAKING OF CÉLINE DION

JEAN BEAUNOYER
with
JEAN BEAULNE

Translated by Don Wilson

THE DUNDURN GROUP
TORONTO

Original title: ET ANGÉLIL CRÉA CÉLINE
Copyright © 2002 by Jean Beaunoyer and Jean Beaulne
Jean Beaunoyer and Jean Beaulne have asserted their moral rights to be identified as the co-authors of the Work.
English translation Copyright © 2004 by Dundurn Press

Copy-Editor: Jennifer Bergeron
Design: Jennifer Scott
Printer: Transcontinental

National Library of Canada Cataloguing in Publication Data

Beaunoyer, Jean
    Rene Angelil : the making of Celine Dion, the unauthorized biography / Jean Beaunoyer with Jean Beaulne.

ISBN 1-55002-489-2

1. Angelil, René, 1942– 2. Dion, Céline. 3. Impresarios — Québec (Province) — Biography. 4. Singers — Spouses — Québec (Province) — Biography. 5. Baronets (Musical group) I. Beaulne, Jean II. Title.

ML429.A582B3813 2004   782.42164'092   C2003-907199-5

1   2   3   4   5   08   07   06   05   04

We acknowledge the support of the **Canada Council for the Arts** and the **Ontario Arts Council** for our publishing program. We also acknowledge the financial support of the **Government of Canada** through the **Book Publishing Industry Development Program** and **The Association for the Export of Canadian Books**, and the **Government of Ontario** through the **Ontario Book Publishers Tax Credit** program, and the **Ontario Media Development Corporation's Ontario Book Initiative.**

Care has been taken to trace the ownership of copyright material used in this book. The author and the publisher welcome any information enabling them to rectify any references or credit in subsequent editions.
                    J. Kirk Howard, President

Printed and bound in Canada.⚚
Printed on recycled paper.

www.dundurn.com

Dundurn Press
8 Market Street
Suite 200
Toronto, Ontario, Canada
M5E 1M6

RENÉ ANGÉLIL

TABLE OF CONTENTS

FOREWORD

I REALLY BELIEVE JEAN BEAULNE has never given up being a Baronet. Three decades have passed since he left the group in 1969, but he still remembers those years of folly and fame, combined with the years of poverty and the difficult process of becoming an artist. Together with René Angélil and Pierre Labelle he lived through the late 1950s and the 1960s with the heedlessness and vulnerability of youth. For a dozen years Jean Beaulne shared his daily existence with René. The two know one another like brothers. Time, and Céline Dion's career, kept them apart for a while, but inevitably the major events of their respective lives brought them together again, almost as if these two old comrades could no longer escape their past.

I met Jean Beaulne in the course of my work as a journalist. I attended the funeral of Pierre Labelle, the third Baronet, and noticed the pains Jean had taken in organizing the moving ceremony, which was attended by René Angélil, who was accompanied by his wife, Céline Dion. Jean Beaulne was able to make the Baronets live again that day. It was the last time the three of them would be together. René and Jean were accompanying Pierre on his last journey, and as they said goodbye to their old friend they were also burying a part of their youth.

Some time later I saw Jean Beaulne again. He was working on a number of projects, including the production of a documentary on the Baronets' story, with the collaboration of his old friend René Angélil. He had also started to write a book that related, without currying any favours, his relations with René from their youthful years at Saint-Viateur Secondary School to the present.

I had also had the idea of telling the René Angélil story, thinking it a logical sequel to the biography of Céline Dion I had written in the late 1990s. I had already begun work on it when Jean Beaulne and I discovered that we were working along the same lines.

It didn't take us very long to realize that we had everything to gain by joining forces and sharing our knowledge, resulting in a more comprehensive book. What is more, Jean Beaulne was intimately familiar with the entertainment milieu and had lived alongside René, while, in addition to my long experience as a writer, I had a good overview of the entertainment world and of Céline's and René's lives.

Initially, Jean and I met to get to know each other and develop our confidence in one another. Jean was even kind enough to invite me several times to a hotel in the Laurentians to discuss the project — the kind of thing every writer dreams of. And it was in an enchanting setting, beside a lake, during part of the summer of 2002, that Jean Beaulne reminisced about his life with the Baronets and his contacts with René Angélil. I noted it all down in a big notebook as we sat beside a refreshing swimming pool. Jean trusted me and confided in me generously. Then we got together again in Montreal and carried on our exchanges in some of the city's less noisy restaurants. Jean Beaulne, who is a frank, direct, and honest human being, never tried to gloss over the truth or dress it up in any way. He had had many disputes with René Angélil. Born leaders both of them, neither would ever knuckle under when their deepest convictions were at stake. They never tried to please one another, but always respected each other.

After leaving the Baronets, Jean Beaulne had followed the career and life of René Angélil very closely. I even noticed that he displayed an almost fatherly attitude towards René. He was concerned about his health and about the furious pace of his existence. He talked to him about this, but René gave him short shrift, just like in the good old days.

There was nothing new about that. It had always been that way between the two old comrades — constantly at loggerheads, but with a hidden concern for the other's well-being. It was a male friendship, and a competitive one — for how could it have been otherwise with René, who can never bear to lose?

Jean Beaulne handed over some papers to me — more than three hundred pages of a manuscript he had written out by hand. I was as amused as I was impressed. Nobody writes with a pen anymore. But Jean had written with heart, feeling, and truth, and these qualities were better expressed that way. He also passed on a box full of old articles, personal accounts, and short biographies he had collected over recent years — an impressive piece of work.

Later he became my inspiration in writing the essential part of this book. Better than anyone he helped me to understand René's development and his relationship with Céline Dion. Jean Beaulne is his own man, and has no professional relationship with René Angélil or his circle. He often guided my hand and provided the necessary tools for writing this book. We have been able to combine our knowledge and talents harmoniously in producing it. However, I have to say that without his collaboration this volume would lack much of its colour and authenticity. I have given Jean Beaulne a special significance and place in the story of the Baronets — I trust the reader will understand this decision. He is entitled to such a place. It is very much deserved, as is his place in the history of Quebec show business after thirty years as a producer. I can vouch for that.

JEAN BEAUNOYER

INTRODUCTION

FROM THE SHADOW CAST BY the most adulated singer on the face of our planet the features of a man gradually emerge, enabling us to discover a fascinating personage. Years have passed since René Angélil discovered Céline Dion in 1981 and made her into the greatest star in pop music. But the man behind the megastar's success has always puzzled, disoriented, and confused the media and the people in his own circle, never revealing himself completely. By taking control of Céline's life and career from the time she was twelve years old, he moulded her life to his, making himself the brains, the image, the driving force, the hope of the Céline Dion enterprise, and, ultimately, forging its success.

In celebrating the talent and ever-increasing fame of his protégée, René Angélil left his personality in the background, out of the spotlight. For a long time he seemed to be no more than a secondary character in Céline's fabulous story, but in fact it was he who crafted the fairy-tale life of Céline Dion, a girl who had started out with nothing to offer the world but her voice and her faith. René Angélil would take control of everything else with an almost religious passion. He applied himself so utterly that he made people forget his own climb up the ladder of success and his real motivations in this frenzied pursuit of fame and fortune.

Naturally, attempts have been made to pin him down and sometimes even ensnare him in the many interviews he has granted, always as part of promoting one of "his" singer's recordings or shows. But René, constantly preoccupied with Céline's image, just played the game, allowing only a glimpse of what America and the whole world wanted to see.

What is more, his story has to be approached in an organized manner. It is by probing behind the scenes of Quebec's nascent show business that we can discover the real René. It is by getting to know his family and making sense of the influence of ethnic groups in the social fabric of Montreal that we can discover the man's true nature. Finally, it is by tracing the recent development of Quebec, and in particular the spirit of entrepreneurship that characterized the 1980s, that we can understand how Céline Dion was able to achieve her international breakthrough.

So what this book has to offer is a trip into René Angélil's world, travelling across the decades and surveying the various stages of his life that are often hidden from the media. The objective of this book is to get to know René Angélil apart from Céline. It is quite a challenge, admittedly, since he has devoted himself utterly to the singer's career from the moment they first met, when he was thirty-eight. But even if his life has been devoted to Céline Dion for more than twenty years, before meeting her René had already spent four decades searching for the magic formula, the trump card that would allow him to win the jackpot.

René Angélil the gambler has always viewed life as a vast lottery, and for forty years he learned to gamble in the world of show business before being dealt the most formidable card of all — Céline Dion. His triumph didn't come easily, and we shall discover a man who was often sad, bedevilled by fate and forgotten by fame and fortune every time he thought he was close to his goal. He is a charming and fascinating individual, despite his obsessive need to control everything, not only in his own circle but in the entire nexus of communications — a control that often confounds the critical sense of the general public and amply justifies the publication of biographies of him and of Céline — preferably unauthorized ones.

If he has lived in the shadow of one of the greatest stars on the face of the earth, it was inevitable that one day the spotlight would shine on him, and today this personage, well known in Quebec, has attracted the interest of the international press. In the history of show business, wherever you look, no manager — not even the legendary Colonel Parker, Elvis Presley's manager — has ever attracted so much media attention or aroused such interest. People acknowledge his talent and even genius in the rare art of guiding an artist to the pinnacle of the profession. People want to learn about his passions, his moods, his strategies, his relationship with Céline, his wealth and success, and they wonder how so much could have been within his reach. Perhaps René Angélil is the true embodiment of the "American dream" — a dream that obsesses a good proportion of our planet's population.

In his rise from modest beginnings to international fame, this man had to overcome material poverty, intellectual snobbery, illness, and racial prejudice. He has suffered from torrents of rarely confirmed rumours about his private life, and has had to defend himself against a bizarre, mysterious accusation of sexual assault brought against him by Yun Kyeong Sung Kwon, a Californian woman of South Korean origin.

This sorry tale has been much recounted and discussed in the media, especially in America and Europe. The interest aroused by this news item showed the true dimensions of René Angélil's image — it was given the kind of treatment usually reserved for the greats of this world. Obviously, his fame is closely linked to Céline Dion's, but even without her he would still be indisputably one of the great managers of his day.

You're so lazy you can never succeed in life.

"Today I smile at these words, for René has become the most prestigious manager on the face of the planet."

— Jean Beaulne

1

A SECOND CHANCE FOR RENÉ ANGÉLIL

Jean Beaulne hadn't seen his old companion René for some time. The two had come together in the building occupied by the Feeling Company in Laval, in suburban Montreal. Beaulne wanted to discuss a documentary he was planning to produce, telling the story of the Baronets, the pop group the two men had belonged to in the 1960s.

The Baronets had considerable success in Quebec and broke up after an existence of twelve years. Beaulne and Angélil enjoyed some great times together back then. They shared the success, the travel, the fame — and even a few girls, all ardent admirers of the most popular group in Quebec. They also had many disagreements. "We were both leaders," recounts Beaulne. It was Beaulne who caused the break-up of the group in December 1969, but the two men remained friends, seeing one another regularly. After a few difficult years René Angélil, who had become an artists' manager, discovered Céline Dion and catapulted her to the top. Jean Beaulne tried his hand at several different occupations — first as a manager of some successful performers, then as a real estate developer, and finally as a producer and scriptwriter in Florida and California. Although he never discovered anything like a Céline Dion, he went on to complete many successful undertakings.

That day, the two men came together again with a certain camaraderie between them. Yet there had always been a lot of things to come between them. René, though high strung, seemed as imperturbable, reflective, and secretive as Jean was edgy and open. While René liked to gorge on both gourmet dishes and fast food, Jean was careful about what he ate, having always been a proponent of a healthy, low-fat diet, and never drank coffee. Indeed, René had nicknamed him, a little mischievously, "cup of hot water." While René was passionately fond of gambling, Jean avoided it like the plague. René would criticize Jean for being too thin, while Jean would reproach René for being overweight. One became very rich, but not the other, for during the economic recession at the time of the Gulf War, Jean lost more than $3 million in the volatile, risky real estate market.

But if the situation between the two men had changed, they came together that day as they had when they were part of the Baronets — as equals.

"Whenever I see René, I forget about his wealth and fame and see him again as the lad from Saint-Viateur and the Baronet I lived alongside for several years. Other people are overwhelmed in his presence, but not me. I've known him for forty-five years. Truth to tell, I know René better than my own brother, and I'm sure he knows me better than his. When I recount our experiences it's as if Paul McCartney was talking about John Lennon. We've a unique relationship, and he knows it. He's never been able to manipulate me. I'm the only one who stood up to him, and we respect one another."

Maybe this is why René felt the need to explain and justify himself to Jean Beaulne. At key moments in his existence he had been able to face squarely up to the truth, even when it was unpleasant for him. On this occasion, Jean could sense that René was weighed down by something he could no longer bear and was feeling an urgent need to confide in someone. The two agreed to meet in the offices of Feeling Productions, in a building right in the centre of the business quarter of the town of Laval, in suburban Montreal.

It was no longer winter but not yet quite spring in that interminable month of March 2002. Jean Beaulne parked his Mercedes, still with its California licence plates, and went up to the seventh floor to meet René

Angélil, who was waiting for him in his office. Entering the Feeling Company building, he passed the dark brown teak walls that endowed the head office occupied by the famous Dion-Angélil couple with a certain dignity, but also an inevitable ponderousness.

Wearing a grey suit and holding a bottle of water in one hand, René seemed to be looking for something. It must be said that he is something of a stranger in his own office, so rarely is he present there, for he has always preferred to do business by phone or fax and, more recently, by e-mail. He hates living a sedentary existence filled with papers and office work. He'd rather be travelling, active, establishing contacts behind the scenes or in restaurants, and at the centre of the action. So he is not very often to be seen in the offices of this company he and Céline founded together. Whenever he puts in an appearance, however, the staff welcome him joyfully, like an old friend.

There are hardly more than six rooms on the premises: an office for the accountant; one for the advisor and lawyer; one for Mario Lefebvre, who looks after the career of a singer named Garou; one for the secretaries; a little kitchen adjoining the conference room; and René's large office down the corridor.

This is where Jean Beaulne took a seat, with the door closed. One wall was lined with trophies awarded to Céline over the previous few years.

Right away, Jean Beaulne, who heads his own production company, Artplus Film TV Production, which produces documentaries for TV and manages the careers of several artists, enthusiastically explained his project for a documentary about the Baronets' career. At first René wasn't particularly taken by the idea. He was skeptical about the possibility of assembling a sufficient quantity of material dealing with this period of their lives. However, Jean answered that he already had more information than required, and that the documentary could be as much as three hours long, if so desired.

René still hesitated, just as he used to do back in the Baronets days when Beaulne put one of his bright ideas to him. But in the end he accepted when Jean told him he wanted to make this documentary to leave a positive image of the Baronets for the Quebec public that had always been so supportive. Above all, the documentary would be a precious memento for their admirers, families, friends, and, of course, for themselves.

Beaulne also told him about his idea of writing a biographical account of their relationship in the Baronets days, and about the path René's life had followed as Céline Dion's agent. René accepted this idea too, for, after all, who was better qualified to tell this story than such an old comrade as Jean? In the end, nostalgia carried the day. As time goes by René feels more and more nostalgic. Jean and René don't come together very often because of their respective occupations, but whenever they do René talks about the good old days and their shared memories. That day he seemed more down than usual, and Jean could feel that his old friend had been shaken by the accusations that were upsetting all his marketing plans and his life. There was a stain on his reputation. Jean could see he was worried and confused by all the publicity about the case for sexual assault brought against him by a mysterious American woman of South Korean descent. Then René told him what he had gone through on the night in question in March 2000.

He was with a friend and his bodyguard at Caesar's Palace, the Las Vegas casino, when an Asian woman beckoned to him and asked to speak to him. Within a few minutes she was imploring him to visit a person suffering from cystic fibrosis who wanted more than anything in the world to meet him before she died. Céline had been a keen supporter of the cause of cystic fibrosis for many years, so René wasn't particularly surprised by the request. Heeding only his kind instincts, he accompanied her out of the casino and across the road, heading for the Imperial Hotel, where the sick woman was supposed to be resting. But when they got into the hotel's elevator the woman's attitude began to change. The entire time they were going up to the top floors, she babbled on about rape and death threats. René couldn't understand any of it, but to discover what was really going on he nevertheless followed her into the room of the alleged patient ... where he came face to face with the husband of the woman he was accompanying! His suspicions had been well founded: the couple had drawn him into an ambush. Now he watched helplessly as the woman threw a hysterical fit, accusing him of having taken advantage of her and making a death threat against her. He left the room in a fury.

A short time later the woman had a lawsuit delivered to his office in which she openly accused René Angélil of rape and making death threats against her. It couldn't have come at a worse time. Céline was about to celebrate her birthday and was pregnant with their baby. On the advice of his wife (to whom he told everything as soon as he got home from the trip) and of his lawyer, René made the decision that any good agent would have reached in a similar situation — to settle the sorry business out of court and prevent it from reaching the ears of the paparazzi with their appetite for scandal. He therefore paid the alleged victim a certain sum of money and signed a written agreement that he would undergo an HIV test.

Thinking the matter had been settled, he neglected to take the test. The result was that two years later the woman, now known to be a compulsive gambler and chronically short of money as a result of her addiction, launched a second suit against René, demanding a further sum of money. Having failed to live up to the terms of the settlement, he had left himself vulnerable. But this time he refused to compromise. He couldn't imagine that this woman could trigger off a scandal that would harm his reputation.

René Angélil was just ending this horrific story when Céline arrived in the office, accompanied by her bodyguards, so the two old companions didn't get to the restaurant where they had been planning to lunch together that afternoon. However, Jean Beaulne never forgot a single word of René's revelations:

> René was obviously disturbed. He'd lost a lot of weight, and for the first time I saw him as a weary guy who had suddenly grown old. I felt sad inside to see him ruin his health for the sake of wealth and fame … I'd never seen him so depressed. I almost told him he was looking a lot older, but I didn't dare. He was going through the nightmare of a lifetime. Before the media he seemed detached, self-assured, and confident, but I saw someone who was devastated and completely stunned by this accusation of sexual assault brought against him by Yun Kyeong Sung Kwon, the American woman of South Korean origin.
>
> For an hour and a half he recounted the events to me, trying to convince me. I don't know how often he told me he'd gone to the woman's room because he

believed some woman was dying of cystic fibrosis there. Yet this wasn't the story the media was telling. He was trying so desperately to convince me. ...

What upset him most about this business wasn't so much the lawsuit itself as seeing his image tainted in the eyes of the public, and, most of all, in Céline's. Until then her picture of him had been a perfect one, but now, suddenly, it no longer was. Being in a room at two in the morning with a woman other than his wife can cast a shadow of doubt — doubt in Céline's mind — and this was something René couldn't bear.

Jean Beaulne knows René Angélil well from sharing his daily life throughout the twelve years of the Baronets' existence. He knew his family, his friends, and his circle. He was also familiar with the man's private life and his values, which have never changed. Beaulne explains:

René was the victim of a real sting operation, and you have to know how people live in Las Vegas to understand the way the rich and famous can fall into a trap there. I've seen tough, ruthless women go to Las Vegas with the sole intent of robbing rich men. They use any means to achieve their objective. There was a reason why Elvis wore a bulletproof waistcoat on stage. There's a reason why the boxer Mike Tyson and even Mario Lemieux the famous hockey player got mixed up in vice cases. Attractive women are used to ensnare celebrities; people even go through the stars' garbage cans looking for compromising documents and information they can sell to the tabloid press. That's the way famous people get blackmailed, so they have to constantly protect their image. René is a regular customer at Caesar's Palace, and this makes him a target for con artists. It's not without a reason that performers live in seclusion, and especially that they keep their children well out of sight. They live in a state of constant paranoia.

By the way, I can understand why René is proud to show off René-Charles like a trophy. But in a big American city like Los Angeles or New York the boy becomes bait. He could be a recognizable target for kidnappers. Madonna and a lot of other artists won't allow their children to be photographed, and it's not just a whim.

The Kwon-Angélil affair is hazy, and will probably remain so, for it will be settled out of court, as happens in 80 percent of such cases. Yun Kyeong Sung Kwon accused René Angélil of sexual assault and gave her version of the events of March 15, 2002, to the civil court of Los Angeles. It had taken almost two years for her to decide to bring the case against Angélil, since, according to Mrs. Kwon, the assault must have taken place on the night of March 19–20, 2000. A close look at the case reveals ever more contradictions. The two parties had supposedly agreed to keep the matter secret in return for an undisclosed sum paid by one of Angélil's companies. Angélil was to apologize and prove he was not infected with AIDS. Later, it emerged that Mrs. Kwon was a compulsive gambler, with unpaid debts, and that she had used bad cheques to pay a casino what she owed. She had spent time in prison. The public lost interest in the whole story, for it seemed to make no sense.

René was never concerned about the legal consequences of the case. But what did concern him was his image as a perfect husband. He has always been obsessed with his image, both public and private — as though he was always putting on a show, even with those close to him. And that's what made it possible for Yun Kyeong Sung Kwon to get to him. That's why he agreed to pay a certain sum to his accuser. Quite independently of the rights and wrongs of the case, René wanted to avoid the damage of bad publicity.

A short time before the accusations made by Yun Kyeong Sung Kwon, René Angélil underwent several treatments for cancer. Suddenly, there was a show of sympathy from all over the world. His life was in danger, and people followed the stages of his remission closely. René was in the headlines, at last appreciated and admired by the public. He felt he was projecting a heroic image, and Céline was pregnant. It was another perfect image — the image of a perfect couple. But then along came a forty-six-year-old trickster to ruin everything. René will never forgive her for that.

"He hired detectives to investigate the South Korean woman's past," Jean Beaulne told me.

Naturally, René was going to defend himself like a cornered animal.

No image, fame, fortune, or misfortune could come between the two men anymore. In his time of trial René Angélil felt the need to go back to his roots. At the age of sixty, he ruled like a patriarch over a clan composed of his children, cousins, and friends. But his mother had passed away just a few years before, his father was dead and gone, and so was one of the Baronets, for Pierre Labelle had succumbed to a long illness on January 18, 2000. Part of his youth vanished that day. Jean Beaulne had organized the funeral. It was like in the old days when Beaulne looked after all the arrangements for the group. In meeting again with someone with whom he had shared so much during the 1960s, René was rediscovering some of his past.

2

CHILDHOOD

R ené Angélil was born in Montreal, in the modest quarter of Villeray, on January 16, 1942. This means he's not a baby boomer, for the Second World War was still in progress at the time. In Quebec, Alys Robi was singing "Tico Tico"; in the United States, Glen Miller was awarded the first golden disk after selling 1.2 million copies of "Chattanooga Choo Choo"; and 513 soldiers of the Montreal Fusiliers died in the raid on Dieppe.

It was cold in the modest home at 7760 Saint-Denis, where Joseph Angélil lived with Alice Sara, the woman he had married three years earlier after his arrival in Montreal. Born in Damascus, Syria, in 1903, Joseph had gone to Beirut, in Lebanon, the country next door, before travelling with one of his brothers all the way to Paris, where he apprenticed as a tailor. He would certainly have preferred to remain in Paris, and would surely have earned a good living in the city of *haute couture*. But in 1939, the war and the Nazi threat in particular caused him suddenly to leave the "city of light." Montreal, Canada's biggest city at the time, attracted him for several reasons. People spoke French there, as they did in Paris, and his command of the language was improving all the time. The garment industry was expanding, and he expected to obtain employment in his field without difficulty. And lastly, the Sara and Angélil families, who had already been very close in Damascus, had arranged a marriage between Joseph and the young Alice Sara, who had already settled in Montreal.

Much could be said about the matrimonial arrangements of those earlier days, but when Joseph first saw this twenty-three-year-old beauty in the Sara family's living room he had no desire to question the agreement between the two families. The first time he saw Alice, who was born in Montreal on May 4, 1915, he fell for her. It was inevitable, for this very lovely young woman with black hair and mysterious eyes was well able to charm and please, and had an obvious intelligence and generous nature. A remarkable mother, she would have a special influence on René's life. Even though there was a gap of sixteen years between them, Joseph swore to be faithful to her and love her for the rest of his life. And so he did, until his death in 1967.

The Angélil couple moved to 7680 Casgrain, where they settled permanently after the birth of a second son, André, three years younger than René.

Joseph had the soul of an artist. If he seemed distant, stern, and uncommunicative, he was nevertheless a sensitive, nostalgic person, torn between the world of his childhood and the one he dealt with every day from his shop on Maisonneuve Street.

"One day I'll take you back to Beirut and show you the finest beaches in the world, and the finest theatres where you'll hear beautiful music," he used to tell his children.

Joseph wasn't making this up. Beirut was once considered the Paris of the Middle East. It was a city full of beauty, art, peace, and entertainment until the civil war destroyed this haven of delight on the shores of the Mediterranean. It was only natural that Paris should have been the next choice of Joseph, always in search of beauty and harmony.

Settling in Montreal, an artist in his spare time, he would play on the *oud*, an instrument resembling a double-stringed guitar with no frets that reminded him of his country of origin. His talents also found an outlet in the choir of Saint-Sauveur church, thanks to his powerful tenor voice. It was in this church that the Melkite Catholics of Montreal — some of Syrian origin, like the Angélil family, but also Lebanese, Palestinian, Jordanian, and Iraqi — came together to share in the religious service on Sundays. This place of worship, situated on the corner of Saint-Denis and

Viger, would be sold in December 2000 for lack of funds to pay for its renovation and turned into an entertainment complex.

But during the post-war years, the parish of Saint-Sauveur welcomed the Christians from the Middle East, who formed a close-knit community around their priest. In 1996 they numbered almost one thousand in Quebec, with nearly thirty-six thousand scattered across Canada.

Joseph Angélil was a man of principles and traditions. A very religious and reticent man, though active, high strung, and quick-tempered, he imposed his Arab culture on his family. René grew up among people who spoke Arabic, English, and French at home, and his mother, Alice, insisted on enrolling him in a French-language primary school. Syrian dishes were served regularly in the home, Arab songs were played on Joseph's record player, and they scrupulously avoided serving alcohol, which was forbidden in the Joseph Angélil household.

René spent his childhood in a secure, traditional environment. The Angélil family was not well off, but Joseph was a responsible, dependable man who provided unfailingly for the needs of his own. This allowed the young René to grow up with something of a carefree attitude, thinking only of having fun and of play, instead of devoting himself exclusively to work like his father and mother, who in fact often had to take in sewing at home to make ends meet at the end of the month.

As he grew up, René would be subject above all to female influences, and especially that of his mother, Alice, the woman of his life, with whom he would develop an unfailing understanding. She was brilliant and generous, and maintained the contact with all the family, whether children or brothers, sisters, and cousins, who gravitated to the house.

René was also influenced by his grandmother Sara, an enthusiastic gambler. The Angélil and Sara families played cards when they came together, but it was the grandmother who stood out for her analytic ability and playing strategy. There were no casinos or provincial lotteries in those days, and the gaming houses were controlled by organized crime. At the Angelils' people enjoyed betting a few cents or candies playing canasta, five hundred, or poker. But gambling fever would emerge in the players during the long winter nights. Determined to defy chance, they would vie with one another, all the family members joining in, each trying to best the others. There was hot blood running in their veins! People got carried away easily in the Angélil household. They would dig in their heels, argue, and sulk, and then make up, soon forgetting all about it — an attitude typical of a culture different from that of the less demonstrative Quebecois. The young René grew up between these two cultures. His youthful imagination was fascinated most of all by adult games, and he learned how to cope with both good and bad luck — the gambler's heaven and hell.

Before he reached adolescence he had already learned a great deal about the adult world — at least, about the adult world as it was in his parents' household. He learned all the card games long before algebra or geometry, and, thanks to the perspicacity common to all children, he knew his world — this world that surrounded him since birth. What is more, he was a bright child who was often bored in school. He took an interest in many other things — real life, the real world, and real stakes. He had already worked out where the real power lay in his family: there was no doubt it was with the women, whom he admired and respected. It was his mother he would confide in when things went wrong or he got off the rails. His mother would always understand him. His father maintained a distance between himself and those around him, and, in any case, René wanted to cross the boundaries Joseph had set for him. "My son will be an accountant or a lawyer," he used to say, while René dreamed of other things. He wanted to change the world in his own way, to challenge fate, to win and to charm, though he didn't yet know how.

It is amazing how knowledgeable children can be about life. They learn so early the parameters of their lives without daring to express it. Destinies are often framed by childhood visions. As a child René already had big ideas and knew that one day this world wouldn't be enough for him. He was neither ungrateful nor unhappy, but was quite simply eager for everything, burning with impatience to take control of his own life and no longer have to obey or respect anyone else's wishes.

He got on well with the women of his childhood, and he behaved like them without sacrificing any of his masculinity. Some people consider him "macho," lacking in respect for women's wishes, controlling and exploiting women's talents, while the path he chose in life proves quite the contrary. Worse still, some suggest he holds women in contempt because of his religion and ancestral customs. Actually, this is a mistaken view of him and of his family's culture. René is not a Muslim, but a Melkite Catholic, and no male in his family has ever imposed the veil, or silence, on women. What is more, Syrians and Lebanese love to live in a community, sharing mealtimes, arguing, sometimes squabbling, and having fun with their relatives, whether close or distant. Such bonds are all the closer in an adopted country.

So René grew up under his mother's influence and learned to play the game of life — for René already knew that life was just a game. He just had to be a winner. At school he took an interest in sports, but never made a serious effort as an athlete, nor did he take part in dangerous activities. He didn't play hockey, yet his idol was Maurice Richard. One sport at which he did excel was table tennis, and we may well think he bet his pocket money on the chance of his winning. And he didn't often lose, for he was good at controlling the ball. That was his special gift.

One day he'd say he had Arab blood in his veins, so he would often fly into a rage over nothing. "I can understand why there's so much fighting back there, in the land of my ancestors. Fighting runs in my blood, and perhaps that's why I've been so successful. I'm an Arab inside, and a Quebecois outside. That sums me up!"

But René discovered America, and above all Quebec, during his teenage years. Television made its appearance in Canadian households in 1952, the American hit parade was played on the radio, and the ostentatious prosperity of America was in evidence in the streets of Montreal. In the 1950s particularly, even though it was the second largest French-speaking city in the world, Montreal resembled a lot of cities in the United States. That was how Americans themselves often saw it. That was why people bought the magazines, records, and food, and why artists like Sammy Davis, Jackie Gleason, Jerry Lewis, and Dean Martin considered Montreal one of the cities on the North American tour. In most cases signs in the department stores were in English only, while in nightclubs, with very few exceptions, only American music was played. Canadian television was bilingual but the cars were American, the cinema more American than ever, and the lifestyle of French Canadians of the time was modelled on that of the Americans. The wealthiest even dreamed of a bungalow designed like the houses in the suburbs of New York or Chicago. This new world could only dazzle a teenager who wanted to change the world and live life to the full.

3

THE THIRD BARONET: PIERRE LABELLE

A T THE AGE OF NINE, René, surely following his father's inspiration, joined the Saint-Vincent-Ferrier School choir. He still had a child's voice, and an unremarkable one, but he had an excellent musical ear and showed a lot of interest in music. It was in this choir that he met Pierre Labelle, aged just ten, who had a talent for music and a very good voice. René had a lot of friends at Saint-Vincent-Ferrier, yet this friendship with Pierre, a harmless, good-natured, naïve, chubby-cheeked little lad, would change his life, as if fate had linked them together.

Pierre Labelle was born in Windsor, Ontario. His father was a professional musician who played cello in the Detroit Symphony Orchestra for several years. His career was going well, but he was homesick for Quebec and wanted his children to live in a French-speaking environment. So he moved to Villeray, where he lived in a house directly opposite the Angélils. Pierre Labelle's childhood was naturally filled with music — all kinds of music. While still very young he learned to play piano, flute, and saxophone. With his classical training, Pierre's father was unable to find work in Montreal. He finally took a post as director of the orchestra of the Théâtre Mercier, which accompanied the artists invited to perform in this big auditorium in the east of Montreal. The Théâtre Mercier also welcomed foreign artists passing through Montreal.

This was a time when nightclubs reigned supreme in Montreal, where there were very few large theatres. People could dream of a Place des Arts, a Comédie-Canadienne, or a renovated Théâtre Saint-Denis, but these were just dreams in the 1950s.

The years went by and the friendship grew between the two school-boys, who, without planning it, found themselves attending the same schools, first at Saint-Vincent-Ferrier, then at Collège André Grasset, and later at Saint-Viateur. A gifted student, René had skipped Grade 7 and earned the great honour of being one of the elite students who began Latin in the first year of the *cours classique*. Brilliant, but not necessarily a scholar, he would leave André Grasset and catch up with Pierre Labelle again at Saint-Viateur.

René got excellent grades at this school without effort. He had an excellent memory and felt he had no need to study. Of course he would boast about this to all his classmates. He preferred to have fun, listen to music, and go out with his friends. However, he did show a lot of interest in a public speaking contest organized by the school. As lackadaisical, passive, and lazy as he could be in dealing with subjects that were of no interest to him, a competition could fire his enthusiasm.

He put his name down for the contest, and with his mother's help he wrote out a long speech. Alice listened to it, encouraged him, and made him rehearse it for days on end. René had never worked so hard on a project. And when the time came, he went up to speak before his schoolmates and won the contest. This gave him great satisfaction, and he would talk about his achievement for years to come, as if this was the real diploma he would need in the life he was going to lead. And maybe he was right.

But usually he lacked direction and wasn't considered serious enough by the school, so he was turned down for president of the student council towards the end of his Grade 12 year. No matter, thought René, who then became campaign organizer for his preferred candidate, Gilles Petit, who, naturally, was elected. René wrote every word Petit uttered to win over the electors and made him rehearse the speech he had crafted so carefully. There was no question of letting Petit improvise and risk throwing away his chance of winning. He had to stick to Angélil's text. We can see a strange likeness between this approach used by René when he was only seventeen and the one he would later adopt in preparing Céline Dion's public statements and press conferences. As a teenager he got his candidate elected, and thirty years later he made sure his singer would win recognition. Events change, life deals us blows, but people remain basically the same throughout their lives.

Control was the important thing: already he was obsessed by the need to control. Petit would be elected president, and he would also become the fourth member of the Baronets. Control and single-mindedness...

All these years Pierre and René saw one another regularly and spent their spare time together. Pierre wasn't particularly taken by the ancient Arab music he heard at the Angélils'. He preferred modern jazz and, above all, rock and roll, which literally exploded at the end of the 1950s — a kind of music for which there was obviously no place in the Angélil household. So Pierre, deciding his friend had to hear it, invited him home, where the atmosphere was more favourable.

Better yet, Pierre brought René to the Théâtre Mercier and helped him discover what went on backstage in the entertainment world. In the 1950s Montreal was one of the prime spots in North America for nightclubs, and there was a phenomenal nightlife in the city. This came as a real revelation for René Angélil, who couldn't get enough of Olivier Guimond, Jacques Desrosiers, La Poune, Gaston Campeau, Yvan Daniel, Claude Blanchard, and all the Quebec artists who earned their entire living performing in cabaret. Television, still in its infancy, ignored them completely. At the time Pierre Labelle had decided to become a draftsman. He had a natural talent for drawing and was also gifted musically. However, his father wouldn't hear of a musical career for his son, so Pierre opted for a career as a poster artist — an occupation one of his uncles was pursuing with considerable success: he painted the posters, usually featuring portraits of the artists, that were pasted on the walls of the Montreal nightclubs. The two teenagers, fifteen and sixteen, were too young to be legally admitted to nightclubs, but from backstage they could be dazzled by shows they were seeing for the first time in their lives. René had no idea what his future would be, and no plans, but he liked what he saw. Tall for his age, and lanky like children who have grown too fast, he would take up his position leaning against a wall behind the backdrops. There, he was fascinated by the world that was revealed to him. Later, his friends would say that it was then he caught the show business bug.

4

AMATEUR TALENT CONTESTS

A NEW KIND OF MUSIC had found its way into René Angélil's ears and heart. When teenagers at the end of the fifties listened after school to the hit parade on CKVL, most of them wanted to hear just one voice: Elvis Presley's. Other more serious ones preferred Pat Boone. Léon Lachance, an already aging disk jockey, found it difficult to conceal his dislike of Elvis's music, but the entire younger generation was electrified by the young rock musician. René and Pierre listened reverently to this music that was about to transform the world. At a time when the music video still had not been heard of and when black and white TV with only rare exceptions ignored rock music entirely, radio was the only medium that occasionally broadcasted it.

Today it isn't easy to imagine the stir caused by the birth of rock and roll in the United States and Canada. Parents organized demonstrations calling for the banning of this "barbarous, decadent music that will pervert our youth" — the cry in small-town America. Montreal wasn't far behind. Elvis Presley was scheduled to perform in the city, at the Delorimier Stadium, in 1956. Everything was in place: he was to come down over the stadium in a helicopter and sing his hits dressed in a shimmering gold lamé suit. Cardinal Léger and Jean Drapeau, the mayor of Montreal at the time, used their influence to have the show cancelled, and in the end it took place in Ottawa. Thousands of Quebec teenagers took the train to attend Elvis's performance in the capital. It is said that Elvis never forgave Montreal for the insult.

Pierre Labelle's father, even though he was open to all kinds of music, couldn't bear Elvis's "barbarism." As for René's father, one has to wonder if he was even aware of the Presley phenomenon.

But Elvis's style would inspire a new generation of singers who would perform a kind of music very similar to their idol's. What is more, they would even go so far as to mimic the King's physical appearance, hair, and casual manner. Ricky Nelson, Buddy Holly, Ritchie Valens, Bobby Darin, Conway Twitty, and almost all the successful young singers of the time took their inspiration, in one way or another, from Elvis Presley.

Pierre and René had changed their hairstyle, wearing quiffs greased with Brylcreem, and hummed rock and roll as they strolled in the streets of Villeray. Pierre's thoughts were of the music, and René's of the girls screaming with delight at the sight of their pop idols. Unfortunately for him, René didn't have his father's tenor voice: he had inherited his mother's reedy one. But maybe if he sang with Pierre Labelle it might work…

"Why don't we enter Billy Monroe's amateur talent contest?" they asked themselves. And that is what they finally did, some time later.

At this point we must say something about Billy Monroe, a musician — an Anglophone composer from Montreal — who had once sold one of his songs to an American producer who happened to be passing through. The song in question was "When My Baby Smiles at Me." The producer paid him twenty-five dollars, and the song went on to be one of the big successes on the American hit parade in the years after Second World War. Monroe never got more than the twenty-five dollars given to him by the producer — whom, incidentally, he never saw again. Monroe never got over this bit of bad luck. He might have been a rich and famous composer, but he had to be satisfied instead with accompanying young singers during amateur talent contests, for a pittance. But at least he was to have the satisfaction of witnessing the first steps of some great Quebec stars, including the Baronets. But for now they were still in the embryonic stage.

In 1958, the popularity of amateur talent contests was comparable to the many "improvs" of today. In Montreal, Quebec City, and elsewhere in the province, all the radio stations had to include in their programming a show during which undiscovered talents competed for the top prize.

We could well call this exploitation in the worst sense of the word, since none of these aspiring talents were paid and the generously sponsored program awarded the winner only a twenty-dollar watch. But what did it matter! All the participants dreamed of fame, and Pierre and René decided to give it their best shot, for, in 1958 and a long time after, amateur talent contests were the prescribed springboard for launching a career. All you had to do was turn up at the audition, bringing a sheet of music you would put down in front of the pianist, and sing. Back then most of the participants sang in English, while others took over the major French hits.

5

THE BARONETS

Life continued its usual course at Saint-Viateur, where René was completing his final high school year with all the carefree attitude of a seventeen-year-old. That was when he met Jean Beaulne.

"It was in 1957, and I was practising basketball with some other students in the school gym. I was new at the school, and René, who was a year older than me, wanted to demonstrate his superiority. He prided himself on being the best player, and, holding out a quarter, challenged me to score more baskets than him. That was how our relationship began."

And over the years there would be many such challenges. But René suddenly took an interest in the young tenderfoot when he discovered that he had the same musical tastes as Pierre and himself. What was more, he sang with his brother's band. He talked about this with Beaulne and Gilles Petit, who was on the same basketball team as René.

But it wasn't just music that the four teenagers had in common: they shared their sense of humour, too.

"It was hilarious to see Pierre and René together," recounts Jean Beaulne. "They carried on like Dean Martin and Jerry Lewis. Without being aware of it they were talented comedians, and perfectly matched. René made up jokes for Pierre, who was already a natural clown. They only thought about making people laugh and having fun, and I was a great audience for them. I laugh easily! And then René was a guy who seemed to like a challenge, and I liked that."

The four new friends would go out together, meeting regularly in a restaurant in Villeray called Chez Marcel. One evening they decided to go hear a popular singer named Tex Lecor perform in a café, La Catastrophe. In the taxi on the way home they spontaneously sang "Bye Bye Love," the Everly Brothers' hit of the moment, which they followed up with other songs by the American duo. It was actually a musical performance that the taxi driver was hearing.

"Yes! Not bad! Let's form a group and enter some talent contests," suggested Beaulne. "Why not a foursome like the Four Aces, the Four Lads, the Four Preps, or the Four Seasons?"

They immediately set about seriously rehearsing a number for a show to be put on at Saint-Viateur. At that time, too, high school students often came together under a teacher's supervision at the local school to celebrate special occasions. It was at one of these that René, Pierre, Jean, and Gilles performed one of the classics of doo-wop music, "In The Still of The Night," by the American foursome The Satans. This time there was no mistake about it: the group created a sensation.

But it still wasn't enough. René was single-minded. So the four youngsters decided to take part in the radio show *Les Découvertes de Billy Monroe*. Beaulne suggested to the other three group members a song he had composed called "Joanne."

The audition was a success, but before starting the broadcast Billy Monroe, at the piano, asked the group's name. He couldn't very well introduce the members individually, so the group needed a name. On the spur of the moment they came up with "The Flyers" for the occasion. It was just a short while later that Gilles Petit, leafing through *Montréal-Matin*, a daily newspaper of the time, came across the name of a hockey team that had the right sound: The Baronets.

There were no objections, for the name worked in both English and French, and so it was the Baronets who sang "Joanne." Their performance won them some attention, and they carried off the first prize. The following Sunday the Baronets went to the Casa Loma nightclub to take part in *Les Découvertes de Jean Simon*, and again carried off the first prize. With Jean Simon again, they went to the El Dorado and won for the third time.

"When I saw them on stage, I knew they were sure to win. They had good voices, but above all a great stage presence, and a lot of confidence in their ability," recounts Jean Simon, who in a career of thirty-seven years has presented almost one hundred thousand acts and thirty-five thousand singers in his legendary amateur talent contest. He was a genuine institution in the world of show business.

Jean Simon was quite right. All the audiences liked the Baronets, and René, Pierre, Jean, and Gilles were exhilarated by these early stage successes.

After their "triumph" René never tired of telling and retelling every detail of this memorable day to his friends at Saint-Viateur. His schoolmates were highly impressed.

When the school year ended, the students graduating from Saint-Viateur were at a crossroads. In 1959 only Grade 12 was needed to launch a career. Pierre Labelle, Jean Beaulne, and Gilles Petit gave up school. Pierre's career path led to drawing, Gilles went into insurance, and Jean enrolled at the Institut Teccart while continuing to work with his father, who owned a business leasing televisions in hospitals.

René was torn by the choices confronting him. He had a burning desire to go into show business and lead a flamboyant life, but he didn't want to disappoint his father, and in the end decided to enrol in a business school, the École des Hautes Études Commerciales (EHEC). At seventeen he was one of the school's youngest students and certainly one of the most talented, but after only a few weeks he knew his heart was not in it. The group was entering contests and regularly carrying off the first prize.

6

THE BARONETS' CAREER

IN 1960 THE BARONETS PERFORMED in evenings and on weekends. This kept them all happy. René was studying, while Jean, Pierre, and Gilles worked in the daytime to earn a little money. But what mattered most to them was their growing popularity with the opposite sex. This made them think about quickly developing a repertoire and giving their group a personality.

Knowing they weren't were musicians, the members of the quartet called on the well-known pianist Georges Tremblay, who would teach them voice projection, the use of different keys, and harmonizing. Tremblay was a competent and demanding teacher and made them work hard. It would be a much more profitable investment for the young men than they realized.

Jean Beaulne made more and more contacts. René wasn't particularly receptive to Jean's many initiatives, and seldom agreed with him — no more than did Pierre, however. René didn't always take things seriously and developed a taste for games of chance at the EHEC. Barely two months after starting there he dropped out. For him there could be no question of wasting his time on schoolwork, studying other people's theories, and being bored in the sphere of abstract notions. He needed concrete, tangible things, like gambling, money, girls, and cars. In no time, without telling his parents, he had found a job at the Bank of Montreal. In his spare time he set off again with the Baronets, who were dreaming of their first single, the sign of recognition at the time.

Unable to announce his decision to his parents, he concealed his hand and went on behaving like a student while taking his first steps in the world of business, learning to be a teller at the Bank of Montreal. For several months his parents had no inkling of what he was up to.

But the Baronets' career turned a corner when the group negotiated its first professional gig. René still remembers it very well, for it marked the true birth of the Baronets. The great event took place at the Feuille d'Érable, a very popular nightclub in the Montreal region.

He took advantage of the event to inform his parents that he had dropped out of his studies at the EHEC for good and was intending to pursue a career in show business. Joseph looked at his son and recognized perfectly that nothing would stand in the way of his pursuit of this unexpected vocation. He had dreamed of a career as a lawyer or accountant for René, and this came as a blow to him — a terrible blow. Show business wasn't a serious business in 1961, particularly in Quebec, thought Joseph. René invited him to the Feuille d'Érable, and he was in the audience for the successful show put on by the Baronets. Although he smiled and applauded, his heart wasn't in it, for his dream had been shattered. Communication between the two would become difficult from then on, and René would suffer from his father's oppressive silence for years without daring to discuss the situation with his friends. Fortunately, his mother would understand.

"Every time we went to pick up René for work there would be an argument between Pierre and me to see who would ring the doorbell. We were always afraid of getting a telling-off from his father," remembers Jean Beaulne. "We could hear him giving off. The father and son would argue. Maybe it was how it always was between them, but in the end Pierre and I decided to wait for René at the corner of the street rather than go to his house anymore."

Gilles Petit staked everything on the insurance business and terminated his six-month adventure with the Baronets. "I'd rather work in insurance. I'm not made for a job with so little security," he told his friends.

He could see that the Baronets' popularity was growing steadily and that he had to make a choice. He was giving up fame and a lot of money, but he never regretted it. He pursued his destiny with all the confidence in the world. As for René, at eighteen he didn't have any doubts either. He was brimming with confidence — confidence in himself first of all, and then in the group.

After their success at the Feuille d'Érable the Baronets received many requests to perform. With so much youthful enthusiasm the three friends didn't hesitate to buckle down seriously, holding onto their day jobs while fulfilling their performing commitments in the evenings and on weekends.

7

PARENTS AND HARD TIMES

THE LAUNCH OF THE BARONETS took place in difficult circumstances. The three teenagers from different cultural backgrounds
had to learn to live together. René's culture was Arab; Pierre's was
Anglophone, for he had spent his childhood in Ontario; and Jean was of
typical Quebecois stock, with fervent nationalists in his family. One of
his cousins, Yvon, was an ambassador; Jean-Pierre was a judge on the
Supreme Court in Ottawa; and Guy was a director at Radio Canada.

All three spoke fluent English. They had to learn to get along and to
respect one another. It wasn't always easy in the beginning. Beaulne
remembers their early struggles:

> I soon found out that René liked to be in charge. He liked
> to dominate. From the outset and during all the years
> when we were Baronets, we used to fight. I can't stand
> being dominated by anyone and neither can he, but we
> did respect one another. It didn't stop us from having
> some good times together. I was the only one who stood
> up to him in his entire life. No one could dominate him.
> Pierre had a docile temperament and went along with
> whatever René said. When René was set on an idea he

could defend it for hours on end, and that's how he developed his debating skills. He always wanted to be a winner. The fear of losing was a constant obsession with him. He never stopped telling us he was going to win, as if it was the end of the world for him to lose.

The Baronets also had to learn to deal with the rather peculiar world of show business in the 1960s, particularly the nightclubs. Also, like all adolescents at the time, they experienced a generational conflict that has no equivalent today. Parents and children are closer now, sometimes sharing the same musical tastes, wearing the same make of jeans, and going to see the same movies. Obviously, age always creates a gap between generations, but the kind of bond you see nowadays between parents and children was unimaginable back then. There wasn't just a generation gap, but a real gulf.

The parents of the three Baronets had lived through the Depression and, above all, the war. All of them had been poor. Joseph, René's father, had been closer to the conflict, for he lived in the Middle East and France and had suffered more. He was having a difficult time in the tailoring business, which wasn't going very well, and he had to work from home, as did his wife, Alice. Jean Beaulne's father was having difficulties in his rental business. Pierre Labelle's father wasn't earning a fortune, and had to struggle to make a living as a musician. In the 1950s and 1960s musicians were poorly paid and had much less protection than today.

As a result, the parents of the three young artists were worried, wanting only a better life for their children. They had spoiled them, despite their limited means. They had made sacrifices to ensure they enjoyed life and were prepared to pay their tuition if it would help them get into a real profession — especially Joseph, who had high hopes for René. And now here were the three lads launching out on an uncertain career and even living for a while the very life of poverty their parents had wanted to spare them. But their parents didn't recognize that this baby boom generation were dreamers, and that they believed in their dreams. It was this ability to dream that created a bond between the three young Baronets. Their parents belonged to a generation that had suffered so much that it had abandoned its dreams and could think only of survival.

So the three young singers went their own way, deciding to break with the past and with tradition, convinced that in life happiness was show business. They even decided, in spite of everyone — which is to say in spite of their parents above all — to pay whatever the cost of their enterprise would be. But it would cost them even more than they imagined.

Jean Beaulne reminisces about how they lived in those early years in the bars where the amateur talent contests were held:

> It was often in third-rate bars, immersed in noise and smoke, before an audience that was drunk most of the time. We'd be asked to turn up at ten p.m. to go on at eleven, but unfortunately we too often had to go on stage at one-thirty or two o'clock, and next day we had to go to school very early. Our parents were angry at us, for we had only had three hours sleep.
>
> When we came off stage at three in the morning there would be no bus to take us home, so we had to take a taxi. When we won the contest, which made us ten dollars, we could afford to take a taxi, but when we didn't we had to dip into our pocket money.
>
> When we were on stage I kept an eye on the entrance all the time because I was afraid my father might come looking for me. He'd told me once that if I didn't stop going to those disgusting bars full of druggies and mafiosi he'd come and haul me off the stage. René and Pierre laughed at my fears, but I didn't find it funny at all. Fortunately, later on my father came to understand that I was too stubborn to change careers.

In the summer of 1961 René Angélil became unable to continue: he had caught mononucleosis and was obliged to stop all his activities. At the age of nineteen he was confined to the bedroom in his parents' house that still belonged to him, and had to resign himself to reading and listening to music.

Pierre Labelle visited him regularly, bringing him records and discussing their work, but René's thoughts were elsewhere. He took advantage of his enforced idleness to draw up a life plan he was completely serious about: to make his fortune by breaking the bank in a casino. Yet he had never set foot in a casino and had never gambled huge sums of money. Before getting seriously into gambling he was preparing a strategy, for he had no intention of making one up as he went along. He did his research, consulting gamblers, observing, reflecting, and making calculations. At home he spent time with his family, who played cards tirelessly, but he had other plans — greater ambitions that would make him a rich man, he hoped. And he was driven by this prospect as much as by the Baronets' career. Gambling is a serious and important business for René. In fact it would take him much further than he ever dreamed when he was nineteen. Entertainment and luck run all through his life story.

IN A LOW VOICE

René really liked to imitate a person who had lost their voice. Sometimes, when a too-insistent fan came up to congratulate us, René would speak to him in a low voice, lowering his head more and more. The individual would bend down with him to hear what he was saying, and end up almost kneeling on the floor, in the most ridiculous posture.

JEAN BEAULNE

REAL GIBBERISH

In the days when the Baronets were on tour, we often ate in restaurants. Even though people recognized him, René never hesitated to play tricks on the waitresses when they came to take his order. He would gabble a few incomprehensible words, ending up with one they could understand, for instance, "Groninigna, bovoro ta du, okay cake." The waitress would say, "Oh! Is it cake you want?" René would answer in gobbledygook again, ending with the word "ashtray." The waitress would say, "Okay, I'll fetch an ashtray." Then he'd say, "No. Houda bout donna fried." At that point the waitress would decide to fetch the manager who, after listening to René, would find he had a strange accent: "It's very odd, I don't understand a thing you're saying. Yet I've no problem understanding you when they interview you on TV," the manager would finally say.

JEAN BEAULNE

8

MEMORY

WHILE HE WAS STILL VERY young René worked on developing his memory. He knew instinctively that by doing so he could succeed in games and get the better of those around him. He had already succeeded in completing his secondary education just on the strength of his memory. Thanks to it he won a public speaking competition. He helped Gilles Petit win the school election by making him memorize the speeches he wrote. But that wasn't enough for him. He wanted to perfect this faculty to help him win at gambling.

During his spare time he would apply himself to remembering the face value and suits of the fifty-two cards of the pack before him. He'd perform this exercise dozens of times, shuffling the cards and starting over again. Sometimes he did this alone and sometimes with a partner, and without seeing them could tell exactly what cards his opponent was holding.

He also learned the phone numbers of all the people he knew. He memorized figures and dates. He was fascinated by statistics — baseball players' averages, the number of goals scored by hockey players, and the scores. He read biographies, memorizing the important dates in the lives of performers, mostly, but of politicians, too. Even today he can retell the details of his own past life and of Céline

Dion's with exemplary precision. When he was nineteen, memory was already as much a source of power for him in his professional life as it was in gambling.

René was never ashamed to say he was a gambler, which is easy enough to explain. Whereas a good proportion of respectable Americans condemn certain games of chance, things are very different in the culture of the Angélil family. It wasn't on the street and in dives that he learned to gamble, but at home, with an honest family around him who had respect for gambling, and for whom it was the principal pastime.

THE JOURNALIST

We were in Boston, in one of the most fashionable nightclubs in the United States. The premises could hold as many as eighteen hundred people, and all the big names of the musical stage, including Frank Sinatra, had performed there. We were appearing in the first part of Connie Francis's show. She was a very popular singer in those days, and we were pleased to see our name was beginning to get some media attention. In fact a journalist had made the trip from Montreal to Boston to write an article on us. However, René was a bit irritated by the familiar attitude of this lady, who he guessed was coming on to him. So he decided to spin her a yarn. It was about a woman who was having a brain operation. The surgeon opened up her head, took her brain, and put it down on the windowsill. But a cat came along and ate it. So his assistant asked the doctor what he should do. "Put in some cotton wool! She's a journalist, so she doesn't need a brain!" When she heard this, our journalist immediately stormed out, fuming. We were worried about what she would say in her article about us after this incident, but to our great surprise it was full of praise! But it was the last time that journalist came on to René!

JEAN BEAULNE

9

AN OPENING FOR A MANAGER

Aﬀter three months spent convalescing René was completely cured and claimed to be in top form. He had spent all summer reflecting on his future, and the time had come to make some big decisions. Such a shower of contracts was being rained down on the group that René soon had to make up his mind to leave his job as a teller with the Bank of Montreal.

The Baronets had become true professionals. The recording industry in Quebec was evolving fast, and new stars were rising to the top of the French-language charts.

The Baronets, inspired by the Four Lads and the Four Aces, also sang sentimental ballads. By 1961 rock and roll had run out of wind. Elvis had obeyed the draft, while the tragic death of Buddy Holly and a few scandals had tarnished the image of rock and roll. People were going back to sentimental songs with singers like Bobby Rydell, Bobby Vee, Connie Francis, and the like.

It was a relief to the Baronets to start on a full-time performing career. No more studying, no more day jobs for them. They were living their new lives as artists to the fullest, enjoying the greatest freedom.

"We didn't have a choice anymore," Jean Beaulne says. "René was falling asleep behind the counter at the bank and making mistakes.

Pierre wasn't being very creative at his drawing board, and my father, with whom I was working, kept telling me I wasn't as efficient as I used to be. With one accord we decided to give up our respective jobs, and we suffered hell for a while, above all from our parents, who were more and more unhappy about our decision."

And of course their parents were right to worry. The Baronets put on a good show, combining comedy and singing, but they still weren't recognized stars. They were serving a difficult apprenticeship performing in nightclubs. Some of these were respectable, others less so. When you start out on a career you have to learn the ropes in some rather disreputable joints and be prepared to sleep in hotels that aren't much better. Jean Beaulne continues:

> It wasn't easy to adapt early in our career, and the nightclub and hotel owners didn't spoil us. We were unknowns at the time, so we had to accept whatever rooms they offered us. We had good parents who until then had seen that we didn't lack for anything, but now, suddenly, we were being given dirty bedrooms and mattresses that sagged so badly our backs would hurt for the next three days. We were used to living in clean houses, so it was difficult to put up with that kind of filth. I remember one place that was so disgusting that I slept in my fur coat so I wouldn't catch something. At Wildwood in New Jersey the owner of the hotel where we performed offered us rooms where the beds had no sheets or blankets. The mattress must have been used by a regiment of soldiers, and they must all have been screwing in that disgusting bed. I was so worn out and disgusted at three in the morning that I slept on the floor.
>
> But we loved our work passionately, and were prepared to make whatever sacrifices were required. The owner of one bar, who had hired us for sixteen shows, was so mean she had us timed and calculated that we'd been on stage thirty-seven minutes less than the contract said — an average of two minutes and a bit per

show. So she subtracted that from our fee. The doorman told us she'd earned enough to buy the club by ripping off her husband's receipts for years. As soon as she'd ruined the poor guy, she bought the bar from him. What a piece of work!

The Baronets found it very difficult to make ends meet. What is more, Jean owed more than six months' rent to his grandmother, in whose house he was living at the time, even though he only had to pay fifteen dollars a month, board included. It's pretty hard to put your future plans into effect in such difficult conditions. Sometimes the Baronets accepted gigs blindly, rarely consulting one another first. It was a problem when they found out they'd made conflicting commitments. Finally they got together in their favourite restaurant, Chez Marcel, and decided to get better organized. Jean suggested they hire a manager for the group: "A guy to find us contracts, and a recording company to make us better known. Someone big, who'd send us down to the States." So he set out to find a manager — no easy job.

In a bar where we worked regularly in the days of the Baronets, a very simple young man — a bit too simple, really — was working as a waiter and lighting technician. But he pestered us so much that one day René decided to play a neat trick on him, with the audience's connivance. So he got him to come to the dressing room by telling him he wanted to make some changes in the lighting. "When I touch my head, turn on the pink light, my nose, the blue, and when I scratch my leg turn everything off." The young man followed these instructions. But when all the lighting went off the audience began to shout and complain. The poor guy didn't know if he was coming or going. To make him even more uncomfortable, René gave more and more signals at an incredible rate, with the result that the room was flashing pink and blue like in a nightclub. We laughed ourselves silly.

JEAN BEAULNE

10

BEN KAYE

THAT YEAR, 1960, THE THREE young artists could see that the Quebec market wasn't particularly favourable to them. Now that Maurice Duplessis was dead and gone, politicians were talking about a "Quiet Revolution" and political renewal. But in René, Pierre, and Jean's universe — or, rather, their bubble — there was nothing in the province to motivate them. They didn't know that Quebec would soon be carried along on a great wave of nationalism. All they could see around them was Radio Canada, which seemed to them an inaccessible universe, unfamiliar, and too highbrow. The newspapers and magazines were all American, as were the recording companies and the top singers. They viewed Quebec music, local showbiz, and the whole Quebec entertainment industry as weak and marginal, and they were thinking seriously of pursuing their careers in the United States. If they were to survive, they thought, it was the only way.

They became increasingly interested in appearing in the U.S., encouraged by the extraordinary success of the Canadian singer Paul Anka. Born in Ottawa, he struck it lucky at the age of fourteen when he recorded a composition of his own called "Diana." It was a phenomenal hit, selling nearly 10 million copies worldwide. In 1960 it became the biggest hit of all time after Bing Crosby's "White Christmas," with 25 million records sold. Jean, accompanied by Pierre, who was a little less enthusiastic about the idea, decided to go to the Palais du Commerce, considered the temple of American music in Montreal at the time. All the great names appeared there regularly: Bobby Rydell, Chubby Checker, Dell Shannon, and Paul Anka himself, who had added his name to the list of stars. Jean wanted to get to know the promoters of these shows. Logically enough, he thought it was the best place for making contact with producers and agents who would open the door to the United States market to them.

Pierre was so intimidated that he hardly dared to climb the few steps to the third floor, where the offices of Ziggy Wiseman, the producer of the *All Stars Dance Party*, playing in the building at the time, were situated. Jean told him they were looking for a manager. Since he wasn't interested in taking on any new performers, he suggested they meet his own promotions assistant, Ben Kaye (real name: Benjamin Kushnir).

Kaye wanted above all to hear a "demo" tape before meeting the group. Knowing he was Jewish, the group decided to record the song "Havah Nagilah" and Jean Beaulne's composition "Joanne." Kaye showed some interest and Beaulne invited him to come to hear the Baronets perform at the Central Hotel in suburban Montreal. After the show Kaye immediately offered them a five-year contract, asking for 25 percent commission. It was the beginning of a long association.

The group was already fantasizing about an international career. Kaye too thought this was a possibility, but that it would take time.

Ben Kaye was fascinated by Elvis Presley's manager, Colonel Tom Parker, and was inspired by his approach. Like Parker, he relied heavily on publicity and marketing to sell the Baronets. He exaggerated and bluffed, and was able to obtain large fees for his protégés. After a while the Baronets realized that Ben Kaye, good salesman though he was, was not the greatest of strategists. So decisions were soon being made by the four of them together.

"Address the women in the audience. You've got to charm them," he told René.

René knew that. Girls followed him when he came offstage, making him tempting invitations he couldn't always resist. René had great charm and never became attached to any girl in particular. For the time being he was free and took full advantage of what life had to offer. Jean Beaulne says:

I know René like my own brother. We've been through some good times together, and difficult ones too. We shared our joys, but we also had one dispute after another. I had my worries and he had his. I needed to plan ahead and know what was supposed to happen five years down the road. René only thought about the present and didn't give a damn about the future. He wanted everything, right away. And when he was having one of his anxiety attacks I was the one he took it out on, because Pierre didn't react. It usually happened in the dressing room or in our hotel rooms. He was losing his hair and he was still very young.

"I'm going to be bald at forty, like my dad," he'd say to me. "I won't have any hair left ... but I'm still better looking than you. You're thin, you've got lines in your face already, and you're nowhere nearly as good-looking as me."

"I am what I am, and I'm proud of it," I'd reply. "I look at my results on stage, and they're as good as yours, or maybe better. I think you've got a big superiority complex that's really an inferiority complex. If you're not proud of who you are, that's your problem. It's not your hair that'll make you a success, but your brains. So forget about your hair while you still have some."

René is such a perfectionist that everything about him must be perfect, including his appearance.

René liked a good laugh, and at twenty he was a real practical joker who came out with trick after trick. His best one was to call a pizzeria, which in the 1960s was usually run by an Italian. His wife, who spoke with a very strong accent, would take the orders over the phone.

René would take great delight in ordering eight pizzas — three large, three medium and two small, each with different toppings. "Anchovies and cheese on the first. Olives and mushrooms on the second. Tomatoes and peppers on the third," and so on. The lady was having a lot of trouble following him, and to confuse her even more he would suddenly change his mind and start over again, changing the toppings for all the pizzas! We would be with him in the room at the time, listening to the conversation on other phones. I don't have to tell you we were all killing ourselves laughing. René would sometimes dare to call back to ask for additional toppings on each of the pizzas, apologizing all the time. This farce could go on for half an hour! The lady, who was a patient soul, would do what he asked without ever losing her temper. But the best part of all was when René would call her back to cancel the order.

JEAN BEAULNE

11

"JOANNE"

B EN KAYE FINALLY CALLED THE members of the group together to announce some good news: they were to record their first single. Back then people thought in terms of a simple 45 rpm with two songs on it. No new artist could hope to record an album. You had to have had a lot of success on the charts before you could think of doing an LP.

Jean suggested they go back to the song he had composed, "Joanne," which the Baronets had performed on the program *Les Découvertes de Billy Monroe*. For the flip side, Ben Kaye chose "Arrêtez ce mariage." Pierre Nolès, who was a leading producer in the early 1960s, was in charge of the recording. The record would soon reach top spot on the hit parade and sell very well.

It took years before the Baronets would admit that the first record of their career was made … in a washroom. To their great surprise, Pierre Nolès, the Stereo Sound Studio's producer, did indeed ask them to turn up in a washroom with their microphone. At first they even thought someone was playing a joke on them. But when funds were short this was the only way a lot of Montreal recording studios of the time had to produce an echo effect.

So they found a washroom nearby where the stone floor produced a nice resonance, and the result was excellent. In the U.S., a lot of rock recordings were made in the showers. But the Baronets kept their technique secret for a long time, for fear of being baptized "washroom singers."

Later, Ben Kaye would come up with a contract that filled his protégés with enthusiasm. It was for a two-week gig in Puerto Rico.

"I was happy, but I went out and bought a map to find out where Puerto Rico was," recounts Jean Beaulne.

Perhaps René didn't know where it was, either, but he knew very well what he could find there: slot machines, blackjack tables, roulette wheels, elegantly dressed croupiers, and a lot of people driven by a passion he shared — namely, gambling.

12

PUERTO RICO

Ben Kaye had obtained a two-week engagement at the Hotel Caribe Hilton, in Puerto Rico. According to the agreement with the owner of the property, the Baronets were to have bed and board and be paid about four hundred dollars a week each. The three young artists, still dreaming of an international career, were euphoric, and couldn't contain themselves. They could see the doors of American show business swinging open for them, with the promise of a grand life in hotel suites, the top clubs, and fame. They had forgotten that the money wasn't particularly impressive and that they still didn't have a lot of stage experience. No matter: that would come. Already Pierre Labelle and Jean Beaulne were thinking of beaches, bikini-clad girls, deluxe restaurants, and their first plane flight. For their families this trip seemed such an adventure that they made a point of accompanying them to the airport. Counting cousins and distant relatives, there were about fifty people there to wish them well before they left.

René had visited a few American towns when he crossed the border by car with his family on Sunday afternoons, but this was the first flight for him, too. It didn't seem to bother him particularly, for he had a firm intention in going to Puerto Rico: not only would this be his first flight, but it also would be his first visit to a casino — a dream come true for the nineteen-year-old. In his room after performances he was already fine-tuning his system and swearing to break the bank. The strategy he'd been working on for months was ready to be put to the test.

Once in Puerto Rico he was raring to go. While their bags were being brought up to the rooms he suddenly disappeared and went down to the hotel casino. For the first time in his life he was setting foot in such a temple of gambling. He spent a long time walking along the aisles, and a shiver went up his spine when he heard the slot machines and the cries of joy that rang out from time to time. He stopped at a blackjack table and bet a few dollars, swearing to keep his wits about him. In no time he had won one hundred dollars, and stopped. It was intoxicating. He had had the good — or bad — luck to win on his first try. Experienced gamblers will tell you that you never forget the strange euphoria of your first winnings. That's when you get hooked, for it makes you suddenly think you can go on winning forever because you are born lucky — never mind the statistics. It is a success, however modest, that gives a strange sense of power — an indescribable feeling, like something produced by a drug.

René cast caution to the winds and forgot Ben Kaye's good advice about the perils of gambling. He went back to his companions in the room to announce that his system had already won him one hundred dollars and that they should take advantage of it too.

Like a past master, immune from doubt about his expertise, he explained to them with infectious enthusiasm that if you doubled your bet every time, you had to win. Basing his theory on the impossibility of losing more than eight times in a row, René persuaded his friends, minus Jean Beaulne, to follow him to the blackjack table. He even dragged Ben Kaye along on his crazy adventure. Full of enthusiasm and assurance, the neophyte gamblers set off for the casino feeling certain their fortunes were all but made.

But chance decided otherwise. It took no time at all for them to lose every penny they had, and René admitted he'd have to revise his system. He had forgotten about runs of good and bad luck. His friends had learned their lesson and left the casino cured. But René was still looking for the flaw in his system.

He would have to find it on an empty stomach, for the Baronets had no money left to pay for meals in the expensive restaurant. They would have to make do with the sandwiches and free meals provided by the hotel. Fortunately, Ben Kaye asked for an advance on his protégés' fee. René would gamble away his share, and the other Baronets' money as well, having borrowed it from them. And he'd lose this time as well.

13

DALLAS

E VEN IF THEY HAD NO luck in the Puerto Rican casinos, the Baronets still had some success on stage — enough to continue what they, with all the naivety of their twenty years, were convinced was their climb to international fame. After the island in the West Indies they went on the road again, this time to Dallas, where they were to perform. Their act included American songs and some French favourites such as "C'est si bon," "Les Feuilles mortes," and "C'est magnifique." They spent the first two weeks after their arrival performing in one of the top clubs in the city. The audience was mainly composed of millionaires who reached out to them and applauded, while well-heeled young women invited the "French guys" to accompany them in their limousine to meet their fabulously rich daddies.

After one of their shows, the Baronets, who never missed a chance to amuse themselves, asked the manager of the establishment to show them where they could find a club with good entertainment. The city had a reputation for having the best shows in the U.S. The Baronets were soon sitting at one of the best tables, and a man began to chat to them, sitting with them for a few minutes. He was pleasant, but some-one came to whisper in René's ear that this individual was a member of the Mafia and probably dangerous.

"Come on! Mafia guys aren't all that dangerous. Up in Quebec we see them every day," answered René, as cool as a cucumber. The man bought the three Baronets a round and then went about his business.

Six months later, René and his companions were shocked to hear about President Kennedy's assassination, on November 22, 1963. Like everybody in America and in the whole world, they were glued to their black and white TV, following the events closely. Suddenly, on live TV, a man took out a handgun and fired at Lee Harvey Oswald, John F. Kennedy's assassin.

The Baronets looked at one another. "But that's him! Don't you remember him, guys?" asked Jean Beaulne.

Of course they remembered him. It was the man they had met in Dallas — Jack Ruby, who would die of cancer in prison a few years later.

So the Baronets discovered the hidden face of America — a face that is never seen on stage. But at the age of twenty you don't try to understand or rebel against plots and treachery. They had their lives to live, and those lives were going to be glamour-filled, far removed from low dives and corruption.

14

THE BEATLES

A LWAYS DEVIL-MAY-CARE, JOKERS on stage and in life, the Baronets performed at the top clubs in Quebec, on the beaches of Wildwood, in Atlantic City, and even on Boston stages. Slowly but surely they were abandoning the repertoire of the Four Lads and turning to the music of the Four Seasons and the Beach Boys.

In December 1963, Tony Roman, who worked with the producer Pierre Nolès, received in the mail a record made by the Beatles, a new group that was already all the rage in England, although still unknown in Canada or in the United States. For the first time the three Baronets listened to what was to become their music. They were beside themselves with joy to discover such a dynamic, explosive, creative repertoire.

Finally, an agreement was reached, and the Baronets chose to translate, not "I Want to Hold Your Hand," or "She Loves You," the first major successes of the Fab Four, but "Hold Me Tight" (as "C'est fou mais c'est tout"), "It Won't Be Long" (as "Ça recommence"), and "Twist and Shout" ("Twiste et chante"). They also translated the Dave Clark Five's hit "Do You Love Me?" ("Est-ce que tu m'aimes?") The 45 was recorded in a few hours, and this was followed by a marketing operation the likes of which Quebec has rarely seen. The media was present to witness the radical transformation of the group by a hairdresser. The Baronets would henceforth wear a Beatles' cut, with the hair falling over their foreheads. They would wear Mao jackets and colourful shirts, and have their pictures taken running and jumping in the streets of Montreal. They toured all the radio stations, organized autographing sessions in department stores, canvassed the media, and in no time at all became the most popular group in Quebec. Very soon hysterical girls were packing the houses where the Baronets were performing, screaming and jockeying for position, some of them fainting at the sight of their idols.

René Angélil was observing the manager, learning a job that would be his own some years later. Their songs climbed to the top of the charts. The Baronets were objects of worship in a way they had not previously known. Girls followed them home and swarmed around their cars, writing "I love you" on them with lipstick. In that year of 1963 the Baronets, who had barely earned sixty dollars a week when they first began, were now raking in more than two thousand dollars each (an enormous sum for the time), and were buying new cars almost every month. Intoxicated by their burgeoning fame, the lads spent madly, without any thought for the future. What did wealth mean to them when they were loved, adulated, and feted everywhere they went, and were even able to provoke riots. Using the Scopitone process — the forerunner of today's videos — they made a short movie that was seen in clubs and places of entertainment. Girls fainted when they heard them sing "C'est fou mais c'est tout" ("Hold Me Tight").

The Epstein family settled in Liverpool early in the twentieth century, after fleeing Poland. They opened a furniture store that prospered from the start. The business was taken over by Harry Epstein, Brian's father.

Brian was born in 1934 into a family that was well off in spite of the serious economic difficulties experienced by pre-war society. His family lived in a neighbourhood on the outskirts of the city, owned two cars, and lacked for nothing. The first school Brian attended, Southport College, was only one of his numerous educational experiences that ended in failure. He was never able to get on with his teachers, and was always a favourite target for them. Later he attended Liverpool College, from which he was finally expelled because of his poor marks. Other schools followed, without any more success. Finally, at the age of sixteen, and without a diploma of any kind, he began working in his father's shop for a wage of five pounds a week.

Just when things were beginning to improve for Brian he was called up for national service. If anyone was ill suited for military life it was this sensitive lad, who still didn't need to shave and who had had so many problems during his school career. A series of minor acts of insubordination ended when he was accused of impersonating an officer in order to ridicule him. He had returned to the base wearing an officer's uniform, a bowler hat on his head and an umbrella under one arm! The military administration released him on medical grounds, while recognizing he was a sensible boy deserving of confidence.

After getting out of the army Brian began to lose interest in the furniture trade. It was at this point he joined an amateur theatre company.

The young man made quite a good impression on his teachers, who recognized he had natural talent. But then he began to detest the actors' lifestyle — a closed little world he found very inward-looking. He realized that he was a businessman after all.

So Brian went back to his family, and took advantage of the growth of the chain of music stores. Still, something in him was giving him the idea he wasn't meant to remain a provincial businessman or salesman. He wanted to do something different, but still didn't know what.

One fine day a man came into the store and asked for a rock version of "My Bonnie." During the two days that followed, more and more people were asking for it. These requests encouraged Brian to investigate. He hated not being able to satisfy his customers, so he undertook some research and discovered that the song had been recorded in Germany by an English group. In fact they were some Liverpool musicians he had once seen in his store a short time before!

Out of curiosity he went to the Cavern Club to hear this local group and find out why people were asking for this famous recording. Brian was amazed to see the number of people who turned out to hear them, and by the noise filling the room. He was immediately drawn to the Beatles, sensing their fantastic stage presence. Then Brian spent a month discovering what exactly the duties of an agent were.

On their first meeting the parties merely exchanged their impressions in order to establish everyone's intentions. On the second meeting, commitments were made: Brian was to get 25 percent of the profits, more than the usual agent's commission. But in exchange he would do everything in his power to guide the Beatles to the pinnacle of fame. The contract was signed at the Casbah, where John, Paul, George, and Pete Best put their signatures at the bottom of the document — but not Brian: he considered his word was enough. It was quite a rash decision, but one that reflects very well the kind of flair Brian always displayed in his dealings with the Beatles.

Thanks to his numerous contacts in the recording world he was able to get them an audition with Decca. The group travelled to London with their old guitars and amplifiers. Unfortunately, some time later the Beatles received a negative answer from Decca.

After this audition they set off on their third tour to Hamburg. They were supposed to earn more money than on previous trips and were to perform in a more upscale club. After they arrived, a telegram came from Brian Epstein: "Congratulations lads. EMI requests recording session. Rehearse new material."

On June 6, 1962, they all turned up in the EMI recording studios in London, in St. John's Wood. There they were welcomed by George Martin, a smartly dressed gentleman who worked for EMI with responsibility for the "artists and repertoire" department. At the end of July, Brian got word from George Martin that Parlophone Records had agreed to record the Beatles!

When the paths of Brian Epstein and the Beatles crossed, they were four sarcastic young musicians who dressed in leather jackets and ate sandwiches and drank beer on stage! Brian laid down certain conditions if he was to work with them. The Beatles had to accept some rules. No more sandwiches and beer. No more leather jackets or pub songs like "She'll be Coming Round the Mountain," either. The only things allowed to survive were the Beatles' haircuts and songs, and their free and easy manner.

Brian pulled off a miracle: he was able to transform four working-class lads into well-dressed young men and cheeky members of high society. Later, John Lennon would criticize Brian for the changes he forced on them, but this showed a lack of understanding on his part. When the Beatles burst onto the pop music scene it was thanks to Brian. With the Beatles he was able to have people accept what were considerable changes for the time.

If later on Brian didn't share their enthusiasm for Eastern philosophy or the rock phenomenon, the young people who did take an interest in this trend owed it largely to Brian, who laid the foundation for it. But the task was more and more difficult, for the Beatles were in demand everywhere in the world. Offers poured in, so that Brian even had to advertise in the newspapers that he couldn't accept any advance engagements. He refused astronomical sums of money offered for them to perform. And he was beginning to have too much responsibility on his shoulders. He was beginning a gradual descent into hell.

At this time, Brian Epstein had everything he needed to be happy. He was thirty years of age, handsome, and led a healthy life, so he had no need to envy anyone. Yet he hadn't found happiness.

His temperament was unstable and he was rather too inclined to sink into depressions and feel bad about himself. In addition, his homosexual inclinations were well known. Indeed his homosexuality was so notorious that a number of his acquaintances behaved distantly towards him. Moreover, John Lennon would admit to having had sexual relations with his manager.

Brian was sinking more and more into a hopeless depression. In 1967, Epstein was preparing to set off for a weekend in the country, but in the end he decided to stay in London. He called some friends, saying he would call back later that weekend. He told them he was tired and not feeling in top form. None of them suspected that these were the Beatles' manager's last days, and his phone call caused no concern. On Sunday, when they still hadn't heard from him, they decided to call Peter Brown, a close friend of Brian's. Peter suggested they ask a secretary to call a doctor. Two hours later, the secretary and the doctor entered his room to find Brian dead.

Officially, the hypothesis of an accidental overdose of barbiturates was put forward. However, ten years later Peter Brown admitted to a British tabloid newspaper that he had visited the scene before the doctor arrived. He revealed that he had cleared away anything pointing to the fact that Brian had been murdered during a sexual encounter. A few weeks later, on August 27, 1967, the results of the police inquiry would be made public by the London prosecutor's office, with conclusions pointing to suicide.

How he really died will probably never be known. Was it suicide, an accidental overdose, or murder? The wider public will never find out what really happened to Brian, the person who was officially designated the "fifth Beatle."

Nothing can alter the fact that Brian, described by some as gentle and generous and by others as quick-tempered, aggressive, and unstable, was a real father to the up-and-coming four lads. They owed him a great deal. If he had not died so soon perhaps he could have saved the group from breaking up.

Brian Epstein is buried in the Jewish cemetery in London.

JEAN BEAULNE

15

WOMEN, SEX, DRUGS, AND
THE BARONETS

VERY QUICKLY AFTER THE BARONETS embarked on their career they
became the most popular young men in Villeray. Later, they would
vie with the most popular Quebec singers for young women's hearts. In
1963 the pill had already come on the scene, women were looking for
greater liberty, and love was becoming more free. The pop music stars
not only made their fortunes, they were also able to benefit from certain
opportunities that came along with their career — opportunities that
usually took the form of attractive young groupies crowding around
stage entrances looking for their favours.

These young women would lie in wait for the Baronets after performances. Indeed, the lads just had too many to choose from.
Sometimes they would take advantage of it, but they rarely embarked on
a lasting relationship with any of the girls, who were only trying to make
a fantasy come true. In time, the pop stars wearied of these brief affairs.

The Baronets didn't resemble the image of the sixties and seventies
rock groups spread by newspapers and magazines. In this special world
of pop music, how many artists succumbed to alcoholism, to drug
addiction, to scandals of a sexual nature, and other such excesses! The
Baronets were no saints, but they still went to Mass every Sunday. They
were often seen together at church, in accordance with their upbringing

and its religious influence. At the time, the influence of the Catholic Church was still strong in Quebec and religious observance was deeply rooted in people's habits. Failure to attend church on Sunday was frowned upon. René, Pierre, and Jean, who were still living with their parents, were no exception to the rule. They wouldn't give up attending Mass until their professional commitments made it impossible.

In spite of the success, the money, and the whirlwind activity of show business, they were amazingly disciplined young men who refused to drink even in nightclubs on the road. When the owner offered them a round they would ask for orange juice. None of them touched alcohol during their years of fame, or later. It was Jean Beaulne who confirmed this to me as I watched him sip a cup of chamomile tea at nine o'clock one morning — he was nicknamed "cup of hot water," for that is what he drank everywhere the group performed. The musicians hired by the Baronets thought Beaulne very strait-laced. For indeed, weary of having to adapt continually to new instrumentalists who were more or less talented according to the location, the group had decided to provide themselves with an experienced band of musicians able to adapt readily to their style. Living in the company of these people led to the discovery of a new reality: drugs. Beaulne explains:

> They called me "straight" because I didn't smoke pot. I'd already tried it with René and Pierre at a party, and I didn't like it.
>
> In fact, a shady-looking guy who often came to our shows once approached me suggesting I sell hash. He said he made a pile of money by mixing it with corn leaves and horse dung. That was his little scam! He did me a big favour that day, because after that I no longer had the slightest desire to touch any drugs whatsoever. When cocaine came on the market, the pushers would mix it with powdered glass, bicarbonate of soda, scouring powder, and even cement, on one occasion. The poor guy who sniffed that mixture went through hell when the cement dust hardened on contact with the mucus in his nose — he ended up in a hospital emergency room.

But drugs didn't spare all the Baronets.

> Pierre Labelle was a sensitive guy, and very impression-
> able. From 1957 till 1965 everything went along just
> fine, until one day a member of the band suggested to
> Pierre that he try a little joint, using the classical argu-
> ment: "Just try it, it's magic, and it's not addictive." Like
> hell! I never believed that, and I still don't believe it.
> Unfortunately, in spite of my advice, Pierre got dragged
> down into drug hell at the time. He made me uneasy
> when he went on stage with glassy eyes. He claimed he
> performed better in that condition, but it wasn't true.

But if René had no problem with drugs or drink, on the other hand he'd been overeating for a long time.

> René has always been obsessed by his waistline. He had
> an ongoing rivalry with Pierre about their weight.
> They'd compete to see who could lose the most, the
> most quickly.
>   I advised Pierre and René to eat healthy food, but it
> upset them to hear me talking like that. I told them the
> body should be treated like a temple, so we shouldn't
> consume so many toxins. We should even find out what
> was in the food we consume.
>   René took an enormous mouthful of cake, looked
> at me laughing, let loose a resounding belch, and then
> said to me: "It's an old Arab custom to belch after a
> meal. It shows you've eaten well. It's good to have a bit
> of gas. Eating junk does the system good."
>   I was offended, and told myself the day of reckon-
> ing would come. And so it did.

At that time, in the 1960s, fans would join the famous fan clubs. All the popular artists, especially the men, could count on having the thou-sands of members of their fan club to keep up their popularity. Elvis

Presley started the trend, and singers in the 1960s went out of their way to cultivate their best audience: their fan clubs. The Baronets had one too, but they also had passionate admirers who asked for nothing better than to be seduced.

However, contrary to what you might expect, the Baronets didn't bed all the local wenches. At least, believe it or not, not in the beginning. Jean Beaulne explains:

> You've got to remember the circumstances. The contraceptive pill came on the scene in 1963. That was a hell of a revolution in morals. Until then, things weren't so easy with girls. You had to think twice before getting laid. We had rather inhibited relations with girls between 1958 and 1963. We had our first experiences in 1963 exactly, at Trois-Rivières. We were no angels, but back then there wasn't the kind of sexual freedom there is today. ...
>
> Before we started our show, we'd take a discreet peep through the curtain, looking all round the hall to spot girls. René and I chose one in the first row. René would say: "I bet you ten bucks I'll leave with the blonde in the front row." And when I was the one that went off with her, I'd say to him: "Don't forget, ten tomorrow morning!" — meaning he had to pay me the next day! I hardly need tell you that all through the show all our attention was focused on the girl the bet was about! The other girls couldn't understand why we ignored them. But we were only thinking of our ten dollars!
>
> René thought he was better looking, and told me I was too skinny. But when all's said and done we were evenly matched.

Basically it was neither love nor lust, but a contest. But Beaulne went much further on the subject of women. They made up the majority of their audience. The more the group's popularity grew, the more numerous and turned on they became.

"In our case, our careers forced us to cultivate them. Evening after evening our show had to seduce them. So we developed tricks with our eyes, sentimental songs, and special movements, and we'd approach some of them during the performance. And this went on every evening for years. At the time, you could have very lovely girls. René preferred the glamorous, luscious ones — the Marilyn Monroe type."

So what about women after all these years? "A woman needs a hero. There are all kinds of women. There are one-man women, women for doctors, for sailors, for crooks and for cops ... We saw the lot."

We could talk about this at length, but what was taking place among the Baronets' fans — and obviously the Beatles' and Elvis's, too — was the phenomenon of collective hysteria. Girls would actually pass out when the Baronets' craze was at its height in Quebec. They would weep and go into a trance. How can you explain that kind of phenomenon? Were these young women, who at the time were so excited by the Baronets, deranged in some way? Can we reach any conclusions about women based on that kind of behaviour?

THE SPIRITS

On one road trip, René made the late Jean Grimaldi (a producer of shows in the 1960s) really angry. Grimaldi, who was a spiritualist, had invited us, along with other artists on the road trip, to a séance at a round table in a dimly lit room. Grimaldi appeared with pencil and paper in hand, and solemnly declared that the spirits would speak through a medium, who was one of us. This individual would fall asleep and allow his hand to be guided over a sheet of paper as he wrote out whatever the spirits dictated to him. Grimaldi began the séance with a few words of gibberish addressed to the invisible powers. Not in the least impressed, René pretended to fall asleep, took the pencil that Grimaldi pushed into his hand, and wrote a few words. Beside himself with joy, Jean Grimaldi exclaimed, "We have a medium! We have a medium!" Then he grabbed the piece of paper and read out loud: "You piss me off!" He immediately left the room, yelling. It hardly needs to be said that he didn't speak to René again for at least three days!

JEAN BEAULNE

PIERRE'S SHOES

During one of our performances in a hall where the stage was higher than usual, our feet were level with the spectator's faces. From the first song the people began to laugh and whisper to one another, pointing at Pierre. When he saw this, René burst out laughing, fell to his knees, and stopped singing. He looked at me and pointed to Pierre Labelle's shoes. Pierre had forgotten to change his shoes after spending the day working in mud. As you can well imagine, they were anything but presentable! When this happened he left the stage in a huff, but we had a good laugh, along with the audience.

JEAN BEAULNE

16

HYSTERIA

During the Baronets' performances, young women reacted in a kind of collective hysteria. This was by no means a new phenomenon, for we saw spectacular manifestations of it during performances by Elvis Presley in his heyday, between 1956 and 1960, by Frank Sinatra in his early years, and, of course, by the Beatles around the same time. In fact the Beatles became victims of it, for they decided to stop performing on stage because the screams of their teenage admirers used drown out the sound system completely. The crowd would go delirious when the Beatles swayed their hips even a little bit, so they became cult figures, reduced to silence by the swarm of female admirers. The music itself had become superfluous.

The Baronets were no Beatles. In spite of this, at the height of the wave, the same behaviour emerged. In fact, during a TV program called *Jeunesse d'aujourd'hui* the fans screamed so loud that the noise covered the playback, so that the singers could no longer tell where they were in the song.

So how can we explain such hysterical behaviour?

The first thing we notice is that from Elvis to the Backstreet Boys it took the same form, invariably involving young girls, pubescent or otherwise, who were discovering unconscious emotional drives, generally of a sexual nature.

Freud, whom a lot of women consider the foremost male chauvinist of modern times, formulated a theory saying that the symptoms of hysteria result from a conflict between the social and ethical restraints placed on the individual and that person's repressed desires. However, it was attributed almost exclusively to women, for it is rarely diagnosed in males. Hysteria is among the least understood psychiatric ailments, and its status as a specific neurosis is often questioned.

The ancient Greeks explained the instability and excitability of somatic symptoms and fits of psychic disturbance found in some women as being a symptom of a supposed displacement of the uterus. This theory of the "wandering uterus" is what gave its name to hysteria — in Greek, *hysteria* means "uterus," the organ associated with pathological phenomena characterized by highly emotional behaviour. In the Middle Ages, but particularly during the Renaissance, hysteria was attributed to demonic possession and witchcraft, leading to the persecution of women.

In time this attitude became more nuanced. The term "collective hysteria" was used to describe situations where a large number of people exhibited the same kind of somatic symptoms without any physical cause. For example, a case of collective hysteria was recorded in the United States in 1977, when fifty-seven members of a school band suffered from headaches, nausea, dizziness, and fainting fits following a sporting event. After looking in vain for a physical cause, scientists concluded that a reaction to the heat suffered by a few members of the band had spread to the others by suggestion. Today people prefer the term "collective stress reaction" to designate this kind of phenomenon.

From these analyses, the idea of a "conflict between the individual's social and ethical constraints and a repressed desire" makes sense. In Quebec, most certainly, Elvis, the Beatles, and the Baronets did move young women to express this "repressed desire" in the form of a revolt they could allow themselves to express collectively — a revolt against the things they felt were stifling them: their parents, school, and society in general. In 1965 the pill was still new on the market, and women's lib was just beginning for many of them. Was it the first step towards a more general liberation? The question can be debated, but in the 1960s the phenomenon of collective hysteria existed on a scale that has no equivalent today. It was remarked on at the time, and discussed. And the phenomenon was a worldwide one, whereas today cases are more isolated.

17

FIRST LOVES

R ENÉ HAS ALWAYS BEEN DISCREET about his love affairs. We are only aware of a few relationships, but they were always lasting ones and played an important part in his life.

It was in 1961 that he met Denyse Duquette, when he was nineteen. She was almost the same age, very pretty and uncomplicated, and gave René a sense of security. She led a wholesome, orderly life, and loved nature.

When the Baronets' popularity exploded in 1963 she was still on the scene, living with René in his parents' home. He was earning a lot of money and would lend his Chrysler to his uncle Georges, but it never occurred to him to set up in an apartment with Denyse. He preferred to remain with his family. It was his world, his haven, where his roots were, and Denyse had to share it. The Angélils and the Saras were as united as ever, and would remain so. René couldn't make up his mind to leave home — particularly since he constantly had to be on the road and didn't have the time, or the wish, to worry about a place of his own. However, he was very much in love with this young woman, who allowed him all the liberty he wanted. She knew he was popular with women and that many of them came on to him, but she understood and accepted the situation. René appreciated Denyse's attitude and shared all his spare time with her.

He believed she was the woman of his life and that he couldn't live without her. But she was his biggest secret, for no one in the Baronets' circle knew of her existence. The two lovebirds were ready to get married, but in the 1960s singing stars couldn't marry without it costing them dearly. The Beau Brummel of the Baronets didn't even dare mention the possibility in front of his companions, and least of all to Ben Kaye, who would probably have thrown a fit.

But Joseph Angélil wasn't in show business and didn't see the situation in the same light. A man of high principles, he had difficulty accepting that his son and his companion were living together without being married — and especially under his roof! With his usual insouciance René went on with his road trips, leading a bachelor's liberated existence with the two other Baronets, allowing himself to be seduced. He had to keep up the pretence with his companions, or someone would have smelled a rat.

18

MARYSE

IN 1965, WHEN THE BARONETS were experiencing their finest hour, René made the acquaintance of a young singer who had tried to pursue a career using the name Maryse Marhall. She had competed in a lot of amateur talent contests, hoping to attract attention and to make some recordings, but there was a lot of competition and she failed to win the attention of any producers. She finally gave up and took work singing in a chorus. She had sung with the top artists in Quebec, on stage or in the recording studio. At the age of only eighteen she was working in the studios of Tony Roman, the producer for the Baronets and a lot of other artists.

René Angélil didn't just attract groupies and girls from the Baronets' fan club. At twenty-three he was a young man endowed with incredible charm who created havoc in the female heart. Maryse fell for him madly, and looked for every opportunity to meet him outside the recording sessions with Tony Roman. Her strategy was so successful that she was finally able to attract the handsome René's attention, for he wasn't indifferent to her charms. Head over heels in love, Maryse made every effort to seduce him, though she knew perfectly well he loved Denyse Duquette. She gave herself to him, tried to hold onto him and make him forget the woman he loved. It was no good. Maryse had a brief affair with this man who continued to fascinate her. She went on to suffer a great deal, doing more and more foolish things, as often happens with people who believe they have lost the great love of their life.

Then she met a new idol of the younger generation, Johnny Farago, who became a real star following his first appearance on the adolescents' favourite show, *Jeunesse d'aujourd'hui*. Johnny Farago sang French versions of Elvis Presley songs, and his first hit, "Je t'aime, je te veux," had already reached number one on the charts. Out of pique, and certainly looking for revenge, Maryse turned on her charm and had a brief affair with him — really as a caprice.

Shortly afterwards, she discovered she was pregnant. She was sure René was the father. What was she to do? Later she would say that she never told René about her condition because she knew he was head over heels in love with Denyse Duquette and would never leave her. Falling into a depression, she gave up her work as a backup singer and decided to bring up by herself the child she was expecting.

She gave birth to a perfectly healthy boy, and he grew up thinking he was René Angélil's son. By a strange coincidence he was born on the very day René Angélil married Denyse Duquette, on December 11, 1966, in Saint-Sauveur church in Montreal.

Her error would have its denouement twenty-nine years later.

"When I was young, I didn't think about any physical resemblance to my father. But as time went by, I began to have doubts," relates her son.

In 1995, Maxime Laplante (his mother's surname), knowing that his mother had had an affair with Johnny Farago, asked the latter to undergo a DNA test. Aware of the importance to him of knowing who his father was, Farago agreed. All doubt was removed: Farago was indeed the father. There was a touching reunion between them, and Johnny even thought of working with his son on a show.

But their time together would be short, for Farago succumbed to a heart attack in July 1997. René Angélil paid the costs of the funeral in memory of the past.

19

THE FIRST MARRIAGE

T HE PREPARATIONS FOR RENÉ ANGÉLIL'S wedding — he was twenty-four at the time — took place in an atmosphere of considerable paranoia. Leaks, indiscreet probing, and above all media attention, had absolutely to be avoided. This was quite an undertaking in the circumstances, for René was hugely popular in Quebec. He was known to the general public, who saw him constantly on television, in clubs, and in the newspapers. René went even further, concealing his marriage from his friends, especially from the other Baronets. This allowed the group's career to continue its normal course. The marriage was celebrated in the strictest privacy, with only his family members present after they had been sworn to complete secrecy.

Even if he was still in love with Denyse Duquette, René didn't see why he had to marry her. But he didn't have any choice. His father, who had never accepted his son's cohabitation, kept up the pressure for the union to be regularized. René had always found excuses to gain time and postpone the day, but he suddenly ran out of arguments. His father was sixty-three years old, and he didn't want to disappoint him yet again. Did he have a premonition that Joseph would be dead within a few months? People often have a presentiment of this kind of fatality without wanting to admit it.

The wedding brought great happiness to Joseph and Alice Angélil, who treated Denyse like their own daughter.

20

THE INTERNATIONAL
MARKET ALREADY

THE BARONETS ENJOYED IMMENSE POPULARITY in Quebec, but this didn't satisfy René, who dreamed of crossing borders and competing with the top American and British groups. René often discussed this with the other Baronets, who finally asked themselves, "Why not us?" Jean Beaulne too was dreaming of an international career, as was their manager, Ben Kaye. But how could they break into the American market? There were hardly any precedents. One Canadian group, The Diamonds, reached the top of the hit parade with "Little Darling," but weren't able to follow up on their success. Another group, the Beau-Marks, this time from Quebec, led by Ray Hutchisson, also managed to reach the top spot on the American charts with their hit single "Clap Your Hands." This group was also unable to produce a follow-up success.

The Baronets had been travelling to the United States to perform, but so far theirs couldn't really be called an international career. The pay was laughable compared to what the great recording artists and American TV performers could get. So it was imperative to make a record down in the U.S.

One day Jean Beaulne met an American producer, Al Kasha, from the Vee Jay record company. He was on the lookout for a group from Quebec. After the success enjoyed by the Beatles, foreign groups were in fashion, and Kasha told himself that a group from Quebec, with a French flavour, might win over the American public. Ben Kaye did not waste any time and set off to New York to meet Kasha.

Kaye, whose talents as a salesman had always impressed René, managed to interest Kasha sufficiently for an agreement to be reached without delay. So the Baronets travelled to New York and were soon preparing to record an album made up entirely of original American songs. It was for the Vee Jay label that the Four Seasons had recorded their greatest hits. In the mid-sixties Beatles frenzy was unleashed on America, bringing with it a host of British groups who took over from most of the American rock artists. Only the Beach Boys and the Four Seasons held their ground. With hits like "Big Girls Don't Cry," "Walk Like a Man," "Ronny," and "I've Got You Under My Skin," their sales surpassed the 50 million mark.

It was the manager of these top American stars, Bob Crew, who produced the Baronets' English-language record, aimed at a worldwide market, backed up by the most prestigious professionals on the New York musical scene (Charlie Calello, arranger and composer of songs; Brooks Arthur, Adam Sandler's present producer; Bob Gaudio, a member of the Four Seasons; and Al Kasha). René and his buddies were on cloud nine, and it looked as if all their dreams were about to come true. This time they seemed to be holding all the cards needed for success in the most lucrative market in the world. They were in New York — the city about which Frank Sinatra sang: "If you can make it there, you can make it anywhere." This made René realize the fundamental role specialists played in creating a good recording, and the value of a song. Once the recording was done the Baronets returned to Montreal to fulfil their engagements, having to wait for things to take their course and, perhaps, for international fame. The American dream was within their reach.

Weeks went by without any news. Suddenly, they learned that the Vee Jay record company had declared bankruptcy and all its operations had been suspended. So much for the Baronets' international career!

Anyone might think they could have repossessed the recording and turned it over to another company to relaunch the album. But it wasn't that simple, for in a bankruptcy all the material is seized, analyzed, and listed. After that, time is needed to recover assets — too much time for the Baronets, who also lacked the necessary financial means to start over again. There still exists an album from this episode that has never been played on the air. However, Jean Beaulne does own a copy, which he is keeping with future projects in mind.

This was a hard blow for the group, particularly René Angélil. But with the benefit of hindsight a lesson could be learned from this debacle. What distinguished René from his buddies and from those close to him was his ability to learn from any kind of event, even the most distressful, and take advantage of it. In his long climb to fame and fortune he would undergo the sternest trials and profit from them. Before winning — before carrying off the big prize — he would be a loser more often than most of his peers. Often, he would almost attain his objective, needing only a final signature or one last meeting, yet still not succeed. I'm not one of those who think René benefited from a lot of luck. A long series of disappointments was the price he paid for his success.

21

A PUNCH IN THE FACE

ONE MIGHT ALMOST THINK New York City was unlucky for René Angélil. It was a city where he was to suffer several disappointments and very unpleasant experiences. Jean Beaulne recalls one incident that testifies to the bad blood that existed between René and himself. Angélil had inspired many infatuations among the female sex, but so had Beaulne. This was New York, and the latter got a phone call from an attractive woman who had come to the Big Apple hoping to spend a few amorous days in his company. Beaulne was delighted, and took the opportunity to show his conquest the city. He hired a record player so that in his room he could play his admirer the recently completed recording for the Vee Jay label. So he set off to recover the machine and demo from René, to whom he had loaned them a few hours before. René refused, saying that he hadn't had time to listen to the recording. Jean insisted, but René still refused to give in. Beaulne picked up the machine, while René grabbed the cord hanging from it and pulled hard.

"Let go!" yelled Beaulne, red with anger. René pulled even harder, as if it was a tug-of-war. Beaulne, knowing that as always René wanted to have the last word and was quite prepared to break the machine, lost his temper and punched him in the face. René staggered, and Pierre and Ben Kaye, who witnessed the incident, quickly separated the two men.

In the end Jean Beaulne got to listen to his music in peace, and the incident was already forgotten by the next day. He explains:

It was the first time René and I came to blows. Even if neither of us was the sort of person to hold a grudge, or naturally aggressive, we did have forceful personalities, and were never stuck for a smart answer. The only other time I saw René fight was in a hotel lobby, with our bass player Gerry Legault, who had become very aggressive about a card game they'd played the night before. However, in the twelve years of our career together we did have several quarrels, for we were both quick-tempered.

At the time, René could only think about having fun, while I dreamed of an international career for the Baronets. I couldn't accept René's devil-may-care attitude. But, years later, when I was living in Santa Monica, in California, and I too was thinking only of having fun riding my bike and in-line skating and living the life of the Hollywood "night file," it would have been his turn to call me lazy!

When René took over Céline's career he became the passionate kind of person I was back then, so much that when people he was dealing with didn't agree with him he'd get angry. During his first years as a manager, he often praised his protégée's enormous talent, knowing all along that a lot of people didn't believe in his plans. People often told him he'd be better to drop the whole thing and that the girl would never succeed, for she had neither the looks nor the personality she would need to get to the top.

Now that René has settled down and Céline become a success, he has a better understanding of the meaning of life — like the person who once said: "Money can't buy happiness ... but only rich people know that!" His first priority is the loved ones around

93

him. He even told a journalist from a major daily how unimportant money and fame had become for him. Céline and René-Charles have become his only priority, and for them he would give up everything at the drop of a hat.

22

AT THE COMÉDIE-CANADIENNE

T HE BARONETS' POPULARITY WAS GROWING, and the group was
packing in the crowds in all the clubs where they performed. René,
Pierre, and Jean took advantage of their fame and were living high on
the hog. Each of them was earning as much as five thousand dollars a
week. They led a life of luxury: driving new cars, wearing the best
clothes, eating at gourmet restaurants, and staying in expensive hotels.
They even decided to buy three new, identical Pontiac Parisiennes. It
was a great marketing ploy, and Ben Kaye, their manager, was all in
favour of it. When the Baronets were doing a show the three cars could
be seen parked together at the door of the club like a trademark or
poster for the Baronets. Strangely, they never had to complain about
acts of vandalism by jealous young men or thieves. People respected the
group, whose members made no secret of their virility and banked on
self-mockery and humour. Everyone seemed to like the Baronets.

There were more and more gigs, and the trio was in demand everywhere — but tension was growing within the group. The three companions that fortune had brought together didn't appreciate the
increasing prevalence of violence in the clubs, or the drug trade, which
was now being carried on more and more openly. In addition, the
Baronets were tiring of their hectic existence, the smoke-filled rooms,

and the repetitious shows. Finally they met with Ben Kaye to discuss a suggestion made by Jean Beaulne: why not put the Classels (a very popular group in 1964) and the Baronets together on the same stage, with other groups as warm-up acts? The participation of the Classels, a group that considered themselves the Quebec equivalent of the Platters, wouldn't be a problem, since Ben Kaye was also their manager.

This was a new concept for Quebec. There was a lengthy discussion around the table, for there was some concern about putting two star groups on stage in the same show, since it could put the profitability of the venture at risk. But they decided to give the idea a try all the same.

No fewer than eighteen thousand people packed the Quebec Coliseum to see the big show. The event was a total success, and the Baronets were ecstatic when they returned to their dressing room after leaving the stage amid cries of "bravo" and applause. The experiment had worked, and it meant they could begin a new, much more profitable and less demanding routine than performing in clubs. It put an end to the lengthy tours, long hours, and the heavy, oppressive atmosphere of the nightclubs.

Still feeling euphoric, the Baronets got ready to share the take. A pile of beautiful green banknotes was put on the table, totalling $52,000. The Baronets were wide-eyed, the triumphant Jean Beaulne more than anyone — for after all the show had been his idea.

Suddenly, someone told Jean Beaulne that half the amount would first have to be paid to a co-producer, who had advanced the publicity and production costs. Beaulne turned pale. He was flabbergasted:

> No one ever said anything to me about this co-producer. They'd plotted behind my back, and the confidence I had had in Pierre, René, and Ben suddenly evaporated. I had been betrayed on the pretext that an investor was needed, and 50 percent of the receipts were going to someone I didn't even know. If at least someone had made me aware of the situation I'd have invested what was needed for the promotion myself, for I had so much faith in our popularity. My whole world collapsed. All those years of sacrifice, and now this! I was

in a terrible rage. They tried to tell me I'd been told about the situation, but there was no way they could convince me.

The Baronets' euphoria very soon evaporated, and an uncomfortable atmosphere pervaded the office in the Coliseum. Beaulne went over to Ben Kaye and said to him, squarely, "Starting from today, I'm going to manage. I'm going to plan my own future on my own. I've no confidence in you anymore. I'm still a Baronet, but I'm not going to be a full-time one. I'm going to keep my commitments, but I won't be putting the group first anymore. I have to think of Jean Beaulne's future."

Beaulne pocketed a much smaller amount than he had counted on and stormed out of the Coliseum without saying goodbye to anyone.

"Alone in my car, as I drove to Montreal, I shed bitter tears for three hundred kilometres, asking the good Lord why they didn't respect me more. I told myself I'd get my revenge by being more successful than they as a manager, and so I was."

If we had to put a date to the end of the Baronets, buddies and comrades in arms since their adolescent years, it would have to be on that night of December 11, 1964, for after that things were very different. People can argue about the events surrounding the production of the Coliseum show and cast new light on it, but the fact remains that one consequence of that evening was that one of the members of the group was severely wounded in his pride and dignity, and in his affections too. He would never recover from it.

Later, Beaulne hurried to rejoin his comrades in Montreal to rehearse for a show at the Comédie-Canadienne. An irony of fate decided that just as the Baronets were going through a tremendous rift, the greatest conflict of their collaboration, they were about to win ultimate recognition on the most prestigious stage in Quebec.

The Comédie-Canadienne, in 1964, was Montreal's Carnegie Hall, the equivalent of the Paris Olympia. It was where Jacques Brel, Gilbert Bécaud, Charles Aznavour, and countless other top artists put on unforgettable shows. It was the temple of French and Quebec song in Montreal. Only the biggest names appeared there. For the Baronets, it was an extraordinary piece of luck, an opportunity to take their place beside the most prestigious artists in the country. It was absolutely essential to forget recent events and rehearse the sketches and songs one last time. The tension between the three members of the group was at its height. But no one around the Baronets' circle was aware of their problems, and they agreed to concentrate on this particularly important show.

Wearing brand new tuxedos, backed up by fifteen musicians under Georges Tremblay, they performed to a particularly enthusiastic audience. Friends and relatives sat in the front rows. People too faint-hearted to go to see them in clubs were there. The Baronets wanted to have class, prestige, and a better reputation in the business, and now their wishes were coming true.

The premiere succeeded beyond their wildest dreams. If Jean Beaulne was sick at heart and secretly licked his wounds, it didn't show on stage. The group was humorous, charming, very professional, well prepared, and the audience couldn't get enough of them.

Anyone would have thought it was all sweetness and light in the Baronets' dressing rooms after the show. Beaulne even allowed himself to make a joke: "It's the first time I haven't heard someone I know from the audience tell me 'Chuck it in. There's no future for you in this line of work'!"

He adds, "It was the best moment in the Baronets' career. My best memory."

René was euphoric: "Recognition at last!" The critics were almost unanimous in their praise, and the group was on top of the world — particularly since a few months later they attracted no less then sixty thousand people to Jarry Park for the celebration of St. Jean Baptiste Day, the Quebec national holiday.

René couldn't imagine that one day there might no longer be any Baronets. He thought the group would be able to adapt to every change in fashion. He wasn't the sort of person to cause a break-up, and that was how he would be for the rest of his life. At twenty-two he was still living in his parents' house and still had the same friends. Jean Beaulne told him he wouldn't be with the group much longer, but René didn't take him seriously.

23

DISCORD

B Y THE END OF 1965 there were reports in the specialized press about the increasingly tense atmosphere between the members of the Baronets. Their disputes could even be overheard in the corridors of the Casa Loma or the National Theatre, where they appeared regularly. Pierre Labelle and René Angélil accused Jean Beaulne of neglecting the group and spending time on the careers of other artists. Jean Beaulne accused Pierre Labelle and above all René Angélil of being lazy, of leaving all the administrative chores to him, and of failing to take the group's career seriously. Jean Beaulne had lost faith in the Baronets.

Ben Kaye attempted to reconcile the members of the group. He listened to the arguments from all sides and made them promise to be more disciplined. It was a promise they wouldn't keep for long, and things fell apart again. As in any conflict, it's hard to know who was really to blame. René Angélil too was interested in managing. He had already taken charge of the career of a young singer named Mugette, and it was he who had discovered the Classels. Ben Kaye became the manager of this group, while Jean Beaulne had discovered the Monstres (of which Marc Hamilton, the first French Canadian to have a number one hit in France, was a member), the Bel Cantos, and the Bel-Airs. René Angélil wasn't the only member of the group to show initiative and leadership qualities. He had a serious rival whose instincts had led him to discover some singers who would enjoy considerable success in the following years. This situation couldn't continue, and a decision had to be taken about the Baronets' future.

Pierre Labelle, who didn't have a mean bone in his body, kept out of the quarrel, but instinctively sided with René, his childhood friend. Ben Kaye didn't know whose side to take, but finally allowed René to convince him it would be best to replace Jean.

But no one had the courage to tell the person in question that he was no longer a Baronet. He was devastated and deeply wounded when he learned it from the newspapers. Truth to tell, he wasn't expecting it, despite the considerable friction within the group.

Jean Beaulne was replaced by the very young guitarist Jean-Guy Chapados, who had already played with the group several times. So that is how the Baronets became the "Nouveaux Baronets." The group went on tour, made a few recordings, and gave itself a new look that didn't seem to appeal. Their female admirers could see that the chemistry had changed and the image of the Baronets been watered down. The Nouveaux Baronets' popularity was in a steady decline, and René was worried.

Things got worse when Jean Beaulne sued his former group for fifty thousand dollars for using the Baronets name without his permission. René, who had once thought of studying law, was asked to deal with the matter. He prepared the case for the defence and tried to discredit his former companion, but the judge decided for the latter. In June 1966, the Nouveaux Baronets were ordered to pay him fifty thousand dollars, or else no longer use the name.

Pierre and René didn't want to pay out that kind of money, particularly since the group wasn't a great success.

It was René who called Jean Beaulne to arrange a meeting. He asked him to rejoin the group and take his place like before.

"We made a mistake," he admitted. "Let's forget the past and start over."

Jean asked for time to think about it. René, who never gives up, went back to see him every week for two months. He promised that he and Pierre would be more disciplined, work harder during rehearsals, and stop turning up late all the time.

Jean did finally agree to come back, on two conditions: that the name "Baronets" become his property, and that he manage the group. Beaulne didn't want to keep any business connections with Ben Kaye, whom he considered a good salesman but a poor strategist.

24

1967

I N 1967, MONTREAL WAS HOSTING Expo. All of Quebec was busily preparing to play host to the millions of visitors expected from around the world. The Quebecois, who had been very inward looking ever since the Conquest, were at last opening their homes to a great number of visitors needing accommodation, for the hotels didn't have enough rooms. Cultures were mingling, getting to know one another, and Quebec was changing and becoming more liberal. Restaurants and clubs closed later at night. Alcohol licences became easier to obtain. People celebrated with all the other nationalities, and the sense of a common humanity was never warmer in Montreal and all over Quebec.

Feeling pride in themselves and eager to attune themselves to international culture, the Quebecois wanted to be seen and heard. They were spending money on the arts and on their own music, and singers like Charlebois, Vigneault, and Léveillée sang about their own people in words and music.

Pop groups also took part in this awakening, and people listened to the Hou-Lops, the Sultans, César et ses Romains, the Sinners, and other groups, each more creative than the next.

The Beatles had revolutionized pop music once and for all, and a new creative generation had taken control of the industry. In 1967 the Fab

Four went even further. The launch of the album *Sgt. Pepper's Lonely Hearts Club Band* made a real cultural impact. One song on the album, "A Day in the Life," announced nothing less than a musical revolution.

The Baronets, who had achieved their fame with versions of the Beatles' early hits, could no longer keep pace with their mentors. Indeed very few could bear comparison with the Beatles in 1967.

In fact, the Baronets had been left behind by the musical tide and by a good number of new groups, even if Jean Beaulne's return gave them a fresh start. But they wouldn't throw in the towel so easily, and gave one of their best performances to celebrate their comeback. At first they had thought of the Comédie-Canadienne, but it was in the Café de l'Est, before a full house, that the three Baronets triumphed in March 1967.

The day after this successful reunion, René, who had celebrated very late into the night, found he couldn't open the door to the bathroom in the family home. Someone inside was very still, giving no signs of life. René stepped back, launched himself, and burst in the door. His father was lying on the floor, no longer breathing. At the age of sixty-four, as unobtrusive as ever, he had quietly taken his leave.

René suddenly realized what a gulf there had been between them, and suffered more than ever to think of it. He blamed himself for disappointing his father, for failing to understand him, and for never having told him he loved him. The loss of a father makes you see things differently.

25

FATHERHOOD

JEAN BEAULNE'S RETURN TO THE Baronets was supposed to mean better times. But in fact the group was slowly falling apart, with René and Pierre keeping to themselves, isolating Jean and clinging to the world of cabaret.

However, 1968 began with some good news. René became a father with the birth of a son, named Patrick. His wife, Denyse Duquette, gave birth on January 28, 1968, and René was beside himself with joy. He was so happy about the event that this time he wanted to share the good news with his friends and acquaintances. This was how everyone learned that René was a father, and that he was in fact a married man. It came as quite a surprise to the Baronets, who hadn't suspected a thing. When you think about it, his wasn't a foolish strategy. How could he have aroused any suspicions, hiding his wife away and living with her in his parents' house? Unlike other young married couples who usually leave home immediately after the wedding, the Angélil couple had stayed put, shielded by the family. René could travel, have fun, and work late, yet he never left his wife on her own.

After Patrick's birth René devoted himself to this new role and spent some time watching his son develop. The tiny infant helped him recover from the loss of his father a year earlier, as if he was regaining his equilibrium and reason for being.

His career with the Baronets went on, but he could see that they couldn't go any further. Routine was already setting in, and there was no major new project on the horizon. Jean Beaulne had announced he was going to leave the group one or two years after rejoining it in 1967, and he did indeed distance himself from it in 1969: "Seeing that my companions lost their ambition and didn't welcome my ideas with any great enthusiasm, I preferred to keep them to myself and use them for the groups I was managing."

And it was at this time that Jean Beaulne said to René, exasperated by his lack of concern and devil-may-care attitude, with his mind entirely on gambling, "You're so lazy you can never succeed in life."

It was a remark he'd regret later, for reasons that are obvious today.

Beaulne's business prospered in 1969, when he was managing the careers of the Bel Cantos and the Bel-Airs, among others, and planning a European tour. The Bel Cantos in particular were having considerable success singing original songs, and this won them an invitation to the Universal Exhibition in Osaka, Japan. The Bel-Airs were able to climb to the top of the charts, and Beaulne was earning four times as much as a personal manager than as a performer. His career would subsequently be littered with successes that won him little recognition, however. Always on the lookout for future stars, he was the first, through his talent show, to discover Mario Pelchat, André-Philippe Gagnon, and Marina Orsini. Beaulne wrote a book on the entertainment industry in Quebec, the only study of its kind in the 1970s, which was recognized by Quebec's Ministry of Cultural Affairs and distributed in school libraries. And, ultimately, it was he who managed the Baronets' career more than it seemed, something René Angélil would never admit, for he shut out Jean Beaulne the way he would later do to Paul Lévesque, Céline Dion's first manager.

26

THE END OF THE BARONETS

I T WAS THE BEGINNING OF the end for the Baronets. A decline was setting in. The group was performing more and more in clubs, and
Beaulne, who now managed the group, squeezed the lemon dry while
there was still time. He had no illusions about his on-stage companions,
who seemed to have no artistic ambitions. Jean Beaulne recalls this time
with nostalgia and resignation:

> I hoped that Peter and René would change, but I didn't
> really believe it. Their bad habits were so ingrained. ...
> My heart was in that group, and I was still foolish
> enough to think we might have a career in the United
> States. I was dreaming. We made a comeback, which
> should have been at the Comédie-Canadienne, but
> since not everyone could agree it took place in the Café
> de l'Est. It was a success and we started working in
> clubs again. There was more of an effort, but the group
> wasn't evolving, and it was the same old routine. My
> presence on stage, even if it didn't change the show, was
> enough to sell the group for a few years more. I wasn't
> happy in this situation, and in the end I could only

think about earning some money until it became impossible to market the group any longer.

The clubs were also in decline after the euphoria of Expo in Montreal. In television, private networks that employed many variety artists were growing. Large theatres were becoming more numerous, and the clubs now attracted only a low-grade clientele, often made up of fringe elements and criminals, so that violence became endemic in most of them.

One evening, in a club, the Baronets were interrupted during the show. A rather unsavoury character seated near the stage was talking at the top of his voice. He was telling anybody willing to listen that he'd just come out of jail. He was in the company of three disreputable-looking young women. He suddenly stood up and aimed a revolver at the Baronets' drummer. The four hundred spectators were frozen in their places, and complete silence fell in the room: "Listen, drummer! If you don't make less noise, I'm going to shoot! Understood?"

Beaulne took the drummer, Michel, by the arm and led him to his dressing room, signalling to the others to carry on. Satisfied with the group's reaction and pleased to have created a disturbance, the gangster sat down and raised his glass of champagne in a toast to his companions.

Other similar incidents occurred throughout 1969. Beaulne recalls one rather sensitive porter who didn't always appreciate his jokes. Seeing Beaulne wearing an expensive fur coat, he said to him, "If you weren't wearing that, I'd steal it from you."

"Watch out! I've got submachine guns!" the Baronet said playfully, opening his coat.

The porter then held his revolver to Jean's right eye.

"Please not in my right eye; it's the better one," Beaulne joked to get out of the scrape.

So then the porter put the weapon against his left eye.

"Oh no!" exclaimed Jean, trying to defuse the situation. "One's no good without the other!"

Then he sat down a little way off, still trembling from this ordeal that could have cost him his life.

In the end no harm was done, and the porter put his weapon back in its holster with a smile. But it's terrible to have to earn your life like that.

Despite all that, explains Beaulne, Pierre and René seemed to be content with their lives:

> It was as if they'd settled in for life. When René came to see me to get me to rejoin the group I knew he was saying whatever came into his head, but I thought that if I became the group's manager I'd be able to change him. I was dreaming. He just wanted to get me back so that the old routine could continue.
>
> But in those days he had no ambition. He only thought about gambling. There was no sign of the genius he would call on in dealing with Céline. If he'd shown that kind of genius with the Baronets we'd have been an extraordinary team and succeeded in the United States. It was in dealing with Céline that his talent would emerge and he'd bring off his big coup.
>
> A group like the Baronets had to be united, but that wasn't the case. René had no faith in the group because he had no faith in himself as a singer.

The Baronets weren't working as much any more, and Jean Beaulne took advantage of this to work on the careers of the groups he was managing. Now and again he'd meet up with his comrades, but the old magic was gone. The Baronets were dying. Pierre and René had rehearsed an act that was supposed to last between five and ten minutes that started out with comedy, but then the two of them launched out on a long improvisation during the act, leaving Beaulne hanging about on stage for fifteen or twenty minutes. They were going too far.

One day René called Beaulne to tell him about a contract they'd been offered to perform at the Rainbow Club in the east of the city, on Rue Notre Dame. It was probably one of the most unsavoury clubs at the time — a real dive that put on low-grade shows for equally low-grade audiences.

Beaulne finally agreed, but with an idea firmly at the back of his mind. On that day, December 12, 1969, a day he would never forget, he went to the Rainbow, where he met the owner shortly before the ten-thirty show. He made a proposal to him.

"I'm leaving the group this evening because I'm due to leave soon on a tour of Europe and Japan with my artists. If you're willing to take on René and Pierre as a twosome you'll save a third of the fee and you'll have just as good a show. They've enough material to last a good hour."

The owner accepted the plan on condition Beaulne stay by him throughout the entire show. If the show was good he'd keep René and Pierre on for the whole week.

Jean Beaulne went down to the other two Baronets in their dressing room to tell them he was leaving, thinking they'd be pleased, for they had become used to working as a duo during the previous few months.

Pierre swallowed and showed no reaction when he heard the news. René jumped up in a rage and, flushed with anger, ordered Jean: "Go and get changed for the show, do you hear me?"

"I don't have to take any orders from you. Nobody can make me do what I don't want."

Beaulne told René in no uncertain terms where to get off, and René went for him. The two almost came to blows before Pierre separated them.

"Afterwards, I watched the show," recounts Beaulne. "For the first time I understood the important place I had in René's life. Even after all the quarrels we had, he was attached to me. He suddenly felt lost. The Baronets were his security blanket. He lacked confidence in himself and in his abilities. As for me, I couldn't imagine how he could be attached to living like this in bars, as if nothing else existed in the world. He couldn't see the degradation, or the miserable future that awaited us with this group that had become unable to evolve."

Then a film suddenly flashed by inside his head. There was a sequence of sad but amusing mental pictures. He saw René and Pierre back again at Saint-Viateur School, imitating their teachers and making him laugh. He saw René, in the heyday of their career, stopping his brand new car on the road at three o'clock one morning and getting out. He prostrated himself in front of the car, which was stopped in the middle of the road, and began to recite prayers in Arabic and sing songs from his country of origin.

"What on earth are you doing?" asked the young Beaulne.

"I'm celebrating my new car's first thousand miles."

That time, Beaulne laughed himself silly.

He saw another scene, on a road in the United States. It was very late at night, and the three Baronets were driving to Montreal. Sitting in the back, René had decided to read out the names of all the companies whose products were advertised on the billboards along the road. "Coke, Maxwell House, Texaco, Wonder Bra, Lipton, Mobil Oil, Chrysler, Pepsi, American Airlines, Orange Crush, *The New York Times*, Chevrolet, Marlboro, Dr. Pepper …"

"Listen, you've been reading out the ads for half an hour now. That'll do, okay?" said Pierre Labelle.

"… Woolworth's, Dodge, Shell, Kentucky, Minute Rice, Austin, A & W, Sony, Neilson, Studebaker …"

"Come on, that makes an hour now," pointed out Beaulne, who had also had enough of it.

"… Kleenex, Seven-Up, *The Wall Street Journal* …"

Pierre and Jean looked at one another in despair, almost driven out of their minds, and then burst out laughing.

"How stubborn he could be," thought Beaulne. "How pigheaded!"

He did some mental calculations. They had been together for almost twelve years, laughing together, tearing one another apart, sometimes feeling a soft spot for one another without ever admitting it — and getting along so badly they would come to detest one another, but soon forget all about it.

Then Jean returned to reality. Pierre and René were funny. Jean laughed, maybe a little too loudly, to influence the owner. But it was over. He didn't want to see the Baronets in such a dump ever again.

After the show the owner agreed to hire the new Baronets duo. Beaulne went to see his former companions for the last time, leaving them his suit. Later, René and Jean would meet and maintain a sort of friendship, but right then René had to think about his future.

René and Pierre decided to go on performing as a duo. From then on there would be just two Baronets.

When she was born on March 30, 1968, Céline came into the world as if on her way to a show. She was constantly immersed in a musical atmosphere, for the Dion clan was a family of performing artists. Her mother, Thérèse, played the violin, and her father, Adhémar, the accordion, while her brothers and sisters, Denise, Clément, Claudette, Liette, Michel, Louise, Jacques, Ghislaine, Linda, Manon, and the twins, Paul and Pauline, were all talented at singing or playing an instrument. By the age of five, Céline already knew several songs and even sang at her brother Michel's wedding. She was so pampered and cosseted by her family that her first day at school couldn't possibly go smoothly.

It was a shock! The little girl didn't take to school. Without music, school didn't interest her. Worse, her schoolmates laughed at her when she told them she wanted to be a singer when she grew up and nick-named her "Vampire" because of her long teeth. The only way her parents could think of to help her per-severe with school was to allow her to sing in their bar, Le Vieux Baril, on condition she promised to rise early the next day to go to school.

Although she didn't attend school for long, Céline has learned a lot in the school of life, surrounded by adults whose gift and love for music she also inherit-ed. Coming from a modest, honest, and exemplary family, she learned from it the admirable values she stands for today.

JEAN BEAULNE

27

RENÉ IN THE MOVIES

Now the two long-standing friends launched out on a new adventure: acting in movies. After the success of *Valérie*, *L'Initiation*, and other films like them, a lot of movies were being made in Quebec — mostly comic or erotic ones. So it was that René and Pierre made their film début in a comedy called *L'Apparition* and in an erotic movie called *Après-ski*.

Roger Cardinal, the director, knew the Baronets by name only. Quebec popular music and groups meant very little to him. Pierre Labelle and René Angélil were to play just minor parts in a comic scene. Being busy on the set, Cardinal didn't waste any time explaining to the two buddies what they had to do: "You, René, are going to be the comic, and you, Pierre, the straight man. I can't talk to you for long, for I've got to get back to shooting."

René and Pierre didn't know what to do: Cardinal was reversing their usual roles. They waited for two hours in a little room set up on the set before Cardinal returned, for he thought they had gone home.

"Can I speak to you, M. Cardinal?" asked Angélil. "You see, on stage, I'm the straight man and Pierre's the comic."

"Well, guys, that's not the way I see it. I'd rather you played the comic," answered Cardinal.

"But that's not what we do professionally," insisted René.

"Okay, then! Do what you like and we'll work something out together."

They made another movie because Cardinal had liked their act and their attitude on the set. This time Cardinal was directing *L'Apparition*, a film for which René and Pierre had written the scenario. René had turned to Roger Vallée for financial backing for the comedy. Camille Adam had initially been the director, and Roger Cardinal was redoing it from the beginning. The production was a continuous laughfest, and Cardinal still remembers the tricks the two buddies used to play on him:

> In cahoots with the technicians, they deliberately screwed up scenes, suddenly forgetting their lines or dropping a reflector during the filming, and I fell for it completely. They were filming me all the time. They were first-rate comedians. At the time, almost nothing was working out for René anymore. He had been through two divorces, and was out of money. I'd lend him money to eat, and even give him somewhere to sleep. But he was always smiling. He always said things would sort themselves out.
>
> His ultimate objective at the time was to go into acting, and I must say René could have done it. He was good-looking and talented, and could very well have acted in dramatic comedies. He really wanted to become an actor, and then he'd have married Barbra Streisand instead of Céline Dion!

The two films Pierre and René acted in didn't have the hoped-for success and were completely savaged by the critics. It was fortunate the two buddies had been paid and had had fun themselves during the filming, because neither of these movies made it into the history books.

This episode in his life didn't last long, and René apparently forgot his dream of becoming an actor.

Next Pierre and René went back on stage for a while. They were singing less and less and turning more and more to comedy.

Now it was Pierre Labelle's turn to complain about his partner's lack of commitment.

Having become a real gambler, René was playing cards and never missed an opportunity to bet on a hockey game or even on bowling. It was a bad time for him. His luck seemed to have run out completely. He even tried to bring off a major coup, assuring Pierre and some of the Baronets' musicians that their fortunes would be made in the Caesar's Palace casino using another of his infallible systems. The Baronets squandered several thousands of dollars on this venture. The group's guitarist, Jacques Crevier, remembers it well:

> René had met someone who told him he had an infallible system for playing roulette. All you had to do was apply the system scrupulously for a certain time, and you were bound to win. René was always very strong in math, and he'd always been a gambler. It all clicked in his mind. He couldn't wait to try out his infallible method, so here in Quebec he bought a roulette wheel like the ones in the casinos. We began to test the system. We were doing a show at the time in a hotel in Saint Jérôme, and after we came off stage we'd practise with the roulette table. René was getting to understand the system better and better, and week after week we got together in the hotel room, thinking that one day the famous system would break down. But no! It worked! We didn't lose! Sometimes the numbers didn't come up, but according to the system you doubled your bet the second time around and then you won. That way you recouped your losses. It was a sure thing, mathematically.
>
> We used René's memory, which was phenomenal. You needed two people to play, one to lay the bets and the other to keep the statistics. René was in charge of the statistics. Since it always worked, we began to fantasize. We told ourselves that with our system we'd do far better than in show business. We thought we'd go and play in all the casinos everywhere: two would travel to

Monaco and two to Las Vegas, and that way we'd make piles of money. One day, René came up with a brilliant idea: we'd take a trip to Las Vegas. Each of us had to put in one thousand dollars, which was a lot of money at the time, making a total of four thousand dollars — the amount required for the scheme. We agreed that two of us would go to begin with. But we had to decide who it would be. René would be one, of course, but who else? Pierre wasn't a gambler, and I was too intimidated to go and bet so much money. So we decided on Carlo, the group's drummer. He often played cards with René, and had never left Montreal. He was excited at the idea of going to Las Vegas and couldn't wait to get going.

Once they arrived the two guys called to tell us they'd won twelve hundred dollars. They went for a week. Back in Montreal, we were telling ourselves: "Don't say we're going to have to start travelling as well. But will we be able to apply the system?" For it was very mathematical, very complicated. Then, after a few days, they started to lose. We couldn't understand it, for the system was supposed to be infallible. What was going on? They'd forgotten one thing: the roulette wheel they were using back home wasn't exactly the same as the one in Las Vegas. We had a roulette wheel with a 0, but there they had one with a 00 as well. That was what we'd missed. So we lost everything. They ended up laughing at it, and at themselves. That was René's baptism of fire in Las Vegas. But when we realized we'd lost so much of money, we freaked out.

One evening, Pierre and René were doing a show in some rather sleazy joint. The magic was completely gone, the two of them were tense and sick of things, so in the end it was Pierre, the likeable, good-natured Pierre, usually so easy-going, who reached a decision and sounded the group's death knell: "It's no use any more, René! That's enough! Let's call it a day!"

René dug in his heels to the very last minute. There is every reason to think he would never have given up on the Baronets. He never does give up, even when it's a lost cause — and that's what it had become.

The break-up of the group became official in 1973, but really the Baronets ceased to exist that very evening. It was a sad one, and a sad show. René, faithful to the end, was the last to cling to the group.

But the thirty-year-old had to accept the inevitable. He didn't have what it took to pursue a performing career. He remembered how he had once been an attraction, idolized by teenage girls, and how sometimes the screams and applause went to his head. But the 1960s were past, like the best of his youth. His mother had paid his gambling debts, and he thought about trying his luck in a different field.

28

GUY CLOUTIER

After the break-up of the Baronets, Pierre Labelle turned to comedy and was already working up a solo act. Jean Beaulne was devoting himself entirely to being a manager, and René Angélil turned to a manager named Guy Cloutier. The two men had known one another for several years, and René was sure that Cloutier had the necessary qualities to initiate him into the profession and help him add to the experience he had already gained from watching Jean Beaulne and Ben Kaye. In addition, Guy was a friend, a good guy, and, above all, someone who made him laugh. He found him as entertaining as Pierre Labelle. But Cloutier was more ambitious, with more get up and go, and that was an asset.

He was one the people who left their mark on René Angélil. So let's take a look at this show business phenomenon, who deserves our attention.

Born in Alma in 1942, Guy Cloutier is a natural organizer. At school, he arranged dances and group outings, and after graduating it didn't take him long to become the owner of a record store, La Maison du Palmarès. By the time he was twenty, his business was one of the most prosperous in Alma. Even without recognizing it, he was already a formidable record promoter. To make his business profitable, he pestered the radio stations in the region to get them to play the new records he was getting from Montreal. He was constantly on the watch for anything new in the way of songs, knew the itinerary of every performer's tour, and kept a huge stock of 45s and albums.

It was at the hotel in Alma that he first met the Baronets in 1963, and soon he became close friends with the group. Fascinated by the entertainment world, Cloutier wanted to get closer to the capital, for his record store had just gone bankrupt. But this wasn't as easy as he thought. Starting over from nothing, for a while Cloutier had to live a life of poverty. He was always with the Baronets; in fact, while times were tough for him he stayed with the band members, first in the Angélil house and then in Pierre and Jean's. Then he found a job in Tony Roman's recording studio. Starting out as a man Friday for the Baronets for pay of $150 a week, Cloutier, who was dynamic and endowed with exceptional initiative, became a promotion man and producer for the Canusa label — a company that issued many hits during the 1960s.

Later, Cloutier wanted to broaden his scope by managing the careers of promising artists. That was how he noticed the young René Simard, who had dazzled everyone on the Quebec TV program *Les Découvertes de Jen Roger*.

Cloutier, who remembered the phenomenal career of Joselito in Europe, thought that René Simard would turn into a real goldmine and had the potential to become a big star in Quebec, if he had a good manager. He didn't waste any time in meeting his parents and signing an agreement with them.

René Simard was only nine at the time, and Cloutier made a star of him in under a year. All that was needed for the young singer to become the darling of the Quebec public was an album, entitled *Ave Maria*, and a hit song, "L'Oiseau." He was in demand for television performances, specials were already being devoted to him, and he even put on a successful performance at the Montreal Forum when just ten years old.

It was with René Simard that Guy Cloutier demonstrated the undeniable qualities as a manager that made such an impression on René Angélil. The history of Quebec show business will relate how Guy Cloutier was able to manage the performing career of a young boy without ever endangering his best interests and without exploiting him financially, the way many other managers did. Quite to the contrary,

Cloutier protected the young René Simard like his own son. All his earnings went into a trust controlled by the Quebec public trustee and frozen until René reached the age of majority, making him a millionaire at the age of eighteen.

Cloutier, along with Beaulne and Kaye, practically invented the profession of artists' manager in Quebec. Never before had a businessman devoted himself to an artist. He not only negotiated his protégé's contracts, but also looked after his education, clothes, food, leisure activities, and budget.

René Angélil watched him and learned. By now he was working for Guy Cloutier, helping him manage the other artists under contract to him, including Patrick Zabé and Johnny Farago. He took a particular interest in the career of Anne Renée, and succumbed to her charm. She was a particularly pretty, vivacious young singer who had some success with her recordings of French-language versions of American songs, including "Band of Gold" (as "Le Jonc d'amitié") and "Puppy Love" (as "Un amour d'adolescent").

The affair had gone on for several years before it occurred to René to get a divorce from Denyse Duquette. He was madly in love with Anne, but he was married and father to Patrick, now aged five. In the end it was Denyse herself who asked for a divorce, on July 21, after René left their conjugal residence in Saint-Léonard on April 14, 1972. It came through on June 12 of the following year. The High Court granted the plaintiff custody of Patrick and sentenced Angélil to pay her alimony of sixty dollars a week, payable in advance each Friday at the plaintiff's residence.

René was only waiting for the official divorce papers to come through to celebrate a civil marriage with Anne-Renée Kirouac a few days later, on June 23, 1973. The bride was twenty-three, and René was thirty-one. A son, Jean-Pierre, was born to this union on March 23, 1974, exactly nine months after the wedding.

So Denyse Duquette disappeared from René Angélil's life. A discreet person, far from the media, she now leads a quiet life with a man from the Drummondville area.

Angélil took more and more interest in the career of another René, René Simard, when he learned that this young darling of Quebec mamas had been invited to take part in the Yamaha World Popular Song

Festival in Tokyo — an event that brings together the most promising young singers from all over the world.

He had received the invitation after scoring a success in Paris, in the first half of Daniel Guichard's show. René Angélil accompanied Cloutier and Simard to Tokyo, where the fourteen-year-old singer triumphed, carrying off first prize in this prestigious competition. The trophy was presented by the great Frank Sinatra, in 1974.

Cloutier and Angélil were on cloud nine. They stayed on a few days in Tokyo to celebrate, and they took advantage of the opportunity to plan a splendid strategy. They couldn't wait to get going on it. "Guy, it's now or never!" exclaimed René. "We've got to think big! Even Sinatra's crazy about him. We've got to try the States, right away. The kid's hot everywhere!"

René Simard made a recording in Japanese, which was played on the air in Tokyo. The lad charmed everyone with his soprano voice and open, happy face. He had just the right image to appeal to the Americans.

The two lost no time getting to work. First of all they told an American journalist that René Simard had sold more records in Quebec than the Beatles and Elvis Presley combined. The article was picked up in the prestigious *Wall Street Journal*, and René Simard was beginning to make a name for himself in American show business circles.

It was mostly Angélil who was behind this campaign, using the style advocated by Ben Kaye, the Baronets' former manager, who had marketed the group as if it was the top one in America. René had learned from Kaye never to hesitate to boast of an artist's qualities. So, René Simard became nothing less than the most promising singer in all America, Frank Sinatra's protégé, and a bigger seller than the Beatles and Elvis. Actually, all Sinatra had done was present the trophy, and over a brief period Simard had indeed sold more records than the Beatles or Elvis. But the important thing was to strike when the iron was hot — and strike hard. And the Americans swallowed it.

Delighted at the success of their publicity campaign, the two managers set off to New York to meet representatives from the recording company CBS. To facilitate negotiations with the company's representatives it occurred to Angélil to employ the services of Walter Haford, the lawyer who represented the Beatles in New York. The two were very pleased with themselves, imagining the deal was in the bag, and that the meeting, scheduled to take place in a New York restaurant, would only be a formality.

Guy Cloutier didn't speak very good English, so it was Angélil who took the initiative in communicating with Haford, the lawyer, to let him know what the young prodigy was asking for.

So Haford informed the representatives of CBS that nothing under $1 million would be needed for the star from Quebec to sign a contract. Angélil had managed to convince his partner that asking for such a large sum would impress the people from CBS. "Think big" — that was René Angélil's secret.

But that wasn't at all how the people from CBS saw things. They finished their meal without reacting, saying they'd think it over … and nothing more was heard from them. Angélil had lost his gamble; the bluff had failed.

However, the two men persisted, deciding to have René Simard make a record in English, aimed at the American market and financed by them. It turned out to be a miserable failure, and as a result a unique opportunity in his life as a performer — the opportunity to become an international star — slipped between René Simard's fingers. Very little would have been needed to bring this about — just a better approach to the major players in American show business and greater familiarity with the international market.

René Simard would make some impact in the U.S. when he appeared in a few TV variety shows, and later with Liberace in Las Vegas. CBS, however, would certainly have opened the doors to a real international career for him, providing original songs and a team that would have propelled him to the top.

It was a bitter defeat, but the lesson would prove useful later on. René Angélil would never forget that an international career is built up gradually, prudently, and even with humility, and with the support of multinational companies.

For the time being, the thirty-two-year-old was at a loss, and things were not going well between him and his partner. The failure to make a breakthrough in America created a chill between the two. The venture had required a substantial investment, which turned out to be a total loss, and there was no other project to breathe fresh life into their collaboration.

In any case, Angélil was beginning to have doubts about their association. After investing everything in Guy Cloutier's business, Angélil thought he deserved to be a full partner and receive 50 percent of the company's profits. It was his wife, already an experienced businesswoman, who encouraged him to demand his slice of the pie.

This part played by Anne Renée allows us to see a René Angélil very different from the powerful, dominating personality he has become today.

When 1975 came to an end, René was still an easy-going, undisciplined individual who was having fun and hadn't yet found his direction. He was Guy Cloutier's employee as well as his friend, and could see that his scope was limited. He didn't have the control over the business he would have liked to have.

In the end Cloutier refused to make him a partner, so he decided to create his own company, to his wife's great satisfaction. She would provide for the family out of her earnings. After giving up her career as a singer on the birth of her son, Jean-Pierre, she hosted a very popular TV program called *Les Tannants*.

When he left Guy Cloutier Productions, René Angélil brought with him Johnny Farago, the artist who had begun his career singing French-language versions of Elvis Presley hits.

29

ELVIS PRESLEY

THERE WERE GOOD REASONS FOR Angélil to take charge of Johnny Farago's career. Of course, the two men had known one another for several years, for Johnny had launched out on his career when René was one of the Baronets. But actually Angélil had been fascinated by everything about Elvis since he was a teenager. It wasn't just the artist himself that appealed to him, but the myth surrounding him.

In 1976, accompanied by his wife, Guy Cloutier, and René Simard, he was in the audience for one of the last of the King's performances. Naturally, they sat in the front row. Angélil and Cloutier were dazzled by the presence of this living legend. However, some others in the audience were much less impressed.

"It was disappointing. Elvis didn't seem to care about the people who had come out to see him, and he had difficulty moving. It didn't leave me with a very good memory," René Simard would say later.

It is true that Elvis had become a mere shadow of his former self. He weighed over 130 kilograms, could barely move about on stage, and would even forget the words of his greatest hits.

But even this decline fascinated Angélil and Cloutier. After the show, Guy Cloutier found a way to meet his idol and shake hands with him while someone in the group took a photo. It was then that

Cloutier said to Elvis, in his best Lac-Saint-Jean English: "Congratulations, Mr. Presley!"

René Simard, who was present when this happened, still laughs about it. In 1976, people went to see Presley the way they would a famous monument. The pop idol could still draw the crowds, but he was no longer selling a lot of records, nor did he have much influence within the music industry.

Johnny Farago's career, which ran parallel to Elvis's, suffered as a consequence. Recognizing he was identified with a singer in decline, Farago attempted to take a different direction and tried out different styles, but without much success. His career was going nowhere, and Angélil was hoping things would improve for him. Angélil was now thirty-five, and he realized Farago wasn't going to make him rich. His income was modest, and he was worried about his future when, on June 12, 1977, he was present at the birth of his second child with Anne Renée — a daughter named Anne-Marie.

Counting Patrick, the child from his first marriage, René was now the father of three children, and wasn't very proud of himself. He was marking time professionally, still dreaming of the artist who would allow him to manage his or her international career. He wasn't a big gun in Quebec show business and enjoyed little respect in the field. But he knew that Quebec was too small a market to provide a decent living for a pop artist. He was finding it confining, even if he felt at home and liked living there. It was the star system that interested him, and it still didn't exist in Quebec. People were pretty restrained in his part of the country. He was no novice in show business, but he was still a dreamer who visualized himself in the company of his idols: Colonel Parker, Frank Sinatra, Barbra Streisand, the producer Phil Spector, the Bee Gees, and the other big names in pop music.

30

ELVIS DIES

O N AUGUST 16, 1977, THE media all over the world announced Elvis Presley's death. Suddenly the defunct monarch was King again. From all around the globe thousands of fans hurried to Memphis to attend the funeral of the most famous singer of his age, the first singer of the atomic era, the real creator of rock and roll. No one spared the superlatives.

René Angélil didn't want to miss this event at any cost. Right away he flew to Memphis with Johnny Farago, and was able to worm his way into the crowd to pay his last respects to his idol's remains. He paid particular attention to the diligent efforts of Colonel Parker, who controlled the situation perfectly. In addition to looking after the funeral arrangement, he was organizing Elvis's "new" career.

RCA Victor, for whom Elvis Presley had recorded since 1956, was no longer able to satisfy the demand. All over the world his records sold out. Despite RCA Victor's best efforts to press new ones, the company just couldn't keep up with the demands of a public eager to get its hands on Elvis Presley's recordings and every available souvenir of him.

In Quebec it wasn't just Elvis's records people were crazy about, but also those of his imitators, including Johnny Farago. Taking advantage of the craze, René Angélil had the bright idea of organizing a tribute to

Elvis with Farago playing the part of the King for the occasion. It was all very well staged and presented in Jarry Park before an audience of ten thousand that was still suffering from the shock of Elvis's death.

Amazingly, the critics, who until then hadn't been easy on Farago, praised his performance, writing about the great show put on by this emulator of the King. René was delighted, and decided to organize a tour throughout the province, which had great success. It seemed as if Presley was back in fashion, since Farago, more like Elvis than ever, was drawing capacity audiences everywhere he went. The tour would be extended to last more than a year.

31

GINETTE RENO

RENÉ KNEW VERY WELL THAT the craze wouldn't last, and that Farago's talent was limited. So he was open to any new proposals and was dreaming of a high-calibre artist he could launch on the international stage. The opportunity arose during the 1977 Christmas season, while he was staying with Anne Renée and the children at the El Presidente Hotel, where Johnny Farago was performing. At the time, Mexico was a favourite destination for the Quebecois to spend their winter vacations, and they supplied the audience for Farago's show. Numerous artists also attended, for the El Presidente Hotel was a favourite spot for people like Dominique Michel, Danielle Ouimet, Michel Girouard, and Ginette Reno.

After her performance, Ginette came to meet René and sat down at his table. They chatted about the holidays, their families, and the entertainment business, which wasn't always easy, and on that score Ginette confided in René that she was looking for a manager because her career was too difficult to manage. With no beating about the bush, she asked him if he would be prepared to look after her.

He was surprised and delighted. Why not? He had known Ginette well since the start of her career in the 1960s. She had been entering amateur talent contests at the same time as the Baronets, and Pierre

Labelle had been her first love. They had shared the stage in several clubs in the Montreal region when he was a Baronet, and they also took part in many TV programs, including *Jeunesse d'aujourd'hui*, on which she was one of the artists most in demand.

René was also very conscious of the fact that this thirty-one-year-old singer was the most popular in Quebec, and the most talented, and that she had all the potential required to aim for an international career.

Born on April 28, 1946, Ginette Reno was already a star at the age of thirteen, when she was singing in Montreal clubs. Before she was twenty she was a great hit at the Place des Arts, alongside Gilbert Bécaud. Two years later she took part with other Quebec artists in the show *Vive le Québec*, at the Paris Olympia. In 1968 she won the title Miss Radio and Television in Quebec, and in 1969 she was awarded the trophy for Best Canadian Artist at the Juno ceremony. Abroad she was just as well established, appearing for two weeks at the Savoy Theatre in London and taking first prize at the Yamaha Festival in Tokyo in 1972, in addition to hosting a TV series with Roger Whittaker for the BBC in London.

She had already recorded three albums in English, and had many hit records. But her best memory, as for many Quebecois, was the magical night of June 24, 1975, when she reached a peak in her career — and what a peak! — singing "Un peu plus haut, un peu plus loin" by Jean Pierre Ferland on Mount Royal in Montreal. More than two hundred thousand people had seen her performance as part of the show held to celebrate Quebec's national day.

René also knew that Ginette Reno had a reputation for changing managers frequently and of not becoming tied to any of them. She was always more faithful to her lovers than to her managers. He accepted her offer because he wanted the challenge of propelling Ginette's career further than she could imagine so that she would never want to terminate their association.

What is more, he had no choice in the matter. He was thinking of his family and future and was convinced that Ginette Reno was the key to winning recognition as a manager and respect from his peers. Indeed, she was the lucky break he'd been waiting for so long.

Back in Montreal he attended one of her performances and felt a strange thrill when he heard Ginette sing "Je ne suis qu'une chanson," which had been part of her repertoire for several years. He couldn't understand why no one had suggested to her that she record this song, in which she was at her best.

"I've never recorded it because it's a song suited to the live stage, not to a recording," she explained.

René didn't give up. "Je ne suis qu'une chanson" had to be recorded, for there was no doubt in his mind that it would be a huge success. With his persistence he finally got the singer into a recording studio, backed up by an impressive band. Ginette still wasn't convinced, but he had worn her down, and she finally decided to record the song.

The results soon came, and "Je ne suis qu'une chanson" made history by selling a total of 350,000 records in Quebec — a figure that has never been surpassed. Ginette was particularly proud of this success, because it was recorded under her own label, Melon-Miel, the recording company she founded in 1977.

René worked actively on his new protégée's career and spared no effort. First came a Quebec tour, some TV appearances, and, already, a plan to conquer France. He made more and more contacts, went to Paris, and played Ginette's recordings to a representative of CBS. He also brought along the video of her performance on Mount Royal, omitting the fact that it was part of a show celebrating the Quebec national holiday. He had learned from Ben Kaye to impress at all costs, to spin the truth a little, and to be very persistent.

Right away the French producers were impressed, as much by Ginette Reno's voice and charisma as by René's obvious enthusiasm in trying to bring off his first international coup as a manager. However, most of them thought the singer didn't have what it would take to win over the French public. She didn't have the right look, and her Quebec accent was too strong. Furthermore, at the time France wasn't particularly interested in singers with good voices, preferring the likes of Jane Birkin or Françoise Hardy. René kept at it, however, and finally someone from CBS suggested he go to see Eddy Marnay.

A sensitive man, a dreamer and something of a bohemian, Eddy Marnay was now a little out of things. Fifty-eight years old, he had written songs for Édith Piaf, Yves Montand, Nana Mouskouri, and Mireille Mathieu, in addition to translating songs sung by Barbra Streisand. But these were all artists whose time was past. He was rich and famous, but tastes had changed, and Eddy Marnay was forgotten. But none of that mattered to him, for he had just gone through a devastating divorce, and in any case was questioning his entire life.

This was the man René Angélil met in a Parisian suburb. Marnay was born in Algeria, and René, the sly fox, made no secret of his Arab origins. The two men soon got on famously together, and Angélil wasted no time in singing the praises of the marvellous Quebec singer Ginette Reno. He took out all the material he had brought along and played Ginette's records to an enthusiastic Marnay. He even showed him the videos. René was already declaring victory, and things were falling quickly into place.

Back home in Quebec, he invited Marnay to come to see the show Ginette Reno was giving in a theatre in Quebec City. Marnay was impressed and immediately decided to write some songs for her. Angélil reached an agreement with producer Claude Pascal to record an album of original Eddy Marnay songs in the Pathé Marconi studios in France. Wasting no time, he arranged a tour for Ginette in Quebec and English Canada, in addition to busying himself with the promotion of her new album in France and Quebec. He found this first great achievement of his career as a manager intoxicating. His objectives — recognition, fame, and maybe fortune — seemed within reach. Now he had the backing of a major record company, a recognized songwriter, and an experienced producer. He had manoeuvred well, and his ship was about to come in. Ginette just had to turn up and win over the French. And Angélil didn't doubt for a moment that she would do exactly that.

Unable to contain himself any longer, he informed the person in question. To his great surprise, Ginette Reno didn't share his enthusiasm. She claimed to be suffering from fatigue and was thinking more about the upcoming holiday with her new boyfriend, Alain Charbonneau, than about pursuing a career in France. She didn't discourage René, however, and told him to continue with the plans. René thought she was genuinely suffering from overwork and went on with his preparations.

When she returned from her holiday everything had changed in Ginette's world. She had found the man of her life and wasn't about to sacrifice him to her career. That was when Alain Charbonneau intervened, demanding a share managing her and in the 20 percent commission that came with it. Ginette tried to negotiate an agreement with Angélil, but he wouldn't hear of it.

Suddenly everything was disappearing into thin air: months of work, his biggest dreams as a manager, his contacts, his job, and his money. All that was left was his wife, who supported him, his children, and a few friends. René, now on the verge of forty, remembered his father, and thought seriously about becoming a student again in order to pursue a career in law.

Eddy Marnay called him to try to make some arrangements and to re-establish contact with Ginette. Alain Charbonneau was willing to pursue the project for which René had laid the foundations, but nothing worked.

It was an irony of fate: René Angélil suffered the worst setback of his career just when he seemed closest to his goal and feeling sure of success. Shortly after the end of their professional association Ginette Reno would win five Felix Awards at the ADISQ ceremony, showing the quality of Angélil's work. In fact, she enjoyed the best years of her career with René as her manager.

"Managers expose their stars too much and only think about getting more and more engagements so they can make as much money as possible. That's the way they burn out their artists and shorten careers," she once told a journalist.

For his part, René had already confided to friends: "Sometimes I think she hired me to carry her bags."

Besides, how can a woman of thirty, in love into the bargain, live in such intimacy with a manager who literally takes over her life? A good number of artists have married their managers, including Petula Clark and Mariah Carey. Ginette Reno wasn't wrong to interest Alain Charbonneau in managing her career, even if he knew nothing about the job. How could it be otherwise when a woman wants to prove her fidelity to the man she loves? Haven't people often asked Ginette Reno or René if they were in love, or if they had slept together, as if this was only to be expected? Yet there was never any question of any such thing.

Furthermore, Ginette complained that she wasn't informed of all René's initiatives. We mustn't forget that he was someone who liked to have complete control over his activities and that Ginette was also, in her own way, a strong woman, particularly where her career was concerned.

With hindsight, it is obvious enough that the association between Ginette Reno and René Angélil couldn't have worked for very long, even if the Quebec singer had recorded that album in Paris.

René would learn an important lesson from this experience: never allow a third party to get involved in the relations between a manager and an artist he represents, particularly in the realm of decision-making. Since artists are often very sensitive people who sometimes suffer from an unhealthy sense of insecurity, the manager must protect them from harmful influences, surrounding them with a protective cocoon that neither the artist's friends nor family can penetrate. Such people, who are completely outside the show business environment, cannot advise the artist well or have as complete a view of the field as the agent. On the other hand, in the ideal case, the performer must have complete confidence in her agent, as would be the case for Céline and René. She would put her whole person in René's hands — he who already had twenty-three years of experience behind him and who didn't belong to the jungle of managers and neophyte backers who invent their roles as they go along instead of having mastered them.

In the 1960s there was not yet any school where people could learn the job of artists' manager, and there were very few examples or models to follow. So it was fate that brought two outstanding artists together.

32

THE DISCOVERY OF CÉLINE DION

I̲T̲ ̲I̲S̲ ̲S̲A̲I̲D̲ ̲T̲H̲A̲T̲ ̲P̲E̲O̲P̲L̲E̲ born under Capricorn succeed late in life. As he watched the rain beat against the window of his little office in Laval, René Angélil no longer believed he would succeed in his chosen profession. He thought he had played his final card and lost. He suddenly realized he was working at an unsatisfying job that had failed to reward his efforts. During this period of his life, lasting several months, he hit rock bottom and couldn't see how he could get back to the surface again. He was thirty-nine, left without an artist to manage, penniless, and with no interest in any of the Quebec pop performers. After Ginette Reno, who could hope for an international career? Such performers aren't a dime a dozen in Quebec.

The rise of Quebec nationalism, the PQ government, and the sovereignty referendum of 1980 made a lot of room for composer-singers like Gilles Vigneault, Félix Leclerc, Robert Charlebois, Jean-Pierre Ferland, and Claude Dubois, and for patriotic singers like Pauline Julien, Diane Dufresne, and Fabienne Thibeault. The time was past for facile popular songs and the American dream. Quebec was feeling good about itself. This was discouraging for Angélil, who had no sympathy with the nationalist, or elitist, singers. What interested him was pop music, and in the early 1980s this was considered a minor art by a lot of people in Quebec. He knew that, but he still thought it had a place in the world and that it was possible to have a successful career in it.

A few months aren't much in an entire existence. But this was 1981, and René wasn't very excited at the idea of going back to school at his age and starting all over again with three children to provide for. He had thought he would make his fortune gambling in casinos, but nothing seemed to work in that area, either. He mulled over his life, reviewed what he had made of the past few years, and saw that he'd had a lot of fun and that things had been easy for him, but that now the good days were over. Nothing would ever be so easy again. He knew he would have to work hard, that nothing would be handed to him on a plate. Much later he would come to understand Ginette Reno's attitude, but at this precise moment he felt deep resentment towards her. He had been hurt and humiliated and felt he was the victim of a terrible injustice because he had put out his best effort on her behalf. He was sure he had what it took to manage a singing career. But what good did that do him?

He had no income, was getting into debt, and was becoming more and more paranoid, when suddenly the phone rang. Someone called Gilles Cadieux wanted to meet him to discuss the production of an album. The artist in question was a young girl from Charlemagne who apparently had an extraordinary voice. René was in no position to refuse anything and agreed to meet the caller. So, a few days later, Cadieux and Paul Lévesque came to René's office and played him a recording of the girl, whose name was Céline Dion, singing two original songs that were written by her mother. Outwardly calm as ever, René asked to see the girl before making a decision.

When he learned she was only twelve, he had some doubts at first. She had a good voice, certainly, and nice songs, in spite of some flaws he noticed on the recording. But was there still room in Quebec for such a young singer? In 1980, a young girl of twelve had sold thousands of records and won the hearts of Quebec children. Nathalie Simard had taken over from her brother, whose voice had changed and who was now turning to musical comedy. Nathalie had overtaken her brother in record sales, and of course Guy Cloutier was her manager. Nathalie Simard's popularity allowed her to perform at Place des Arts, make numerous albums, and appear regularly on TV. After breaking off his professional association with Guy Cloutier, would René Angélil now come up against him as a competitor? It was a possibility that occurred to him after hearing this angelic voice.

Paul Lévesque informed him that he was managing the young singer but that he preferred to entrust her to an experienced producer for the recording of her first album. René was delighted to learn that people hadn't forgotten him, and wondered what the young singer's personality was like. It wasn't long before the twelve-year-old turned up in René's office. The story has been told just about everywhere about how that day he asked her to pick up a pencil as if it were a microphone and sing as if she were performing in Place des Arts. Céline Dion sang with all the vocal power at her command, while the man opposite her raised his head and felt shivers run up and down his spine.

Céline looked at him questioningly, and René seemed lost in thought. A marvellous voice, a restrained passion, and a desire to sing … but she was a child of twelve, gripped by a morbid shyness that surfaced when she stopped singing, preventing her from expressing herself or appearing to her best advantage. What was more, she had neither the appearance nor the poise of a singer. But René, relying on his instinct, was impressed. He knew he had stumbled upon an uncut gem, a real jewel that would have to be polished and polished again. No matter, he would devote his time to it — and the money he didn't have but felt certain he could find. What did it matter if she had terrible teeth, was skinny, modest, poor, and uncultured; he would make a queen of her.

"What do you think, M. Angélil?"

"I'd like to meet your family."

Maybe he shed a tear. Perhaps he was dazzled, bowled over, and astounded. The important thing was the magic of this girl who had come along to heal the worst wound ever inflicted on him.

He lost no time in going to Charlemagne to see Céline's parents, accompanied by his wife. The Dion family, which had assembled in its entirety, hadn't been expecting so much — René Angélil, the former member of the Baronets, a record producer, and Anne Renée, the star of *Les Tannants* on TV, right there in their house — what an honour!

René the seducer set to work and charmed all Céline's family members, especially her mother, Thérèse, who had written the songs on the cassette. He chatted with all the family members: her father, Adhémar, and her brothers, including Michel, who belonged to a group. In the meantime Anne Renée chatted with Céline's sisters, who still considered her the baby of the family.

Throughout the evening René talked business with Mme. Dion at one corner of the table.

33

PAUL LÉVESQUE

PAUL LÉVESQUE WAS UNKNOWN TO the general public until several biographies of Céline came out in 1997. Previously, it had been thought that René Angélil had discovered Céline Dion and guided her first steps in the world of show business. This was not quite correct. René had deliberately omitted to mention that Paul Lévesque was Céline's first agent, who had signed a five-year agreement with her mother. Lévesque had a different conception of Céline's career, one that obviously didn't suit either Mme. Dion or René.

Paul Lévesque had managed the careers of Mahogany Rush and Luba, who had considerable success in Quebec and elsewhere. He also had an interest in another, less well known group that was first called Eclipse and later The Show. Michel Dion, Céline's older brother, was a member of this group and had insisted that Lévesque go to the Vieux Baril, a little nightclub in Legardeur, to hear his little sister, who had an exceptional voice, singing. Lévesque finally gave in and had to agree that Michel was right. He signed a contract with Mme. Dion.

Thérèse Tanguay-Dion was an ambitious and impatient woman. She constantly nagged Lévesque to launch her daughter into show business as quickly as possible. But weeks and months went by without Lévesque showing much sign of life. Finally, he got in touch with her to announce that he had found a studio in Longueuil, a suburb of Montreal, where Céline was to record a demo. He asked Michel to help him find musicians and requested some original songs. A musician since childhood, Mme. Dion didn't hesitate to offer her services. In no time at all she wrote "Ce n'était qu'un rêve" in a big exercise book, sitting at the family table. A few days later the musicians in the family accompanied Céline, who one Sunday recorded five songs in the Pélo recording studios in Longueuil.

"They didn't come on the Saturday because that day a fire burned down the building containing Le Vieux Baril where Céline sang and which belonged to her parents. There were seven of them in the studio," remembers the producer, Luc Lavallé. "Jacques, Céline's brother, played piano. Sometimes the singing and accompaniment weren't quite together, but on the whole it was quite well done.

"In very short order, Céline recorded 'Je ne suis qu'une chanson,' 'Ce n'était qu'un rêve,' 'Grand-maman,' 'Je m'envole,' and 'Chante-la, ta chanson.' I kept four songs, since 'Je ne suis qu'une chanson' was cut. Just four copies were made, and I gave them to Paul Lévesque and the producer Michel Bélanger. I kept the master, without touching it, for many years."

In 1997 it occurred to Lavallé to sell this recording, which must surely have great value for fans and collectors, since it was Céline's very first.

"I first thought of giving this recording to René Angélil, and then I decided to ask $300,000 for it," he confided. "Sony refused, and I haven't heard from them since. Some Japanese seem interested, but for now the recording still hasn't been sold. I also have 116 negatives of the recording session. Obviously it's all unpublished material."

Paul Lévesque considered René Angélil the best-qualified producer to record Céline's first album, an important first step in her career. However, Lévesque was still her manager. He wanted to proceed slowly and protect the twelve-year-old.

"I wanted to manage Céline's career, but not to the detriment of her personal life. I thought that at her age she should be in school. But that didn't seem to bother her mother, who wanted to push her daughter into show business. It didn't seem right to me. So I insisted Céline go back to school, so she returned to Polyvalente Paul Arsenault."

René could see perfectly that Céline had no interest in school and wanted only to be a singer. This suited him very well, for it meant he could shape a budding artist in his own image, exerting total control over her career without ever having to put up with interference from lovers or possessive husbands. It was very close to the fantasy of many middle-aged men who dream of preparing, rearing, and moulding a very young girl to be their masterpiece — a dream that haunted Arnolphe, Molière's character in his play *The School for Wives*; George Bernard Shaw, who created a lady in the play that became the movie *My Fair Lady* with Audrey Hepburn; and even Elvis Presley, René's idol, who "brought up" the young Priscilla Beaulieu, aged fourteen, in his Graceland property.

Paul Lévesque was quite right to be concerned about Céline's intellectual development, for the time would come when she would complain about her ignorance of the simplest things. But strictly on a professional level, in a show business world that is often compared to a jungle, René was right to think only of recording a first album and of the young girl's appearance, which had to be changed right away, as well as of all the money that would have to be invested. He would worry about her education later, so in the meantime his wife, Anne Renée, would teach her proper behaviour and deportment, and how to dress and speak in public.

René Angélil had been marked by the humiliation he suffered at the conclusion of his association with Ginette Reno. He had no intention of experiencing that kind of frustration with another performer, so he became implacable in his negotiations and in his attitude towards the competition. Céline was an artist with a clean sheet who didn't bring any past baggage with her. For the time being she had only an exceptional voice and a passion for the stage. He possessed the rest.

34

THE MANAGER'S JOB

JEAN BEAULNE WAS A PROSPEROUS businessman involved in numerous enterprises in Quebec and in the United States, particularly in the early 1980s. Since he broke off from the Baronets he had remained in contact with René, though without the opportunity to see him regularly. However, he followed the career of his former partner with interest. Despite the passing years and the break-up of the group, the Baronets were still the Baronets, after all.

Beaulne, better than anyone, could appreciate the great change that had come about in René's life: "René woke up at the age of thirty-eight." At the time, he had come up against a brick wall. He had lost Ginette, was in debt to the tune of two hundred thousand dollars, and had no one to help him. He had always been able to count on someone in his life, but now he was completely on his own. Jean Beaulne's memory is that René behaved more like a gambler than a businessman in the Baronets days. Life was a game for him, and he had to take maximum advantage of it. Beaulne even recalled that at the time he often told him he was too lazy and that he would never get anywhere in life — a comment that makes him smile today in the light of René's tremendous success since then. He recalls:

René no longer had any choice, and suddenly he did something extraordinary: he took a grip on himself. I was the happiest guy to see someone I'd known so well change like that and make that kind of leap to finally win recognition all round the world. I know the profession well enough — one of the most difficult and thankless there is — to appreciate his achievement with Céline Dion. But Céline was also a great source of motivation for him ever since the beginning of their association.

Brian Epstein, the Beatles' manager, committed suicide. Paul Vincent, who managed Roch Voisine, one of the biggest stars in the French-speaking world, died of an overdose. René has had three heart attacks and suffered from cancer. There's a reason for that. Being an artist's manager isn't just one job, it's many jobs rolled into one. You have to be an administrator, a promoter, a public relations person, a diplomat, an organizer, a copywriter, an artist yourself, a planner, an advisor on all kinds of matters, a conciliator, and be enterprising, understanding, and visionary ... all that and even more, and all in a very short time, because it's a world that changes very fast — at lightning speed, in fact.

When the artist you're handling has some success your phone starts ringing off the hook. Some days René had to deal with more than two hundred messages at his office. Among them would be urgent matters, requests from important people and appointments impossible to postpone. In addition, there's pressure from all sides. You find yourself surrounded by journalists, producers of shows, the performer's friends and family, his or her companion, and the manager is always being cornered. And that's not taking into account the wants, needs, health, and constraints of the performer herself.

In a very short time your small business turns into a multinational. Imagine a tiny company that has so much success that within a few months it becomes a prestigious chain with international standing. That's what happened to René almost overnight, with no one to help him except a secretary and five telephone lines. Lacking the time to prepare a dynamic, coherent structure, and unable to delegate work to anyone else, he was under incredible stress, knowing that the slightest false step could be fatal and a single tiny error destroy Céline's image. Imagine the amount of work! René reacts to his stress by gambling and eating, the way others indulge in drinking or drugs, like Brian Epstein, the Beatles' manager, who died of an overdose.

I know Ginette Reno and I think she's the greatest as a singer. But there again, once you know the kind of person she is, you can see how difficult the manager's job is. René was humiliated when she dropped him. It was terrible for him. I remember one incident in particular. Ginette Reno was invited to appear on Johnny Carson's talk show, so she went to New York to record the show. But the other guests took too long, and there wasn't time for Ginette to appear. They excused themselves to her, and by way of compensation she was offered not one but three appearances on the show. But with her nose out of joint at having made the trip for nothing, Ginette rejected the offer. What could a manager do in a situation like that? That's what the job is like.

Jean Beaulne has managed the career of several groups of artists for years, and he knows how temperamental people aiming at stardom can be:

In general, the very talented artists — the ones you notice right away and for whom you can predict an international career, are highly emotional people. Talent and emotions go together. And artists like that are easily influenced. It's very important who's close to them. How often have I seen careers ruined because of drugs? I managed France Castel, who was also talented enough to have an international career. We know the problems she has had in the past — she's talked about them herself. There was every probability she'd be a winner at the Athens Festival, in Greece, but it didn't happen because she wasn't in a fit state to take part in the competition. Yet it cost me more than six months work to send her to the event, one of the top ones in the world at the time.

When Céline entered René's life it was the exception that proved the rule. She was still a twelve-year-old, without a past or any bad habits, who just wanted guidance, and who had a wholesome lifestyle — not forgetting her extraordinary voice, of course. René, who wanted to control everything, could see she was a gold mine. Céline wasn't and isn't a problem artist. She is balanced, has her feet on the ground, and is ambitious. Yes, his turn had come.

During a trip to Japan he went on with Céline and Ben Kaye, one of his close collaborators, René noticed the photo of a dangerous wanted criminal posted on a wall not far from a police station. Then he had the idea of playing a trick on a policeman by showing him the photograph and pointing to his friend Ben, who didn't in the least resemble the individual in question. The policeman, who didn't speak a single word of French or English, tried to explain to René that he didn't believe him. Once the group reached the police station, an officer who spoke English told him, word for word, that he should get some glasses, since Ben wasn't the wanted man. Céline, who was patiently waiting for the two men to come back, was in fits of laughter on the sidewalk.

JEAN BEAULNE

35

THE FIRST ALBUM

"GIVE ME FIVE YEARS, AND I'll make a star of your daughter in Quebec and in France," René Angélil promised Céline's mother, to her great delight. This was exactly what she was hoping for.

Encouraged by her support, he set to work and decided to eliminate the only obstacle standing in his way: Paul Lévesque. Paul Lévesque had a contract with the Dion family and didn't hesitate to stand up for his rights.

He sued René Angélil, and it would be years before the case was finally settled out of court. René was never too concerned about this. He knew very well that possession is nine-tenths of the law, and behaved from the outset as if he alone were Céline's manager. He had total contempt for Paul Lévesque, as if he was a minor obstacle, and left his name out of his protégée's official story. But René wasn't indifferent — far from it. It was just that he had learned never to allow a rival any publicity.

He was perfectly aware that to get Céline Dion's career really off the ground he had to carefully plan the recording of a high-quality first album, with original songs. The day was already long past when all the young Baronets had to do to be a resounding success on the TV show *Jeunesse d'aujourd'hui* was to record as quickly as possible a few French versions of American or British hits. Now you had to offer original material and compete with all the pop music in the world.

René first called on Eddy Marnay, who had put Ginette Reno behind him and left the songs he had written for her in a drawer. He initially agreed to come and meet the Dion family, once René had told him about Céline's phenomenal talent. Marnay trusted René and his judgement, and was already convinced this young Canadian artist must be worth going to see.

Marnay was delighted to meet the entire Dion family at Charlemagne, and undertook to write some songs reflecting the dreams of a girl of her age. René wasn't surprised by his reaction. This old fox knew very well that Eddy Marnay had written the biggest hits of Mireille Mathieu, the young marvel from Avignon who had started her career at the age of fifteen and would replace Édith Piaf in the hearts of the French. She was the eldest of a family of thirteen children. Her manager, Johnny Stark, behaved like a real emperor in the world of show business and made her into the greatest star of her time in France. Marnay was on familiar ground.

By agreeing to join the team and write songs for him, Marnay was becoming René's right-hand man and one of the principal architects of Céline Dion's international, or at least European, career. Not only was he a famous songwriter, but he was also familiar with the musical milieu and would open doors for René in Europe.

Furthermore, Marnay was a likeable man who loved Quebec. Indeed, in 1979 he met Mia Dumont at a conference on the future of French song at which he was representing France. Mia Dumont was promoting a boxed set containing one hundred and one Quebec songs. They quickly got to know one another, for it was love at first sight between these two sensitive, romantic individuals. They wouldn't allow an ocean and an age difference of twenty-five years to come between them. By 1981 they had become one of the most likeable, genuine couples in musical circles. Mia Dumont worked in public relations in Montreal and was to become Céline Dion's first publicity agent. She was the most pleasant publicity agent I had the good fortune to work with when I was a young journalist with the entertainment section of the newspaper *La Presse*.

René thought that with Eddy Marnay's support he would have no difficulty raising fifty thousand dollars, the sum he felt would be needed to finance Céline's first album. The rumour was that he mortgaged his house to obtain this amount, and he allowed the legend to grow. I've already explained in full detail in another book about Céline Dion, *Céline Dion, une femme au destin exceptionnel*, that this wasn't possible, since his house was already heavily mortgaged. Worse still, the bank decided he was insolvent and refused to lend him the funds he needed so urgently. He was sick at heart at this situation, particularly since his creditors were becoming impatient. For the first time in his life he thought of declaring bankruptcy to get out from under his debt.

He was distraught and devastated for a while, fearing the worst — losing the opportunity to manage Céline Dion because he was penniless, and also losing face before his family and friends. No! It was unthinkable! He met the host of a popular talk show at the time, Michel Jasmin, and said to him: "If you don't invite Céline Dion to appear on your show I'm going to throw in the towel. We're doing an album and we need visibility."

Jasmin believed him. René, who would never have left Céline in the lurch for all the money in the world, had learned from Ben Kaye that you often have to spin the truth a little in order to sell your product.

After knocking on several doors without any result, René finally met someone who deserved to be better known to the general public. Denys Bergeron, head of Trans-Canada Records, provided the funds needed for the recording. It wasn't easy, however, for company policy limited the production cost of an album to twenty-five thousand dollars. So Bergeron decided to record *two* albums to cover the costs, one with songs by Eddy Marnay and the other with Christmas songs. Everyone in the business knew that these sold well in Quebec.

So Céline would make a Christmas record even before her career began, and René had no objection. In fact, he was jubilant, and would never forget the man who allowed him to get Céline's career off the ground, for she would later record five albums with Trans-Canada. Denys Bergeron recounts:

> It's true René Angélil was having a difficult time financially. He didn't mortgage his house, for I was the one who let him have the money to produce Céline's album. He had no business in his own name, and was so broke

I had to buy him a pair of jeans when he travelled to France with Céline. But I believed in his plan, first of all because he's a marketing genius, and also because he had an ace up his sleeve: Eddy Marnay. Marnay was a songwriter with a big reputation. In Europe, songwriters have much more influence than they do here, so I knew he could really help Céline's career in Europe. I knew him well, for he'd already composed a song for my wife, Christine Lamer. At the time he saw Céline as a future Barbra Streisand.

While Eddy Marnay was finishing writing the songs for Céline's first album, Michel Jasmin invited the young singer to appear on his show on June 20, 1981. Céline was only thirteen, and this was to be her first television appearance. Jasmin didn't want to miss the opportunity to have a great future star on his show, and that is how he introduced her. Overcoming her stage fright, she sang "Ce n' était qu'un rêve" with every ounce of the talent she has, and everything went off as planned until the host invited her to come and sit beside him. Now Céline couldn't control herself, and, being born under Aries, charged head first! When Jasmin asked her if she was taking singing lessons, she answered with a categorical "no," saying she didn't need to. People said she was almost arrogant, when really she was just scared stiff. The show was recorded in the daytime, and that evening the entire Dion family gathered around the TV to watch the young Céline's performance.

Céline didn't like what she saw. Her teeth were too long, her eyebrows too thick, her nose too big, and she didn't project a particularly warm image. René listened to her without saying anything and asked Anne Renée to work on Céline's image for TV interviews. It would be the start of a long transformation, and of Céline Dion's real schooling.

Another guest on Jasmin's show was Rodger Brulotte, the public relations man for the Montreal Expos, who invited Céline to sing the national anthems before a ball game at the Olympic Stadium.

It was a great offer, but it wasn't exactly the start to her career she had imagined. René explained the situation to her: "They're giving you a great opportunity. You'll be seen by almost a million people in

Quebec, and even beyond. And you must never forget the guy who's offering you this opportunity. In this business we must never forget the people that help us, so when Rodger Brulotte asks us for something later on, we'll have to agree."

It was René's first lesson, and there were many more to come.

The two albums, *La Voix du bon Dieu* and *Céline Dion chante Noël*, were recorded over three days in the Saint-Charles studio in Longueuil. Eddy Marnay, like René Angélil, took part in every stage of the production. The launch of *La Voix du bon Dieu* took place on November 9 in an elegant room in the Hotel Bonaventure. All the media were invited, even if Céline was still relatively unknown to the general public. René was already setting the tone for Céline's career by surrounding her with the best he could find. It had class, as Mother Dion said — a lot of class!

A few weeks later René launched the Christmas album. The sales were satisfactory, enabling the producer to cover his costs right away and even make a profit. *La Voix du bon Dieu* and *Céline Dion chante Noël* were doing very well, with sales rising above the one hundred thousand mark.

René had learned from his stay in New York that it is the song that makes the singer, not the reverse. This recognition would be extremely useful to him during his career as a manager, and Céline would benefit from it later. If the quality of the performance is important, the appeal of the words, the dynamics of the melody, and a professional team all play a part in a song's success. What is more, the top-selling artists in history, including the Beatles, the Bee Gees, Elvis Presley, and Michael Jackson, were either talented songwriters themselves or could call on top-calibre composers.

But that is not to take anything away from the talent and charisma of the singers. Many singers of limited ability owe their success to high-quality material, without which they would never have been able to develop a proper career. That is why René chose Céline: she combined the vocal and human qualities necessary to any great performer. But in spite of everything, the song is still the central factor in any success. After all, think of all the artists who won international recognition thanks to a single song! Bing Crosby is one example. At first sight there was nothing about him to attract a large public. He was bald and had very prominent ears, but the song "White Christmas" made him popular. In no time at all he had sold 25 million copies, and since then it has been sung by many artists. His attractive voice and talent as an actor allowed him to have an outstanding career. There was also Frankie Avalon and "Why?" Paul Anka, who didn't have an exceptional personality either, had a hit with "Diana" that set a record by selling 9 million copies, an enormous figure for the time. With his manager's guidance, Anka brushed up his image — he was

a little overweight and had an indifferent hairstyle —
and his talent as a songwriter allowed him to pursue a
successful career with songs like "Put Your Head on
My Shoulder," "Lonely Boy," and "My Way," later sung
by Frank Sinatra among others.

René Angélil understood this dynamic from the outset, and that is why Céline Dion had hit after hit. Among
his favourite composers were lyricists like Eddie Marnay
and Luc Plamondon. When she entered the American
market with texts by songwriter and composer David
Foster, by Diane Warren and Aldo Nova, Céline's success was practically assured. But she was also so talented, with such an attractive personality and such determination, that she did perfect justice to the great songs
they provided for her. So she became a real star in
North America. Very few artists, apart from the Beatles,
the Bee Gees, and Elvis Presley, have had a lot of hits.
From the outset, songs like "Where Does My Heart
Beat Now," "The Power of Love," "Because You Love
Me," "My Heart Will Go On," and many others have
kept her constantly at the top of the hit parade. Jean
Beaulne told us that she was surprised when he told her
one day that a lot of her songs would be around for at
least twenty-five years, like the marvellous "It's All
Coming Back to Me Now," now considered a classic on
a level with the Beatles' "Yesterday."

René always protected his performer and her
image. No one will ever see Céline endorsing a product
that doesn't correspond to that image, or that might not
please the age groups that admire her. When an artist
has a good song to perform, the first requirement is for
a good producer, and then for a record company prepared to make an effort to promote the product. The
manager must give his artist visibility, something René
does intelligently and painstakingly. In the early days, he
had the idea of having Céline sing duets with other

artists, like with Clive Griffin for the song "When I Fall in Love," the theme song of the movie *Sleepless in Seattle*. Another of René's successful strategies was to use her as a warm-up act for Michael Bolton, who catered to the kind of audience Céline wanted to reach. This initiative enabled her to tour the major American cities and gave her the opportunity to meet the media and become better known to the American public. Her participation in significant events like the papal visit to Quebec in 1984 and the Olympic Games in Atlanta (more than 1.5 billion viewers saw the telecast!) propelled her towards success. But it was really with "Because You Loved Me," the theme song of the movie *Up Close and Personal,* and "My Heart Will Go On," from *Titanic,* that her fame was consummated.

In her association with Sony Records, one of the world's major record companies (and without doubt the most dynamic, with people like Bill Rotary, the first to recognize Céline as a great international star by having her sign her first contract with Sony), the singer now has a very effective promotion team, in addition to having Vito Luprano as "A and R (Artist and Repertoire) man." Indeed, he played a major part in the singer's career, for he has enormous talent for picking songs. Very few international companies possess such visionary teams. This is why Sony Records dominates a large share of the market with Céline and René. Fate and their sound instinct guided them towards this company, as if the road had been traced out in advance.

JEAN BEAULNE

36

TBS

René Angélil invested all the money Céline earned in the magnificent career he was planning for her, and this was the way it would be for several years. This meant he wasn't exempt from need, and his debts built up. What is more, the French market didn't turn out to be as ready to accept Céline as he had hoped. France was in no hurry to welcome her with open arms. There was some readiness to launch Céline's first album, but things became complicated when Pathé Marconi claimed a share in managing the artist on French soil. A share was already too much for René, who had no intention of giving up his control.

Pathé Marconi finally agreed to launch "Ce n' était qu'un rêve" as a single in France. When the record was completely ignored by the public it came as no surprise to René or to Eddy Marnay, who was already thinking about another album made to measure for Céline.

While this was going on, René Angélil had to put his own affairs in order. And the most urgent thing was the dispute with Paul Lévesque, which was dragging on and becoming a threat to his career plans. Lévesque had a five-year contract with Céline Dion, and claimed still to be Céline's official manager until she reached the age of majority. He considered René Angélil's role in Céline Dion's career to be limited to that of producer — a role he fulfilled magnificently, he was ready to admit.

Obviously this wasn't how René saw things, and, accompanied by their lawyers, the two men met to settle their ongoing dispute. Lévesque was asking for a lump sum and half the manager's commission; René threatened to pull out, but finally offered a quarter of the 25 percent he was paid on all the fees received during the remainder of the contract Lévesque had signed with Céline's parents. Lévesque had no alternative but to accept.

René also decided to clear up his situation and, with Anne Renée, he created a company called TBS, on March 30, 1982, the day Céline Dion celebrated her fourteenth birthday. Oddly, Anne Renée was the president and sole owner of this company while René was just an employee. She gave up her job as host of the TV show *Les Tannants*, intending to devote herself to production and managing artists. Moreover, she was close friends with Céline Dion, to whom she taught the rudiments of fashion, makeup, and poise, while advising her in her dealings with the media. In the end she would have a large influence on the singer's career, greatly increasing her self-confidence.

But no one was taken in by René's strategy, the purpose of which was to put his protégée out of reach of his creditors.

The third album was recorded in Paris and Longueuil in the summer of 1982, and Eddy Marnay was proud of his work. He had long observed Céline at home with her family and friends and even steeped himself in her memories to compose songs made to measure for her. This time around the French musical world was more receptive. People were so impressed by the song "Tellement j'ai d'amour" that Céline Dion was chosen to represent France at the famous Yamaha competition in Tokyo. René Angélil could hardly believe it.

He had managed Ginette Reno, who had won the Yamaha competition in 1972. Then he was involved with the career of René Simard, who also won the Yamaha competition in 1974, and now, at the end of October 1982, Céline Dion was to sing in front of an audience of twelve thousand in Tokyo. She had never sung before such a large audience. René awaited the judges' decision. He was composed, his eyes fixed, as always, on the young girl whose reputation, future, and life were at stake. His or hers? It was one and the same. They were already bound together by fate. René asked for a phone and, talking above the applause of the delirious crowd, he told Eddy Marnay that Céline had won the

Yamaha competition in a tie with the Mexican singer Yoshio. As a bonus, she carried off the special prize awarded by the sixty-two musicians.

As Félix Leclerc used to say, "Quebec artists need endorsement from abroad." And now Céline had won the endorsement of the Japanese, who chose her out of more than one thousand competitors!

Nothing more was required for Quebec to adopt her instantly. In November 1982, as Quebec discovered her, she appeared on the front pages of all the newspapers. Even the prime minister wanted to meet her in person. René had triumphed at last. It was the first of a series of victories.

He launched Céline's third album, called *Tellement j'ai d'amour*, and in no time the sales topped 150,000 copies. But France was still reticent. The first album, *La Voix du bon Dieu*, had never been launched there, the singles it was hoped would be played on the radio weren't, and the French weren't impressed by the Quebec singer's win in Tokyo. Fortunately she was chosen to represent Canada at MIDEM (Marché International de la Musique/International Music Market) in January, and was subsequently invited to appear on Michel Drucker's show, *Champs Élysées*. This time, René was nervous — more nervous than ever. Céline would sing "D'Amour et d'amitié," and 14 million viewers would see and hear her for the first time.

Céline was still awkward, with some rough corners remaining, but she seduced Drucker, a friend to Quebec, who said after she sang, "Remember this name: Céline Dion. She'll go a long way." This was all that was needed for her to reach the hit parade, selling three hundred thousand copies of "D'amour et d'amitié" in France.

If observers thought she had already been able to make a breakthrough in France and that money would rain down on the fifteen-year-old, René saw things differently.

His refusal to surrender a share in managing her to producers in that country and his own investment in the French adventure didn't make him rich — far from it. He had lived up to his commitments by providing Céline and her entourage with all the luxury and comfort they needed and had invested everything he possessed in promoting his artist in Paris. It was an irony of fate that while she was a rising star in France and had become a big hit in Quebec in less than two years, on

January 23, 1983, René Angélil was obliged to declare personal bank-ruptcy with debts of $257,510.23.

It became obvious then why he had put TBS in Anne Renée's name: the company hadn't incurred any debts and wasn't connected to René Angélil, who was merely his wife's unpaid employee, working for a symbolic salary of sixty dollars a week.

That same year, Céline accumulated more and more successes. To begin with, she performed at Place des Arts, the first show produced in Quebec by the Cystic Fibrosis Association. René wanted people to know that his protégée's niece, Karine, was a sufferer of the disease. Céline was deeply affected by it, and René wanted the singer's fans to share in her pain and join in her battle for the child's survival.

Next she sang at Lac des Dauphins in the La Ronde amusement park in Montreal, before an audience of forty-five thousand. Thanks to this event, she developed a great affinity with her public. She learned how to cope with the media and give the right answers, avoiding journalists' traps.

"I'm taking private lessons, because school is important — as important as my singing career," she would say. Actually, Céline was dazzled by her new career and had no interest in her studies, but to avoid creating a controversy she was careful not to reveal what she really thought. Above all, no controversy! That was what René had taught her.

A nice surprise for the Dion clan came when Pathé Marconi award-ed Céline a golden disk for selling five hundred thousand copies of her song "D'amour et d'amitié," and another for the fifty thousand copies sold of the album *Tellement j'ai d'amour pour toi*. In September Radio Canada devoted a special to her, and the year ended with four Felix trophies awarded to her at the ADISQ gala, for LP of the Year, Performer of the Year, the Most Successful Artist outside Quebec, and, of course, Discovery of the Year.

37

A STRANGE BANKRUPTCY

CÉLINE'S SUCCESS MADE HER FAMILY and her entourage happy, but really intrigued René's creditors, including the Canadian Imperial Bank of Commerce. An inspector for the bank's special loans departments, Gilles Gaigle, sent a letter to the receivers Samson Bélair in which he wrote the following remarks:

> At the first meeting of the creditors M. Angélil indicated that he was not an employee of Productions TBS Inc. (a company belonging to his wife), but that he provided services on a voluntary basis, for which he received no remuneration. Between the assignment of his debt and the first meeting, M. Angélil went on a trip to Europe, supposedly to accompany his wife, who is purportedly Céline Dion's manager. But it so happens that this young woman stated during a TV show (Michel Jasmin's), that René Angélil was her manager. Furthermore, all the expenses for the trip were charged to TBS Productions Inc. At the moment, M. Angélil's salary of $60 per month is paid by cheque signed by his wife, Anne Renée. In our opinion, while he is in fact the

driving force behind TBS Productions Inc., M. Angélil uses his wife to sign cheques and other documents to avoid paying out substantial sums to his creditors. Furthermore, during an examination under Article 543 C.C.P. which took place in late October and early November 1982, M. Angélil stated that he worked for TBS Productions Inc. and that he was unpaid, and when Maître Pierre Audet, of the firm Baker, Baker, Nudleman et Lamontagne attempted to have M. Angélil's remuneration evaluated by the court, he assigned his property. In November 1982 a newspaper article indicated that M. Angélil was Mlle Dion's manager, and that he had accompanied her to a Tokyo music festival.

This document does not leave much doubt about René Angélil's strategy. And indeed, logically, how could he have done otherwise? If the bank considered him insolvent when he tried to obtain a loan of fifty thousand dollars to cover the recording costs of Céline Dion's first album, how could he later hope to invest in promoting the artist in Europe and support her entourage financially?

In fact, René Angélil never mortgaged his house to launch Céline Dion's career, but nevertheless he did a great deal, investing money he didn't have and, above all, mortgaging his business reputation. If Céline had not had such rapid success as a performer, René Angélil would have been blacklisted by every bank in Quebec.

But where that was concerned he also stuck to the course he had chosen. Although in 1983 he was being offered lucrative contracts totalling a quarter of a million dollars for a major tour by Céline, he turned them down. Yet in the short term that kind of money would have allowed him to eliminate a good few of his debts. But Angélil was thinking only of the long term where his protégée's career was concerned.

"She's not ready yet," he decided. Céline was appearing in a few TV variety programs and performing in some shows, but her career was still in the embryonic stage. A youngster of fifteen, she was still learning about show business. René taught her everything he knew about the entertainment world. Not only did he tell her about his own experiences in the field, he also introduced her to the lives of the great stars of song and screen. He liked to read the biographies of stars of his time, and his memory was always remarkable. He gave her details about the private and professional lives of Elvis Presley, Frank Sinatra, Barbra Streisand, and many other famous artists with whom Céline would later rub shoulders.

Gradually he was shaping his protégée through long conversations at the Dion's table or in their living room. René became almost a member of the family and behaved as if he was at home in the little house in Charlemagne.

Céline's mother decided to accompany her daughter on all her travels, now that the Vieux Baril had gone up in flames.

The insurance company had paid her a substantial sum to cover the loss, and Mme Dion had retired from business. She had travelled with Céline to Paris and Tokyo, with evident pleasure. Since Céline was still a minor, her mother was happy to play the role of chaperone.

The young girl confided to her mother that she had boyfriends, including a certain Sylvain, a rather shy boy of her own age who lived in the Charlemagne area, and the hockey player Gilbert Delorme. René Angélil didn't seem to like the idea of her going out with boys, not because he had any hidden intentions of his own but because he couldn't tolerate any kind of distraction from her career.

It is pointless to attempt to probe his subconscious or attribute dishonourable intentions to him. A man who had known and seduced some very beautiful women could hardly have been attracted by a little girl of fifteen, still growing up and lacking in physical attraction. Still, René was obsessed by his discovery. He spoke, lived, and dreamed of nothing but her career. His passion was touching, and in dealing with the media he often took over, praising her outrageously. Overwhelmed by all these compliments, Céline would contradict her manager, denying she was that much of a phenomenon. He scolded her: "Listen, Céline! You mustn't sell yourself short in front of the press. You should never be afraid to dazzle or impress. Let me take care of it, and you act as if you haven't heard what I said." She understood, and kept quiet. He told her this very gently. Though he was so quick-tempered, he never raised his voice to her. Any reproaches were expressed in private, and he initiated his protégée into the rudiments of show business with most uncharacteristic patience. He was well aware that she was still very shy and self-conscious about her appearance, which she thought was unattractive, and knew she was making every effort to please. What a jewel he had found! Very few young artists can resist the temptations that come with early success. A lot of them become intolerable, capricious, conceited, and sink into all kinds of excess, whether drugs or alcohol. They abandon all discipline and rebel against their entourage.

This was anything but the case with Céline, who was an uncomplicated, wholesome, ambitious, conscientious, and almost athletic teenager. She was also a dreamer, alone in her bedroom. She listened to American music. She adored Michael Jackson, the Bee Gees, Boy George, and the new British groups. She watched TV variety shows from the U.S., and even if she still hadn't learned English she was attracted and fascinated by this world. Seeing the singers at the Oscars or the famous Emmy Awards ceremony, she told René she would like to be among them one day. She dreamed of a career in America.

René listened to her with pleasure, and wondered if she wasn't even crazier than he. Of course, he was also dreaming of a career in the United States, but the Americans are powerful and not very willing to open their market.

René thought it wiser to concentrate all their efforts on Europe for the time being: first France and then Germany, which was, according to him, the key. Germany was a wealthy, hospitable country, and the German mark was a safe currency — and it was the country of European show business.

In 1984 Céline recorded another album, called *Mélanie*, in Paris and at the Saint-Charles studio in Longueuil, again with the collaboration of Eddy Marnay, who was now composing exclusively for her. Enormous resources were available for this recording. The technical quality was impressive, and Céline's popularity continued to grow in France.

In Montreal an important event was being planned, to take place at the Olympic Stadium. More than sixty thousand young people were to attend an impressive show to be held in the presence of Pope John Paul II. For the occasion Paul Baillargeon composed a special song, "Une colombe" ("A Dove"), with words by Marcel Lefebvre, a hymn to worldwide peace and love. They were looking for a performer to represent Quebec youth. René Simard was mentioned, then Martine Saint-Clair, and a certain Martine Chevrier.

René was in Paris when he heard that Céline Dion had been chosen to sing "Une colombe" at the Olympic Stadium. Inwardly, he was jubilant. Outwardly, he remained composed and asked to hear Baillargeon and Lefebvre's song. A few days later he accepted on his singer's behalf, saying it was "an honour to be invited to sing for the Pope." He couldn't have hoped for anything better. He remembered one of Céline's first performances when she had sung the national anthems in this same stadium before a Montreal Expos game, and now she was to return there to sing for the Pope, as well as for millions of TV viewers all over the world. "What a showpiece!" he thought to himself.

When René discovered her, the little girl from Charlemagne had just given up playing with her dolls. At twelve Céline made her debut on Quebec television, at fifteen she was chosen to sing for the Pope, and at sixteen she made her first appearance on French TV with Michel Drucker.

But her career was unlike that of most child stars, and now Céline is a healthy, well-balanced woman who pursues her life as an artist, wife, and mother with gentle resolve. Hers is the lifestyle of an athlete! From her early years she has followed a demanding routine of daily physical conditioning, healthy eating, and abstinence from alcohol and cigarettes, and especially from drugs. With the loving support of her family and professional entourage, she has also been able to rely on René Angélil, who has guided her as a father would his own child.

Unfortunately, youthful stars have not always been so well looked after!

Shirley Temple. Shirley Temple was born on April 23, 1928, within a stone's throw of the film studios in Santa Monica, California. She was still under four years of age when she appeared in *Baby Burlesque,* mimicking Marlene Dietrich and other idols of the time. Well supervised by her mother, Gertrude, who would take care that their fortune grew, in 1934 she signed a long-term contract with Twentieth Century Fox that saved the company from bankruptcy.

The same Fox showed her the door in 1940. She was twelve, and had filled the studio's coffers, but was considered a has-been in a town that has a reputation for turning sour on artists from one day to the next.

In her golden years she became a national institution and was awarded a special Oscar by the Academy to recognize her contribution to the American people and the movie industry.

Divorced from the actor John Agar in 1949 after a difficult marriage, she married the businessman Charles Black the following year. Under the name Shirley Temple Black, she launched out on a political career. She was appointed United States Ambassador to the United Nations in 1968, Ambassador to Ghana in 1974, Chief of Protocol in 1976, and Ambassador to Czechoslovakia in 1989. She has three children.

Gary Coleman. The tiny Gary Coleman is somewhat reminiscent of the late lamented Jackie Coogan, whose character "The Kid" has entered the collective cinematic memory. Coogan, discovered by Charles Chaplin, amassed a colossal fortune during the 1920s and 1930s, but his parents very soon spent it all. He sued them. The California Child Actors' Bill, commonly called the "Coogan Act," which prevents the repetition of such abuses, was born out of his misfortunes. But despite the Coogan Act, Coleman had to take his parents and accountants to court for mismanaging his affairs. Today he is penniless and works as a security guard in studios that refuse to take him on as an actor or will do so only occasionally and for basically minor parts.

Born on February 8, 1968, in Zion, Illinois, Gary Coleman owes his fame to the series *Diff'rent Strokes*. He played the likeable Arnold opposite an older brother acted by Todd Bridges. The series ran from 1978 to 1986. By the end of the 1985–1986 season Coleman had banked a capital of $18 million — or so he thought. Instead, he learned that he was penniless and up to his ears in debt. He rebelled against his adoptive parents and his managers, who were ordered to pay him back $3.8 million. Today nothing of all this fame and fortune remains.

The series didn't bring any better luck to Todd Bridges and Dana Plato, his two opposite numbers. Plato and Bridges both had drug problems. Dana Plato died of an overdose on May 8, 1999, aged thirty-five. Bridges, in his late thirties, a recovered cocaine addict, works in electronics, far from the studios that almost destroyed him.

Drew Barrymore. "She'll be more famous than her famous parents," proclaimed Steven Spielberg, her godfather, who launched her career in his cult movie *E.T.,* while Francis Ford Coppola, who dreamed of directing her in a film that would consecrate her as a star, added that she was "without question the best actress of her generation."

The granddaughter of the great John Barrymore and Dolores Costello, great-niece of Ethel and Lionel Barrymore, and daughter of John Blythe Barrymore, all actors, Drew Barrymore, who was born in Culver City on February 22, 1975, inherited the ability and the weakness of the Barrymores, all (except for Ethel) well-known alcoholics.

Her talent, which was quickly recognized, allowed her to "play with the big kids," and in their company she had a wild time in fashionable nightclubs, developing a dependency on alcohol and drugs. An alcoholic at twelve and addicted to cocaine at thirteen, she published her autobiography at the age of fourteen. A few years later she appeared nude in the pages of *Playboy,* at a time when she was admitting she was bisexual. At the same time she was acting in often mediocre movies that were sometimes saved by her unquestionable ability.

She has worn the producer's hat in addition to that of an actor, and was behind *Charlie's Angels* and *Charlie's Angels 2*.

"The most reliable of actresses," in the words of the director Mike Nichols, she is also one of the most unstable. This is demonstrated by her first marriage to a bar owner named Jeremy Thomas, which lasted just over a month, from March 20, 1994, to April 28 of the same year, and her second marriage, to Canadian comedian Tom Green, which lasted only from July 7 to December 17, 2001.

Michael Jackson. Now here is the kind of decline no one would wish for Céline Dion! The idol of idols, Michael Jackson, who proclaimed himself the "King of Pop," is a fallen star today. The most gifted of the Jackson children and the foremost star of the Jackson Five first saw the light of day on August 29, 1958, in Gary, Indiana. He was less than six years old when his father formed a family group that would prove enormously successful. But Michael could soon see that his brothers were standing in the way of his personal development.

He launched out on a career as a soloist, and literally reached the summit with *Thriller,* an album that sold more than 46 million copies — an all-time record, which was followed by *Dangerous* (30 million) and *Bad* (30 million). In the mid-1980s he was as popular as Elvis Presley in his heyday. In the firmament of the stars he was the highest and most distant, so he could only fall, as one of his critics has observed.

This descent into hell began with a charge of gross indecency about which everything, or almost everything, that could be written has been. He would always protest his innocence, but would settle out of court for an amount approaching $18 million. Around the same time he admitted to an addiction to painkillers that would put him in a London clinic, and he lost most of his backers.

Then there would be his unconsummated marriage with Lisa Marie Presley, the King's daughter, on May 18, 1994, and a second marriage to a nurse named Debbie Rowe, on November 15, 1996, that would produce two children. They divorced in October 1999.

The album *History,* coming after a long silence, broke no records, for its sales failed to surpass the 10 million level. It was a disappointing flop for him. As for his last production, with the provocative and definitely questionable title *Invincible,* only 4 million copies were sold — another monumental flop.

Instead of recognizing his error, or that the public's taste had changed, he chose to cast the blame on Sony Music and attack its president, Tommy Motolla, whom he called mean, racist, and devilish.

In November 2002 Michael Jackson was a mere shadow of his former self. He decided to put his career as a singer and performer on the back burner. The construction of a children's theme park he had undertaken was abandoned for lack of financing. He owes Sony Music more than $200 million. For five years he has been showing some interest in the cinema, but so far none of his projects has gone anywhere. Michael Jackson, the "gloved one" as he is known to his fans, or "Wacko Jacko" as his denigrators call him, is in decline. It will be difficult, but not impossible, for him to recover.

Macaulay Culkin. Born in New York on August 26, 1980, Macaulay Culkin owes his success to a single role and his wealth to a merciless manager: his father, Kit Culkin, a failed actor. For it was indeed by playing the imaginative Kevin McAllister (a kind of Denis the Menace) in *Home Alone* (1990) that the young Culkin entered the spotlight and became known worldwide.

He was managed by his father, Kit, who, recognizing his son's ability, showed no quarter in dealing with producers. He wanted $5 million for *Home Alone 2,* and ended up getting it. He wanted $12 million for *Home Alone 3,* which ended up being made without Macaulay.

At that point Kit Culkin declared war on Hollywood, and it was Macaulay who suffered the most. *Richie Rich,* made in 1994, was followed by an eclipse of eight years.

So what happened to shut the young Culkin out of movies? He suffered, it is true, from his father's tyranny, but he had also lost the purity, innocence, and naivety that had so appealed to the public. For the producers and the public Macaulay Culkin was no longer Kevin McAllister. His case is far from unique.

Macaulay's parents separated in 1997, and he fired his father. On June 22, 1998, he married the young actress Rachel Miner, whom he divorced on August 5, 2000. He returned to the stage in 2001 in *Madame Melville,* in London, and returned to the movie set in 2002 to play a very antipathetic role in the drama *Party Monster,* in an attempt to escape type-casting.

JEAN BEAULNE

38

1984

IN 1984 QUEBEC WAS BOOMING, and in a festive mood. Now business had replaced politics as people's primary preoccupation. If the Quebecois couldn't have their own country, at least they'd be prosperous, and more and more companies were growing up. "Québec libre" had been replaced by "Quebec Inc.," and in the entertainment world young entrepreneurs were vying in originality and daring as they created spectacular artistic events. Alain Simard started the Montreal International Jazz Festival, Gilbert Rozon went after Charles Trenet to launch his first "Just for Laughs" festival, and in Quebec City they celebrated Jacques Cartier's arrival. Also, some important visitors were expected; in addition to Pope John Paul II, Michael Jackson, the most popular star in the world, was coming with his brothers to put on his show *Mystery Tour*, at the Olympic Stadium, naturally.

René Angélil chose the month of August to launch the album *Mélanie*, while the festivities were in full swing in Montreal, and particularly in Quebec City.

People had been long getting ready for the great occasion of *Québec 1534–1984*. Everyone wanted to get in on the act — artists, producers, promoters, businessmen, and inventors. All of them thought they'd make their fortunes and be part of an event without precedent in

Quebec. The singers would be disappointed, the producers would lose money, and the businessmen would have little business, but Céline Dion would emerge a winner. René Angélil thought it was time for his protégée to participate in major events, and it was with this in mind that he agreed to introduce Céline on the big stage in the Vieux Port. The moment couldn't have been better chosen to launch the sixteen-year-old on the entertainment scene. After her album came out and before her participation at the stadium in the celebrations for the youth festival, Céline was ready for her first big concert, alongside the greats of Quebec show business.

On the occasion of the 450th anniversary celebrations, they had even brought back the most popular group of the 1970s, Beau Dommage. This was the most eagerly awaited event of the festivities.

In the meantime some of the performers were organizing a circus. In the framework of the celebrations, clowns, jugglers, and actors from the Club des Talons Hauts in Baie-Saint-Paul planned a provincial tour they baptized Le Grand Tour. Led by Guy Laliberté, the group of performers visited forty-eight towns from Gaspé to Montreal, including, of course, Quebec City. It was a very popular success, but it wasn't at all comparable to the performance of the greats of Quebec show business. But these were the very humble beginnings of the Cirque du Soleil. Céline and the Cirque du Soleil have nothing whatsoever in common. One day, twenty years later, they would meet again, in Las Vegas. For the time being, however, René had no interest in these acrobats on stilts. His mind was entirely on what was to be the most important show of Céline's youthful career.

He was absolutely determined not to miss this opportunity to get the spotlight on his protégée, and decided to invest a considerable amount of money in the show, hiring twenty-three musicians and four back-up singers. Until then he had turned down all major tours, major concerts, or travel over excessive distances. He had taught the young singer the rudiments of the trade, critiquing each of her performances in small halls or benefit shows given before audiences already won over. Now her turn had come.

She played her hand so well that she galvanized a crowd of forty thousand jammed onto the stands of the Vieux Port — almost ten thousand more than for the comeback by Beau Dommage. The critics called it her best stage performance.

René Angélil lost a sizeable sum of money in this venture, but that didn't matter to him. Céline had triumphed, her popularity had grown, and his plan had succeeded.

This was a particularly hectic period, and events came fast and furious — the album's debut, the memorable performance in the Quebec Vieux Port, a TV special on Céline scheduled for the fall, the performance before the Pope at the stadium, a show in Paris ... The gods were smiling on Céline and René. But there would be a price to pay. A woman was shouting at the other end of the line, accusing her husband of neglecting her and his two children. Anne Renée was seeing almost nothing of her husband, who was completely immersed in his work. Things were becoming acrimonious between the couple. She didn't understand that her husband was experiencing the best time of his career as an artists' agent, that his great gamble was coming off, and that he was making Céline known throughout the entire world. The neglected woman did not and could not understand. She only knew she was losing the man she loved and the father of her children.

In the meantime, René watched Céline come out onto the vast field of the Olympic Stadium and heard her voice soar over the sixty-five thousand young Catholics gathered for the occasion. She sang "Une colombe" with tears in her eyes. Dressed all in white, virginal, pure, and innocent — such was the picture she would leave in the minds of the Quebecois.

As 1984 came to an end, Céline's image was associated with that of the Pope, with purity, and with sport. She was often photographed with the Olympic athlete Sylvie Bernier, who had won a gold medal for diving at the Los Angeles Olympics. René was satisfied. Now he resumed his offensive on France. So Céline left Quebec on October 15 for the greatest attempt at seduction of her whole career, as René dreamed of propelling her into the ranks of the great stars. Her success in the Vieux Port of Quebec, her performance in the Olympic Stadium before the Pope, and the promotion in France of the album *Mélanie* encouraged him to attempt a major coup.

But René was not driving this extensive project on his own. The Pathé Marconi company invested its largest budget of the season into promoting the album and putting on a series of shows. The door to Paris was wide open, and René finally opted for Céline to appear in the first half of the show put on by the comedian and singer Patrick Sébastien at the Paris Olympia. Accompanied by her mother, as usual, Céline was to spend two months in France.

"They offered to present her as the main star in Paris, but we don't want to move too fast and harm her career," Angélil explained to the journalists. "It's important to move forward one step at a time to avoid burnout from early on. To tell you the truth, we were offered a lot of money for a solo show or with some major stars, but money isn't all that's important."

Angélil knew very well that the fans of Johnny Halliday or Julien Clerc would be impatient to see their idol, actually going so far as to demand his appearance during the warm-up part of the show, utterly disregarding the artist on stage. René would never have stood for such a humiliation. Patrick Sébastien wasn't a barn-burner and wouldn't arouse such fan frenzy. As for Céline, she acquitted herself very well throughout her Paris engagement as she patiently mastered her trade. Still, it wasn't a decisive event. It couldn't really be called a failure, but it didn't make her a star in France. Yet a lot had been staked on it. René tried to play it down, speaking of a "necessary stage in her career," of an "introduction to the French stage," but actually it didn't go down as well with the transatlantic cousins as had been hoped.

39

A RUN OF BAD LUCK

WITHOUT EITHER RENÉ ANGÉLIL OR Eddy Marnay or anyone knowing exactly why, Céline Dion's popularity waned in Europe towards the end of the year. She had sold almost a million records in Europe up till then, but then, suddenly, sales fell off dramatically. What was happening? Eddy Marnay, who was being paid substantial rights as a songwriter, was becoming uneasy. René pretended to ignore the situation and concentrated on the first major tour being arranged in Quebec. Fortunately the artist's popularity never flagged in her own country.

But René was aware of the situation. If he could easily lull and control the media, deep down he knew very well that his "game plan," to use one of his favourite expressions, had not worked in France, Switzerland, and Belgium, or in Germany, either. He had counted on using Europe as a springboard to conquer the American market, but this wasn't to be. What could he do? Nothing, or almost nothing. First return to Quebec and complete a lengthy tour, and then wait and see.

So he put his philosophy of life into practice — one mainly inspired by the philosophy he applied to gambling. He had often spoken about this to the media, and to his biographer, Georges-Hébert Germain.

"In gambling, like in life, there are good runs and bad ones. When you find yourself having a good run of luck you've got to play for high stakes, invest your money, work hard, and profit from it to the maximum. On the other hand, when you're going through a bad patch, you have to risk very little or nothing, but just stand back and wait for the storm to end. Bad things never come singly, and neither do good." It's a defensible theory, but the problem is to decide when the good or bad run of luck is beginning or ending. Maybe that is René's real talent: to be able to recognize the moment when the wind changes direction.

The events that followed the lukewarm reception in Europe clearly pointed to a bad patch in René's life, one that would last for several years — a run of bad luck, you could say, that would provide an opportunity for the man to show his mettle.

40

PAUL LÉVESQUE AGAIN

L IKE MOST QUEBECOIS, PAUL LÉVESQUE was aware of the phenomenal way Céline Dion's career had taken off. In less than three years
Quebec was at her feet, she had appeared in Paris, carried off several
Felix awards, sold more albums than anyone else in Quebec, and obviously had a promising future ahead of her.

Lévesque's original contract with her went back to 1980, and he had
reached an agreement with René Angélil in 1982 that gave him 6.5 percent of her earnings in return for giving up his entitlement to manage
her. He suddenly asked himself, in November 1984, if he hadn't made
the mistake of his life when he surrendered his rights to the most promising singer in Quebec.

Lévesque felt he had got the short end of the stick in this agreement
that he had been pressured into signing, and on November 9, 1984, he
decided to have his lawyer, Jean-Jacques Beauchamp, submit a formal
demand to TBS and René Angélil.

The lawyer demanded to see all the documents confirming Céline
Dion's engagements since the 1982 agreement between TBS Productions
and Paul Lévesque, and questioned the validity of the contract between
TBS and the organizing committee for the 450th anniversary celebrations.
The lawyer wasn't satisfied with the fee of seventy-five hundred dollars

allowed Céline Dion, and also complained he hadn't been sent copies of the contracts for a number of appearances on TV and in shopping malls. He went even further, challenging René Angélil's management rights. An injunction was issued, and the two parties went to court again.

Strangely, there was no mention of this lawsuit in the media. Paul Lévesque was still unknown to the public, which had no idea he had been Céline Dion's original agent and was still closely connected to the singer, since he was still being paid a percentage of all she earned. But this was just the problem: he felt he wasn't being told the truth about her fees, and that the financial reports he was being given were falsified. In other words he was concerned that Céline, now a genuine singing star in Quebec, wasn't being paid the fees due to a star.

Before Paul Lévesque appeared in court, on January 4, 1985, Thérèse Tanguay-Dion, her daughter Céline, and René Angélil submitted affidavits to the court, on December 28 and 29, 1984.

In summary, Mme Thérèse Tanguay-Dion declared: "[Paul Lévesque] did almost nothing to advance my daughter's career subsequent to our first meeting and the signing of the contract. ... If Paul Lévesque were to resume responsibility for managing my daughter I would be afraid that the career managed in such a masterly fashion by M. Angélil would be put at risk. ... I have complete confidence in M. Angélil, who has succeeded magnificently where M. Lévesque failed."

Where the fees were concerned, Mme Dion added: "I confirm that TBS Productions report to me regularly on all the professional activities of my daughter Céline Dion, that these reports are submitted by me to my accountant, who is preparing the report required by the Public Trustee so that I can submit them to his office in my capacity as my daughter's guardian."

Céline's declaration confirmed her mother's, adding, "Without the presence of M. Angélil, who leads the team around me, this team would fall apart and my career suffer as a consequence."

René Angélil's statement was obviously much more detailed and longer than Thérèse's and Céline's, as he responded point by point, in eighty-seven clauses, to Paul Lévesque's allegations.

We should mention certain clarifications contained in this document regarding the agreed amounts for Céline Dion's engagement in the Vieux Port of Quebec: "TBS Productions was granted $50,000 to put on two performances by Céline Dion on the occasion of *Québec 1534–1984*. This performance cost TBS Productions Inc. the sum of $46,954.60, including Céline Dion's fee ($7,500), leaving a balance of $3,045.40. After paying the royalties on $50,000 to Paul Lévesque, namely $3,125, TBS was left with a deficit of $79.60."

Angélil went on to point out that "a change of management would be disastrous for all involved," and, lower down, assured Paul Lévesque that "TBS Productions has every intention of respecting its commitments to Paul Lévesque until the expiration of the contract on December 5, 1985."

On January 4, 1985, Louis Crête, the brilliant lawyer picked by René Angélil, defended TBS Productions so skilfully that he was able to run rings round Lévesque, if the transcript is anything to go by. But that meant very little to René Angélil, who was absolutely determined to put an end to this matter. He invited Lévesque to reach a final agreement — an amicable one, the kind he preferred — without any amount being made public. He was above all determined to avoid any negative publicity about the case, which was kept secret.

41

ON TOUR

ONCE THE PROBLEM OF THE contract with Paul Lévesque was settled once and for all, René Angélil could breathe more easily and set to work on the next step in Céline's career: performances in major theatres and tours. So far, she had given stage performances in aid of various causes — for cystic fibrosis, for instance, a disease from which her young niece suffered, and on behalf of the employees of Québecair. She had also promoted the cause of peace, liberty, and youth before the Pope. Now she would be advancing only her own cause on the stages of Quebec, setting off on March 26, 1985, on a tour that would take her to twenty-four towns in the province, ending with the Salle Wilfrid-Pelletier in the Montreal Place des Arts, now considered the most prestigious hall in Quebec.

As disciplined as ever, full of healthy energy, Céline was preparing carefully for this demanding tour, taking singing and dancing lessons from Peter George, and leading an austere existence. At sixteen she was never seen in discos or at parties with friends of her own age except on very rare occasions, and people remarked how totally she was under her agent's control.

She confessed quite frankly to journalists she met at a press conference to announce the tour: "I admit I'd have liked to have really performed on stage during the past four years. For me it was an incredible sacrifice not to give live performances, but I recognize now that I still didn't have all the tools I needed, and I understand why my agent imposed such restrictions on me." René, who was nearby when she said this, immediately added with his usual conviction and passion, "Until now, all our efforts have gone into getting out her recordings. We were aiming at exceptional quality, and we achieved it. Now we're moving on to live shows, and we're aiming at the same quality there. Two years ago, a producer offered us thirty-five thousand dollars to do this tour and we refused. Céline wasn't ready for it yet."

A journalist asked if she would continue her tour in France. He answered, "There's no question of her performing in France for the time being. She's not ready for France yet, and we'll have to wait a year or eighteen months. Here she has put out seven LPs while over there she only has two. But don't be too impatient. Two or three years from now she'll be one of the top singers in the world."

So it was out at last — the great prediction had been made to the media! She would be one of the top singers in the world! Later he would say that she would be *the* top singer in the world. Yet René was broke. He had invested his all in the career of his precious artist without any thought of the expense. No matter: she was his trump card, and her value was growing all the time. That is the way a gambler thinks, constantly doubling his stake. Of course he bought a house in Laval to give his wife and two children a proper roof over their heads, and he was no longer at the mercy of his creditors, but there was no question of making his fortune out of Céline's career — not yet, anyway. He kept watch over his protégée as if she were a precious gem. He was ambitious, but some members of her family say they sometimes felt she was even more so.

She was already thinking about the United States and dreaming of a career like Michael Jackson's, her hero. In 1984 she wanted to perform rock — music that was a bit "heavier." René thought she had to take things more slowly in order to win over a broad public. And of course he was right.

Supported by eight musicians and two backup singers led by Paul Baillargeon, she set out on a tour that turned out to be much more successful than expected. Extra performances were added, and instead of twenty-four shows she soon reached the forty-second in May. The young singer had changed. Her teeth had been straightened, and she could now smile broadly for the photographers. She looked after her figure, for she wanted to be attractive, and for the first time she told a journalist that a woman should be "sexy." She was no longer the shy, fragile, too pure young girl who had sung before the Pope.

She hadn't let the word slip out unintentionally. Indeed, Céline never lets anything slip out in the presence of a journalist, for René is never very far away, and controls every interview. Before appearing before the media, the master and his pupil would have a long discussion and the pupil would be taught what and what not to say.

In performance, she moved a lot, really attacked the song, and was now aiming at an adult public.

René remembered some hits from the previous year, of course, but he also remembered the scorn the Quebec intelligentsia had shown the singer. In 1984, she was too over-emotional, too loud, and sang songs that were too obvious, too sentimental, and — why not say it right out — the "in" crowd (the same who would sing her praises ten or so years later) saw her as just another popular, and even kitschy, singer.

Oddly, Céline suffered from this less than René. Despite his protégée's successes, he was quite aware that opinions about her were divided, that she was considered to be too "commercial," and that her image would have to be changed little by little.

Day and night he thought of her career. He was obsessed by this talent that was developing under his eyes, the way he might have been by a winning streak at the gambling table. He had forgotten everything else — his wife and children in particular.

42

ANNE RENÉE CHANGES HER TUNE

I N HIS UTTER DEVOTION TO Céline Dion's career, during interviews René Angélil never mentioned the name of his wife, Anne Renée, or did so only rarely. Yet she was officially the president of TBS Productions and had worked very hard to create the young singer's image and shape her personality. In time the two women had grown close, becoming friends and bonding like sisters. In 1985, however, Anne Renée took her distance and devoted herself to another up-and-coming star named Peter Pringle.

Pringle, an English Canadian, reached the peak of his popularity in 1985, thanks to Anne's unsparing efforts. He was visible everywhere, and his albums appeared on the Quebec charts. A highly cultured individual, he distinguished himself from the other pop stars by playing the harp or the lute in his shows and speaking seven languages, including Japanese. This was someone who cooked oriental dishes, visited art galleries, and practised meditation. Like René and Céline, Peter and Anne were constantly in one another's company. There were already rumours going around in entertainment circles suggesting they were having an affair. Anne Renée often asked her husband for a little more attention, and above all that he be home more often. But he was caught up in a constant whirlwind of activity, and his wife realized she no longer had any hold over him.

She was hanging on, badgering and reproaching him, but he didn't listen: with Céline he was playing the most important card in his whole life.

Feeling lonely and neglected, Anne Renée confided, not in Peter Pringle, but in one of his musicians, Michel Fauteux, to whom she was attracted. Fauteux was a drummer in the combo that accompanied Pringle, but he was also a member of Céline Dion's group of musicians. Fauteux belonged to that species of free men, very often nomadic, bon vivant, and particularly charming. He was a flamboyant individual, very "jet-set," and Anne Renée was strongly attracted to him.

I met Michel Fauteux while I was writing the unauthorized biography of Céline Dion. He was no longer a musician and didn't seem in very good health. That day he felt the need to get some painful memories off his chest. I had the impression I was the therapist who had entered his life providentially. He confided:

> I remember the date. It was February 21, 1985, one evening after Peter Pringle's show. We were on tour in a quiet little town, and Anne Renée, who seemed depressed, confided in me and made advances to me. She said her husband was neglecting her. Quite frankly, I have to say she didn't interest me just then. I know I could have resisted and kept out of her way, but she wanted to get laid, and so did I, so … you see what I'm saying.
>
> We went on seeing one another, fell passionately in love, and one day Peter Pringle caught us in bed together. I'd never seen him in such a state. He was yelling like crazy, and I suppose he must have been thinking of René Angélil.
>
> I was thinking of him, too, and I wanted to be above-board with him. I arranged to meet him in March to tell him about the situation. At first he didn't want to believe me, thinking it was a bad joke, but seeing I was serious he told me we were finished for good. I wanted to be straight with René because he was someone I admired, and that I've always admired. He's a fair person, very honest, and extremely faithful, in both love and friendship.

Anne Renée, whose real name is Anne-Renée Kirouac, sued for divorce on March 11, 1985. She first asked for legal custody of the children, Jean-Pierre and Anne-Marie. She wanted alimony of eighteen hundred dollars a month, "a sum the respondent is able to pay," and a lump sum of seventy-five thousand dollars "as compensation for my contribution in goods and services to the respondent's personal wealth."

Angélil was stupefied, stunned, and devastated when he saw the document. He couldn't understand. It was he who had been betrayed and deceived, but it was she who wanted to leave him — it was there in black and white. His universe suddenly collapsed around him: his wife loved someone else, and it was serious. Nor was she concealing the fact, for she even confided her problems to the journalist Claire Cyril: "I couldn't be my husband's wife and business partner at the same time. René just saw me as his professional associate. The children were never used to being with both of us at the same time, for we took turns travelling on business."

The person in question changed. He was so preoccupied by his conjugal problems that his heart and mind were no longer in his work. The album *C'est pour toi* wasn't produced with the same attention or enthusiasm as Céline's other recordings. Moreover, it didn't meet with great success.

Tension was rising, and a tempest broke out between the couple. People had been hurt, and René couldn't accept the situation. In addition to being threatened with the loss of his wife and children, he was also afraid of losing TBS Productions — and Céline Dion. We mustn't forget that 100 percent of TBS belonged to Anne Renée, so legally all the power was in her hands. He was merely an employee she could let go whenever she wanted. There was no documentary proof that she had any such intention, but he feared the reactions of a woman scorned. He had never forgotten how he had lost Ginette Reno because of another man. And then he was about to lose his children.

So what happened on that night of March 12, 1985? Anne Renée would tell about it a little later in her official divorce suit:

> After my day's work, at about 3:30, I came home, where
> the children were with their governess. It was only

towards midnight that the respondent entered, when I was in bed. He woke me and began a violent domestic scene, absolutely refusing to let me get to sleep.

When the respondent's harassment became more and more persistent I had to phone the police, for I was afraid of being physically abused.

After a first visit from the police, who seemed to have restored calm, I went back to bed. But the respondent recommenced his harassment and violence and abused me physically, striking me several times, so that I had to call the police again. As a result I had to leave the conjugal home under police protection at around 2:30 a.m., with my children, to take refuge in my mother's home.

On March 13, 1985, the respondent appeared at my mother's home illegally in an attempt to take the children. My mother, concerned, called the police shortly before I myself came home and took back the children.

I returned with them to the conjugal home, where the governess also was, after the respondent promised me not to harass or argue with me anymore.

But despite these promises he continued to insult, threaten and intimidate me and submit me to psychological abuse, making our life together completely impossible.

Anne Renée later declared that she was the sole owner of the shares in the company TBS Productions Inc., and that by a resolution of March 30, 1984, she had hired the respondent, René Angélil, as manager, at a net salary of five hundred dollars a week.

"In May 1984," she states in the suit, "I transferred 51% of the ordinary shares of the company to the respondent, without any financial compensation."

Now we come to March 14, when René Angélil became aware of his wife's true intentions. Anne Renée continues:

On March 14 or 15, after threatening me with the loss of my children and my career and to destroy those I work with, the respondent told me he was going to unilaterally remove the right to sign company cheques from me, and that he was withdrawing my salary.

The respondent told me that, if I continued divorce proceedings, I would find myself in the street with the children, for it would be a simple matter for him to incorporate a new company, paying himself a minimal salary, and so make himself incapable of paying alimony.

After asking my lawyer to suspend proceedings, I therefore moved out, leaving my children, who continued to live with a governess and the respondent in the former conjugal home, which was jointly owned.

Subsequently the respondent forced me, without any financial compensation, to transfer, by notarized deed, my joint share of the former conjugal home out of my name, even though the said property had been purchased a short time after the respondent declared personal bankruptcy.

Furthermore, the respondent insisted that I transfer to him all the shares in the company TBS Productions Inc., without any financial compensation, this despite the fact that the said company was contracted to manage the Quebec artist Céline Dion and consequently produced substantial revenues.

After Peter Pringle's spring tour, Anne Renée lived out her new passion in her apartment on Île des Soeurs during the summer of 1985. In the meantime, Céline Dion put on the most important performance of her tour in the Salle Wilfrid-Pelletier, at the Place des Arts in Montreal, on May 31. It was a performance that held out the promise of a new Céline Dion, more confident in her abilities, more incisive on stage, and more of a rock singer. The critics, of whom I was one in that spring of 1985, heaped praise on the young singer, who even allowed herself to sing a medley of songs by Michel Legrand. Definitely, the young Céline had undergone a sea change.

The flames of passion had subsided by the end of 1985, and Anne Renée wanted a change. She missed family life and wondered if she hadn't made a mistake by leaving her husband and children. She suddenly realized that she was overworked after the long tour with Peter Pringle — as indeed was her husband. And, too, she was a strong and domineering woman in her own way — a woman with a heart, but with a good head on her shoulders as well, quite able to organize a career and impose her ideas. She could stand up to anyone. She could be provocative, and could handle herself well when a storm was brewing.

After thirteen years as René Angélil's wife she could not accept the idea that their relationship had deteriorated so suddenly. She sincerely believed that everything could change if she put enough effort into it and demonstrated some goodwill. So she decided to abandon her career as an artists' agent to devote herself solely to her family. René let her know that things would be different if she returned home. So the couple was reconciled after a period of long, painful quarrels.

Anne was preparing to return home when Céline and René met the Pope again in October 1985.

43

A ROSE FOR THE POPE

I T WAS GILLES CHAMPAGNE, THE president of a commemorative park and a well-known businessman in the Mauricie region, who offered René Angélil a trip to Rome along with Céline Dion and her mother to meet the Pope.

With the help of his horticulturalists, Champagne, who owned a cemetery, had bred a rose intended for the Pope and wanted to present it to him personally. A man of large vision, he decided to bring the media along, as well as the singer of "Une colombe," to ensure he got wide media coverage.

René couldn't resist for very long the prospect of seeing his star's pictures on the front page of the newspapers. And then, after his marital disputes, he thought this trip to Rome might do him a lot of good. He experienced some peace of mind throughout the journey, in the course of which Champagne gave Dr. Ponti, the director of the papal gardens, the famous rose named after John Paul II.

Céline shook hands with the pontiff, who recalled the Olympic stadium and all the ceremonies. The cameras followed Céline everywhere she went.

"However it may seem, there was nothing mercenary about the Rome trip," René Angélil explained to the Quebec press, "particularly since Céline's latest record had reached its sales ceiling on the Quebec market. Meeting the Pope was an extraordinary mystical and human experience for Céline and me."

44

AT HOME AGAIN

ANNE RENÉE RETURNED TO THE conjugal home on October 21, 1985. She shared the joy of their reunion with René. She resumed her place in the little family and was reunited with her children, whom she had greatly missed. With her husband she was hoping to experience a new beginning as a couple.

To make this possible she had agreed to several personal sacrifices. She had thought about the matter at length and realized that two artists' agents were perhaps one too many in a single family, and that it would be best for her to give up her career and her financial freedom. She also wanted to prove to him that she was really determined to resume life as a couple. She obviously hoped he was driven by the same resolve.

To start with he seemed to live up to his wife's expectations, and the couple seemed united, happy, and at peace. The newspapers even announced their reconciliation. It was all very fine and touching, but it didn't mean René could neglect Céline's career. He had to go to Paris for the promotion of the album *C'est pour toi*. Anne did not accompany him, for she had to take care of the children. René met Michel Drucker and Eddy Marnay again, and the whirlwind of activity started up again — like before.

He imagined that his wife had returned home once and for all, and that there was no longer any danger. He stayed on in Paris, while Anne, who had nothing to do but wait for him, was more bored than ever. Back home again, René planned another trip, this time to Las Vegas, to visit the casinos with some friends. He asked his wife to join them, but she refused. He couldn't believe his ears, and on that December 14, 1985, she abandoned all hope of recovering the peaceful, tranquil family existence she had dreamed of. Business, celebrating with friends, the show business lies, the tours, the sleepless nights, and life without her children seemed intolerable to her. She suddenly hated an occupation that was so destructive to life as a couple.

So she stayed home on her own while her husband went off to the casinos. She finally left their home and recommenced her divorce proceedings on December 15, 1985. This time there was no going back.

In her suit, made to the Supreme Court, Anne-Renée Kirouac relates what transpired:

> On around October 21, 1985, I returned to live with my children in the former conjugal home, deciding to end my career as an artists' agent, and in particular to no longer look after the career of Peter Pringle with whom I had a contract, in order to devote myself entirely to my children.
>
> From that moment I had in effect ceased working and so, given my regular and constant presence with my children, I dismissed the governess in the last week of November 1985.
>
> The respondent, for his part, indicated clearly to me that he was happy and pleased that I was taking over the care of the children, who could not have a better mother.
>
> When I returned to live with the children in the conjugal home, around October 21, 1985, the respondent and I attempted a reconciliation, but the situation deteriorated in a few days because of the attitude,

behaviour, and harassment of me by the respondent, and life in common became intolerable.

In fact, the respondent travels regularly, being required by his functions to be out of the city and the country on a monthly basis, and is capable of settling anywhere without difficulty.

Furthermore, the respondent, who returned from a business trip to Paris on December 9, 1985, informed me that he was setting out again with some friends on December 14, 1985, to gamble in the casino in Las Vegas. He asked me to accompany him, but I refused.

The plaintiff added to paragraph thirty-nine of her suit: "Furthermore, the respondent constantly repeated to me in March 1985 and during the final weeks that if I reached an amicable agreement without legal representation I would lack for nothing, but that if I retained the services of a lawyer he would make it seem that he was penniless."

It was a woman in deep distress who was reunited with Michel Fauteux, the lover she thought she had left forever. She had lost everything in these proceedings — family, house, husband, employment, and financial freedom — and was literally on the verge of collapse. Michael Fauteux explains:

I found her a troubled and profoundly unstable woman. I experienced a love affair with her that went from the heights to the depths, like a rollercoaster. I tried to end our relationship, but she held me hostage with threats and suicide attempts on two occasions at least: once in front of the Verdun hospital and the other time in Maine, at Ogunquit. The ambulance men found her hiding in a cupboard. She didn't know what she was doing anymore.

In October I was glad to see her go back to her husband and children. She returned to me later because her attempt at reconciliation failed. And then, after a certain time, she decided to take a holiday to think things out, away from me. While she was absent I suddenly realized I was in love with her. But it was too late, because at a Club Med she met an American Airlines pilot who asked her to go and live with him in California. It was over between us, and I was hurting a lot. Even so, we remained friends for a while, and the couple even invited me to spend holidays on their yacht, but I declined.

And that was how Mark McClellan came into Anne Renée's life and helped her regain her equilibrium and the security she so desperately needed. The couple would live for several years in California.

At the time he granted me an interview, Michel Fauteux left the apartment where he had experienced his mad passion with Anne. He had one final thought before leaving the scene: "I was responsible for a lot of things, and in the end I was the one who made René and Céline's marriage possible. If his wife hadn't left him, he'd never have left her for Céline. He was a man of principle and a faithful one, and I say that knowing he'll detest me as long as he lives."

45

A FRESH START

A NNE RENÉE BEGAN A NEW life in 1986. At the end of January her marriage was officially at an end when the divorce settlement came through. It was with a certain degree of serenity and certainly with considerable weariness that the two parties agreed to the following:

> The two parties will have joint legal custody of the two children of the marriage;
>
> The plaintiff will have physical custody of both children;
>
> The parties agree to sell the former conjugal home with a minimum of delay, and agree to share the product of the sale;
>
> The parties agree to an amicable sharing of the furniture and other effects contained in the former conjugal home.
>
> Furthermore, the respondent agrees to pay the plaintiff a weekly alimony of $300 for herself and the children, until the conjugal home is sold and the plaintiff moves out.

Photo: Jean Beaulne's private collection.

Jean Beaulne in his elementary school class in Montreal in the late 1940s.

Jean Beaulne's private collection.

At school, René and Pierre were already comics who
entertained their schoolmates by imitating their teachers,
and especially Dean Martin and Jerry Lewis.

Early in their career the Baronets formed a foursome. From left to right: Gilles Petit, Pierre Labelle, Jean Beaulne, and René Angélil. Petit soon left the group for a career in insurance. The Baronets' first appearance was in an amateur talent contest, *Les Découvertes de Billy Monroe*, in 1957.

An early photograph of the Baronets in their
dressing room at the Bellevue Casino in Montreal.

The Baronets perform a novelty song at Jean Beaulne's brother's wedding.

In their early days the Baronets appeared in
Quebec and the U.S. in superclubs.

Denyse Duquette, René Angélil's first wife.

The three Baronets were obliged to adopt
Beatles haircuts to please their fans.

Jean Beaulne meets the Beatles' manager, Brian Epstein, during the famous group's visit to Toronto in 1965.

Announcement of René's father's death in 1967.

Jean Beaulne

A publicity photograph of Jean Beaulne after he left
the Baronets to sing on his own. He had some hit records.

In 1982, in a press conference, René Angélil introduces
a new singing prodigy, Céline Dion.

In 1983, Céline Dion, Denys Bergeron, Anne Renée, and René Angélil
celebrate the golden disk awarded for Céline's first album.

Photo: *La Presse*.

Dion Chante Plamondon was gold even before it
arrived in record stores in 1991.

Jean Beaulne's private collection.

René and Céline's "royal wedding" is celebrated in the
Church of Notre Dame on December 17, 1994.

René-Charles Dion-Angélil, born January 25, 2001: the couple's future.

Jean Beaulne, who shared in writing this biography,
and Céline Dion, the woman who transformed René.

The Baronets are reunited almost thirty years after their break-up, in the company of Céline and her father, Adhémar.

> As soon as the plaintiff obtains paid employment, the alimony will be set for the two children alone at $750 per month, with the respondent also being directly responsible for their medical and dental expenses.
>
> As a result of the present agreement, the parties grant each other general and final indemnity from any further claim. Signed by the parties at Montreal, this 30th day of January, 1986.

Anne Renée had lost six kilograms, and admits she went through a period of depression, but in the spring of 1986 she gradually recovered her strength and embarked on a career as a producer in the new video department of JPL Productions, a subsidiary of Télé-Métropole. Not for a moment did it occur to her to return to the whirlwind activity of an artists' manager. Show business was in the past for her.

Her relations with René Angélil remained serene as friendship gradually replaced her feelings about a man who wasn't right for her. She realized this suddenly when she was blessed with a new love. She would live in Laval for a good part of 1986 while working with JPL Productions, and would even produce a video of Céline Dion, proving beyond doubt that Anne Renée and René Angélil had ended their differences and wished to maintain good relations for their children's sake.

She finally left Quebec to live with Mark McClellan in California, where she would live for more than fifteen years. In May 1988 she married McClellan in Marie Immaculée Conception Church. She wanted this marriage to be celebrated in a Catholic Church because of her religious beliefs. It was not until 2002 that she returned to Quebec.

46

RENÉ'S SELF-QUESTIONING

THERE WAS NO END IN sight to René's run of bad luck. Céline Dion's most recent album, *C'est pour toi*, didn't enjoy the hoped-for success. At the beginning of 1986, he started thinking about her next album. He was quite aware that the latest LP wasn't her best. He never deceived himself. If he was good at telling incredible stories and skilfully skirting the truth in order to promote the product he had to sell, he never lost sight of reality. He knew that musically Céline Dion had exhausted all her youthful adolescent emotions. A period of transition was beginning. But now at the beginning of 1986 he had to decide how this transition would take place. The first step entailed negotiating a new agreement with Trans-Canada Records.

In this very competitive environment, a loss of momentum wasn't easily overlooked. At Trans-Canada they were fully aware that the sales of Céline's latest record hadn't been very strong, so they refused to invest in a new recording. Yet René was asking for just fifty thousand dollars. After album sales in the millions, he couldn't understand their attitude.

"One day she'll be the most popular singer in the world," he proclaimed. He was wasting his breath, for Trans-Canada had lost confidence. René saw their attitude as a real insult — aimed not at him but at the most promising entertainer in Quebec. He would never forgive

Trans-Canada for the lack of respect it had shown Céline. He felt shattered and humiliated.

He thought over his career again, and once again decided to risk everything to bring off a major coup. In his office he reread the press cuttings, looked over the newspaper reviews, mentally reviewing every stage in his protégée's career, and saw that her image had to be altered radically. People had to be made to forget about "Une colombe," the naive, over-emotional songs, the nasal intonation, and family matters.

Céline would be eighteen on March 30, and he marked the event by founding a company called Feeling. The singer, who had now reached the age of majority, ended her contractual arrangement with Paul Lévesque and was no longer under her mother's guardianship. René signed a new management contract with his protégée, giving each of them 50 percent, as Colonel Parker had done once with Elvis Presley. Henceforth Feeling would look after her interests.

But in order to introduce a new Céline Dion to the general public, numerous changes would have to be made. Some of these would be painful. René saw that Eddy Marnay's songs could no longer be used if this transformation was to come about. But the friendship between Angélil and the likeable, thoughtful Eddy Marnay was still a real one. It was tempting to maintain his association with a man who had opened the doors to the European market for him, but Céline's new career required a new direction. He didn't want to hurt Marnay by completely breaking off their professional relationship, so he allowed him to write a few more songs, but they were only transitional ones, bridging the gap between the old Céline Dion and the new. So the Marnay period ended in 1986, as the singer left the stage and gradually faded from sight.

47

A SABBATICAL YEAR

A NGÉLIL WASN'T RICH AT THE time, but it didn't show. He had to
protect the image of success. Since Céline's career began he had
always been able to put up a smokescreen by spending money on very
costly launches, hiring outstanding musicians to back up the singer, and
travelling in first-class conditions. He never spared expense.

"Since we first met, René always behaved like a millionaire with
class, elegance, and a lot of intelligence, and my mother liked that,"
Céline Dion would say.

However, Céline wasn't generating as much income at the end of
1985. The strategy was a long-term one, but in the short term the situation was a bit precarious where finances were concerned.

René the strategist saw perfectly that the new direction of Céline's
career would have to go beyond superficial details. He was embarking
on a major turnaround for her, and decided to devote the time required
for the young singer's transformation to making contact with new songwriters. Early in 1986 he decided first to let things take their course and
spend some time at the gambling tables.

He became a full-time gambler in Las Vegas, winning a lot of
money, and even winning a few blackjack tournaments. But he lost
money, too. He soon found himself in debt to the tune of two hundred

thousand dollars, a sum he managed to win back a short time later, with a lot of luck. This episode was another source of stress for him.

"I just had to earn my living during Céline's sabbatical year," he would say later.

48

THE GAMBLER

R ENÉ ANGÉLIL HAS ALWAYS BEEN fascinated by gambling. It was in his genes and in his culture. He has never made any excuses for indulging in games of chance, and has never tried to conceal the fact that he gambled. Quite to the contrary, he likes to speak of life's risks and the runs of luck in people's lives, as if life were a big roulette game, with its odd or even or red or black days. Some days everything goes well, or nothing does. In the 1980s he was already joking with journalists about his runs of good or bad luck in the Las Vegas casinos, as if these were most entertaining things that happened to him. He never dramatized things when speaking about gambling. Win or lose, according to him it was all part of the game and there was no reason to cry over his losses because there'd always be a next time.

Even Céline supported him, in public at least. "René is a gambler, and I'm glad. It's precisely because he's a gambler that I've been successful in my career. In the beginning he bet his shirt on me, and in the end he won. I know he still gambles, but he's sensible about it. Every day when we're staying in Las Vegas we make up little envelopes into which we slip a few hundred dollars for René to gamble with."

Actually, there is nothing sensible about René. He has always done things to excess and been extreme in everything he has undertaken. Ever since his first visit to a casino in Puerto Rico he has regularly frequented gaming houses, particularly Caesar's Palace in Las Vegas. Usually his visits to the Mecca of gambling are discreet, and he registers in the hotels under a false name. Pierre Sara is the one he uses most often.

Jean Beaulne and Pierre Labelle never shared their comrade's enthusiasm for gambling back in the Baronets days. However, the three of them lived in such close proximity that they knew one another like the backs of their hands. They shared everything, even René's moods and his dreams. Jean Beaulne recounts:

> I very soon recognized that gambling was important to him when I saw him practising with a roulette wheel in his room every day we were on tour. He was able take a lot of things lightly, but never anything to do with gambling. I told him that with all the money he was going to make I hoped he'd remember me and buy me lots of things, but he'd look me as if I'd committed a blasphemy.
>
> Later, I'd come to understand very well that his real objective in life was to break the bank. He was obsessed with the idea. I went to casinos without ever becoming a real gambler. I had enough detachment to see how it worked.
>
> One time I saw him at a blackjack table in Las Vegas. He'd decided to play alone at the table, replacing seven players who each had to bet $3,000. So he was staking $21,000 on each hand, and each lasted barely five minutes. At that rate it doesn't take you long to lose a pile of money in an evening.
>
> René competed in tournaments in 1986, and I have to tell you that gamblers from all over the world took part in these tournaments. That was very exciting for René, for it meant he could compete against the best. He never could resist a challenge. People gambled for high stakes in those tournaments, and they could require a minimum stake of somewhere between $10,000 and more than $100,000. Some slot machines are even set up

to accept $1,000 chips, meaning you can lose the astronomical sum of $100,000 in less than half an hour. The tension is tremendous. There are huge sums of money on the table and fortunes are won and lost in these tournaments. In Las Vegas they often tell the story of a rich Chinese businessman who lost his entire fortune, nearly three hundred million dollars. To help him recover from the disaster the casino hired him to bring in more customers. He had to attract other very rich businessmen from China to their gambling establishment. That's the way they do things in Las Vegas.

I estimate that after having seen René gambling throughout all those years and knowing how casinos work — and they never lose money — he must have lost, I would think, a total of ten million dollars at the gambling table. He's stubborn and persistent, and he doesn't give up easily. In his work that's a quality, but at the gambling table maybe it's a major weakness. One day I asked a croupier what was the best way to win at the casino, and his answer was: "Stay home!" So that's just what I did from then on.

But René claimed to have earned a good living while patronizing the casinos in the gambling capital for months, and it was probably true — for a while, at least. But he didn't forget Céline. She acquired a new look and style during this first sabbatical year of her career. The public hadn't completely forgotten her — far from it. Rumours were rife. She was said to have secretly married Angélil in Las Vegas. Others said she had given birth to a baby in Egypt, also in secret, assisted by René's mother. And, of course — the classic story in the circumstances — she was supposed to be hooked on cocaine, which explained why she was so skinny. A lot of other rumours were put about during this time, and even later, heaping all the sins and vices imaginable on the unfortunate woman.

The truth was much simpler and more romantic. She was madly in love with the man who had been fashioning her life for the past few years, and who wanted to push her all the way to the top.

Céline is a grateful person. She never thought of the strategies, skulduggery, marketing effort, and seductive lies of show business. She thought of the little girl from Charlemagne, skinny, not very attractive, rejected by her friends, without any education, who in a few years had become the idol of an entire population. She thought of the life she would have had without him. In fact, that was the only thing she thought about, and she wanted to prove her gratitude to him by becoming a desirable, sexy, fascinating woman he'd be unable to resist.

While René was preparing for the second phase of Céline Dion's career, she was preparing to experience her first love. If she devoted so much energy to developing a new look, developing her flexibility with dance lessons, and learning English with lessons from Berlitz, it was less for the public than for the love of her life. During this sabbatical year, she was working on her plan to seduce — for the seduction of René first of all, and later of the rest of the world.

"She was changing physically, and I didn't see her the same way anymore," René Angélil would later admit.

But in 1986 René drove all such thoughts out of his mind and embarked on an inner struggle. He was now forty-four years of age, his divorce had just been made official by the Supreme Court, and as far as anyone knew he had not had any affairs. His first son, Patrick, was Céline's age, and he just could not imagine himself announcing to the press that he was in love with a girl of eighteen. Besides, the painful split with Anne Renée had left him deeply wounded, with no desire for another love affair, least of all under media scrutiny. In his mind the slightest indication of a possible relationship between himself and Céline would mean the end for his protégée and ruin for him personally. But did he have any idea of the way Céline felt about him? Probably he did, since for the album *C'est pour toi* Eddy Marnay had easily plumbed the young woman's state of mind and written songs that were revealing, to say the least. But René pretended not to notice anything, and concentrated on the next step.

49

CBS

AFTER MONTHS OF WAITING AND reflecting, René met Bill Rotari, the top man at CBS. It could hardly be called a chance encounter. He had been trying for a long time to get together with Rotari, whom he had known back in the Baronets days. His plan had been laid out for a long time already: he wanted to record Céline's new album with CBS. This multinational company was easily the most dynamic in Quebec, and had the biggest names in show business on its list, including Michael Jackson, who had made a strong impression on Céline and René during his last visit to Montreal.

Summoning up all his famous gift of the gab, René made every effort to convince Rotari to offer a contract to the most popular singer in Quebec. "Listen, Bill, I haven't got the resources to produce Céline's next albums. She's become something big, and now it's time for her to record with a major company," he argued.

"But haven't you got a contract with Trans-Canada?" asked Rotari.

"No! That's all ancient history. Céline has to move on, to a new atmosphere, to a different environment. And Trans-Canada wouldn't be right for her. We're thinking big, you see, for Céline is the best," insisted Angélil.

"I'll see what I can do and get back to you."

But René never gives up. He phoned Rotari at every opportunity, and kept on doing so. He had his mind set on CBS and was keeping his fingers crossed.

Rotari consulted his artistic director, Vito Luprano, who initially didn't want to hear of Céline Dion. This wasn't surprising, for Luprano was particularly enthusiastic about the new music. He went to clubs in Montreal and New York, listening to the music young people preferred and trying to spot the latest trends. He was familiar with Céline's hits and had no interest in a kind of music he considered saccharine, naive, and outmoded. But René insisted and urged Vito to go to see Céline perform. It was a good idea, for she had excellent stage command and sang "What a Feeling" like a genuine rock singer. Surprised, and even astonished, Luprano agreed to work with her and was already thinking of turning to songwriter Aldo Nova to write some songs for her. René couldn't contain himself. Now he had to raise things another notch by convincing the most popular songwriter in Quebec to write songs for his protégée. The person René had in mind was none other than Luc Plamondon.

50

LUC PLAMONDON

THE ENCOUNTER BETWEEN RENÉ ANGÉLIL and Luc Plamondon was a strange one. In that summer of 1986 the two men seemed to have nothing in common. They seemed a world apart. René the gambler, the lover of fast food, the golfer and champion of marketing, was turning to Luc Plamondon, a refined, sensitive, and cultured literary individual.

But Plamondon knew his artists well, and had a nose for talent. Not only was he the most sought after songwriter among Quebec artists, he was also the person who had revamped the careers of Julien Clerc, Catherine Lara, Barbara, and Robert Charlebois.

Since 1980, *Starmania*, the musical comedy he wrote with Michel Berger, had literally transformed Francophone music. Until he came along, people said it was impossible to sing rock in French. With *Starmania*, French music emerged into the modern world, and since then young people have been swinging, rocking, and swaying in French to songs like "Coeur de rocker," "Je t'aime comme un fou," "Oxygène," and "Nuit magique," to mention just a few hits equally well known in France and Quebec.

In his house in Outremont Plamondon often hosted and provided a bed for French artists visiting Quebec, such as France Gall, Julien Clerc, Renaud, and Fred Mellan of the Compagnons de la chanson. His house, overlooking Outremont Park and furnished in art deco style, was a veritable embassy and a real haven for people who lived music and talked about it well into the night.

Céline and René had met Plamondon several times at his home and had got to know him. They had seen *Starmania*, and Céline had a dream of one day acting in a musical. "Obviously," said René, "we could put on a musical in the great cities of the world."

In 1986 some people though Angélil had gone out of his mind. His claims that his protégée would become the greatest singer in the world, achieve international stardom, and triumph in a musical — and playing the leading role into the bargain — didn't seem very credible to some. She hadn't yet made the grade in the U.S. and wasn't considered a star in France or anywhere else in Europe. But Luc Plamondon wasn't among the skeptics. He was gradually discovering Céline's extraordinary talent and the passion that was just waiting to erupt.

"I've never heard anyone sing like that in French. She's going to be one of the world's greats," Plamondon, who had never had any time for scorn or snobbery, would say. He was also highly impressed by René's determination, for René had met him many times and absolutely insisted on his collaboration on the next record.

Plamondon finally agreed to write some songs for the young artist on condition he could converse with her several times to get to know her better. As he listened to her he recognized her newfound sensuality, her need to love and to assert herself. And so he wrote first "Lolita" and then "Incognito," the album's title song, to music by Daniel Lavoie.

These were two works that stood out clearly against all the songs the young singer had previously recorded or performed. "Lolita" probed deeply into the profound desire of a young woman whose desire "consumes her body to the tips of her fingers" and who wasn't "*trop jeune pour se donner*" — too young to give herself. When he reread the text of the song to take it in better René didn't turn a hair, and didn't ask for any changes. He wanted Céline Dion's image to change, and this text by Plamondon provided that.

"René Angélil allowed me carte blanche, and gave me a lot of respect and courtesy," Plamondon confided after putting the finishing touches to his work.

René reached an agreement with CBS that called for a substantial investment in the record's production, and included one final detail — an almost negligible one, in fact: merely a clause stating that a budget of thirty thousand dollars would be available to make a record in English! It was accepted, and once again René was jubilant. Yet it was an insignificant amount for anyone with knowledge of the recording industry. But René knew what he was doing and often outlined his strategy to anyone prepared to listen. "It's just a matter of getting a foot in the door of the English-speaking market. The amount, and CBS's interpretation, didn't matter; I knew the clause would be renegotiated one day."

51

THE MACHINE BREAKS DOWN

F INALLY RENÉ ANGÉLIL COULD ENJOY a little respite while this contract with CBS allowed him to dream. He had already spent five years working with Céline — five years during which he had given his all in every respect. How often had he travelled to Paris, Switzerland, Belgium, California, and inside Quebec? He could no longer keep count. How many shows had been given on tour? How many initiatives, deals, and promotions had he launched? And for all that he nothing to show but the insignificant sum remaining in his bank account. He wasn't always rolling in money. He aimed high, always insisting on the best musicians, technicians, and producers, on staying in the best hotels and surrounding Céline with the best possible care. In short, he spent every penny he earned.

On the personal level the previous year had been difficult for him. His break-up with Anne Renée had been one of the most dramatic events in his life, and the rift had left its mark on him. If we add to that the fatigue caused by Céline's tour and the difficulty of breaking into the European market, it is easy to understand why he was so tired.

The carefree lad of the Baronets days had become a man weighed down by responsibilities, who was mortgaging his life again and again on the chance of a fabulous future. He was a man continually living beyond his means.

"René always seemed to live on the edge, to the maximum. He never counted his time, or his money. He was a generous person," Céline Dion often repeats — and she knows him better than anyone.

Sometimes he tried to find an outlet, whether at Las Vegas or playing golf — a passion he developed late in life. In the fall of 1986, when he was enjoying a brief respite, René Angélil was on a golf course at Sainte-Adèle along with his two old friends, Marc Verreault and Guy Cloutier, with whom he had renewed his friendship a few years earlier. His children Jean-Pierre and Anne-Marie had also accompanied him on this day off, which promised to be a happy one. The friends were joking and teasing one another about their bad shots, looking forward to having a great time. But Guy Cloutier suddenly noticed that René was missing his shots, having difficulty walking, and seemed to be having trouble breathing. He immediately decided to drive his friend to the Hôtel-Dieu in Saint-Jérôme, fifty kilometres from Montreal, where he was kept for two days. The doctors considered his case serious enough to send him to the Montreal Heart Institute. A thallium scan showed that he had no blocked arteries and that his heart was holding up, but he needed rest and a holiday.

This was his first health warning, and it obviously left him shaken. Leaving the institute, he had already made a multitude of good resolutions. "I consider myself lucky to have got off so lightly. Now I have to look after my health, and most of all be careful about what I eat," he told reporters. "I like to eat a lot, and I don't eat at regular times. Recently I've put on twenty-five pounds and I know I have to lose weight. I don't smoke or drink, but food is my vice."

Worried and distressed to see their father in hospital, Jean-Pierre and Anne-Marie immediately informed their mother, Anne Renée, who arrived to look after the children and her ex-husband. "I was very scared," she told the press. "René is someone I love very much, and I'm glad it all turned out all right. I spent two days at his side, and did my best to help him."

Once he felt reassured about his condition, René decided to lose weight. He visibly melted away and took a holiday in — where else — Las Vegas!

52

INCOGNITO

T HE ALBUM *INCOGNITO* WAS RECORDED early in 1987, at the studio in Saint-Charles-sur-Richelieu. To reach a wide public and diversify the musical colours of the album, three directors were called on: Jean-Alain Roussel, Aldo Nova, and Pierre Bazinet, along with three songwriters: Eddy Marnay, Luc Plamondon, and Isa Minoke. The recording was carried out with special care, and every resource was made available to the singer to enable her to turn the most important corner of her musical career.

The launch took place in April 1987, and it was then that the media discovered the new Céline Dion. René had kindled the journalists' curiosity by speaking of a new phase, turning a corner, and a new image and sound. The press was paying attention, but not the folk in radio, who didn't have any time for Céline's records. The with-it young stations like CKOI or CKMF never played her records, which didn't have the right "sound."

So the whole Angélil and CBS public relations team undertook a vast campaign to convince them first to attend the album's launch and then to air some of the tracks. When they saw and heard the star singing "Incognito" and "Lolita" during the showcase presented as part of the launch, several of the disk jockeys were astounded. They could hardly believe their ears. Once again René's bet had succeeded. From that moment on, all the with-it stations in Quebec began to play her songs. What was more, the more romantic, traditional songs continued to be played on other stations. Céline's image had changed, too. Previously she had brought tears to the eyes of mothers and older people. Now she had the young dancing to "Incognito" and was surprising people with "Lolita" and "On traverse un miroir." Her image as a saccharine pop singer, and people's disdain for her, were replaced by admiration for an astonishing artist who had the courage to change, putting her career at risk and trying out a different kind of music — rock and dance — and above all tackle new themes.

In Quebec the sales of the album soared, and very quickly passed the one hundred thousand mark. This left René well placed to negotiate a new recording in English.

But first he had to orchestrate the promotion of the new album in France. Eddy Marnay was being careful, and now a French producer strongly suggested that "Incognito" and "Lolita," songs considered too suggestive for the French market, be eliminated from the album. Marnay obviously had something to do with this decision, which René went along with even though he was quite aware of the consequences. He knew that Luc Plamondon would take it badly. It meant the prolific lyric writer would lose substantial royalties and the prestige of a hit recording.

That wasn't quite how Marnay saw things. He knew the French public and claimed that it wouldn't readily accept this new departure by Céline Dion. She was less well known in France, where people prefer to preserve singers' images. People remembered Céline as the fourteenth child born into a nice Quebec family, and liked her freshness, her Quebecois accent, and her shyness. Maybe Marnay was right, but he wasn't thinking enough about Céline's career, for this was exactly the style and kind of music she had to adopt if she wanted to make a break-through in the United States. René saw this perfectly, but his long friendship with Marnay and gratitude for everything the man had done prevented him from insisting. Even his severest critics agree that René has always been true to his friends and never forgets a favour.

The album had moderate success as far as its sales in France were concerned, but nothing like its enormous success in Quebec, even though it quickly sold two hundred thousand copies.

53

CÉLINE SINGS IN ENGLISH

R ENÉ DECIDED TO FORGET ABOUT France for the time being. The
French public still loved a Céline who no longer existed, one they
saw as the successor to Mireille Mathieu — a sweet young girl who
would grow up well-behaved under the guidance of Eddy Marnay,
singing the same kind of song again and again. But this wasn't what
either Céline or René wanted. He had understood and didn't resist. And,
besides, the Quebec public had made him the best of presents by immediately accepting the new Céline. This was an enormous relief for René,
who had suffered anguish over his protégée's transformation.

It was a dangerous metamorphosis, to say the least. The public, it
must be said, is conservative by nature, and doesn't easily accept changes
in its favourite singer's image, style, appearance, and — above all —
repertoire. René knew perfectly well that he was taking an enormous risk
by making Céline change. He went about it with all the diplomacy he
could muster. A little Plamondon here, a little Marnay there; a Céline
who was a bit of a rocker and a little sentimental, a little bit of a rebel and
a little bit of a good girl. And the results proved how right he was. Céline's
public was more vast than ever, and René took advantage of this to
organize a tour throughout Quebec. Claude Lemay, nicknamed "Mégot,"
became the new leader of the orchestra accompanying Céline. René

chose him not only because he was an excellent musician but above all because he had faith: he believed in the extraordinary potential of this Quebec singer. This was exactly what René wanted.

As he prepared for Céline's tour, accompanied by an impressive team directed on stage by Jean Bissonnette, one of the best Quebec directors, René's mind was constantly on her next album. He was preparing for an important step in the singer's career: her first record in English. It was an obsession for René, who was now friendly with the people from CBS. He was just waiting for the right opportunity. This presented itself at CBS's national conference, which took place in June 1987 in the Laurentians. Céline was invited to perform some numbers from *Incognito*, but René thought this wasn't enough. He insisted she should sing "Can we try" by Dan Hill. It caused great surprise among the recording industry people in the auditorium, who were bowled over by Céline's performance.

But René still wasn't satisfied. When Céline was invited to the Junos, the Canadian record industry's prestigious gala in Toronto, he imposed a condition: she had to sing in English. Those around Céline set about preparing an original song. It was to be "Have a Heart," and Céline sang it with all her heart and soul. René shed tears as he listened to her. Céline earned a standing ovation. The English media called it the best performance of the evening, and a new world opened its doors to Céline — and to René — in November 1987.

That evening the general public in English Canada, the media, and the industry feted the girl from Quebec.

René Angélil had brought off a masterstroke, and deserves kudos for being so astute. He was well aware of Canada's "two solitudes." He knew that it would be useless for Céline to outdo herself, to reach the pinnacle of her art, or to give the best interpretation of her lifetime if she sang only in French. He wanted her to sing in English because he knew it would mean breaking down the barrier, once and for all. And so it was. The day after the show, René was in the office of Berni di Matteo, the top man in CBS. There wasn't a moment's hesitation: Céline Dion would make her first recording in the English language.

"I began at $30,000," René Angélil would often relate. "Then, after Céline's 'showcase' at L'Esterel, the budget allowed for the English record rose to $100,000, and then, after the Junos, to $300,000, and in the end the sky was the limit."

The streak of bad luck seemed to be over. René the strategist savoured his triumph. Talent wouldn't have been enough. He had to be wily and negotiate skilfully and respectfully to get what he wanted. The gaffes committed in New York — René's and Guy Cloutier's presumptuous demand for $1 million for René Simard's services — were now a distant memory, as was the failure of the Baronets, eager to enter the American market, also in New York. This time he had pulled it off! Of course luck played a part, but perhaps not as much as people think. René had already paid for this success with his failures.

And he had no intention of stepping aside and letting CBS look after Céline's career. He had already thought of a producer for Céline's album, namely David Foster. He knew that Foster, who was originally Canadian, was the composer of the moment in the United States. He had worked with Céline's idol, Barbra Streisand, as well as Nathalie Cole, Neil Diamond, and a lot of other established artists. Once again René was starting on another stage of Céline's career by paying court to the best in the business. After Eddy Marnay, Michel Drucker on French TV, CBS, and Luc Plamondon, now it was David Foster's turn. He had settled down in Los Angeles, and René sent him all Céline's material there, and in particular a video of her performance at the Junos. Foster was convinced.

54

THE *INCOGNITO* TOUR

WHILE ALL THIS WAS HAPPENING, Céline set out on her *Incognito* tour in Quebec. Once again René hadn't spared any expense, and didn't expect to make a profit from the undertaking. There were no less than fifteen musicians to back up the singer, including the very rock-oriented Breen Leboeuf, a former member of the group Offenbach. The starry-eyed young singer and the papal dove had been left far behind. Céline was intent on giving her all and electrifying the public everywhere in Quebec. Even more, she wanted to make her broader audience laugh, and the comedians' favourite writer, Jean-Pierre Plante, was hired to write the linking speeches.

We should point out that comedy was all the rage in Quebec in the 1980s. Ever since the unforgettable *Lundis des Ha! Ha!* hosted by Serge Thériault and Claude Meunier at Club Soda, the Quebecois were big fans of comedians, who had become even more popular than Quebec singers. It wasn't any surprise that René hired Jean Bissonnette, the producer of many comedy shows on Radio-Canada, to handle the staging of the show.

In the summer of 1988 I was in Quebec City as a reporter for *La Presse* to cover an international theatre festival. As I was strolling along Rue Saint-Jean, directly opposite the Palais Montcalm, René Angélil caught me by the arm and asked me to come to Céline's show, due to begin in a few minutes. He would even keep me a seat beside him. I explained to him that I had to attend a play, and that I was very busy, but in the end I gave in. It's true it's not easy to resist René Angélil.

I had liked Céline's last show, put on at the Théâtre Saint-Denis, and René remembered the very positive review I had given it. He told me this one was even better, so I shouldn't miss it.

The show began and, like any good reviewer, I was studying Céline's every movement — the way she projected her voice, the lighting, and her backup — when I turned my head and saw René's demeanour. Even though he had seen his protégée on stage hundreds of times, I saw him sitting there silently, rapt, almost in a trance, throughout Céline's performance. I didn't dare speak to him, he was focussing so hard. It wasn't an act: he was genuinely enthralled.

Of course after the show he asked me what I thought of Céline's performance, which had played to a full house.

In general, the reviews were enthusiastic, but not mine. To tell the truth, I didn't understand why Céline was indulging in a lot of imitations of people like Michael Jackson, Marjo, Julien Clerc, Édith Butler, and even Mireille Mathieu. What was more, there was far too much comedy in the show, with Céline even going so far as to make fun of herself, at her over-emotionalism and her former image. I pointed out to René that Céline's voice was too good for her to need to imitate others. I couldn't understand.

Strangely, René didn't seem to be offended by what I said, and I actually began to think he shared my opinion. He explained to me that she still didn't have enough songs to make up a new repertoire, and insisted I go to see Céline in her dressing room. To tell the truth, I still regret turning down the invitation. As a good strategist and a clever diplomat, René didn't dare contradict or get on the wrong side of the representative of an important newspaper, but he was very aware of the impact of Céline's show. What he wanted to show the Quebec public was a consummate artist who was breaking with her past image. He was using humour to introduce a new singer of her time, one who was very "with it" and diverse, who would soon take on the Canadian English-speaking market, and, inevitably, the United States market, too. It was already written in the stars — in both Céline's and René's, which are the same. Furthermore, Céline was learning her trade as a performer, serving her stage apprenticeship and committing herself to all types of music — a real "work in progress" in which she was constantly being transformed. In the wings, René was unable to conceal his satisfaction, as he already imagined Céline singing on the world's top stages.

The final agreement still hadn't been signed with CBS, even if René was behaving as if everything was settled. Indeed, no possible doubt remained in his mind, and it was now only a question of time before a complete team of collaborators would be put in place. In parallel with this tour, however, in April 1988, something happened that would transform Céline's life and career.

55

EUROVISION

A S WE HAVE SEEN, CÉLINE Dion's career didn't take off very well in Germany, and this was one of René's failures, one about which he has never said very much. But in 1988 the sun came out again, and even failure began to taste like success. A producer René had met in Germany told him that Nella Martinelli, a successful Swiss songwriter, had written a song especially for Céline and wanted to enter it in the Eurovision Song Contest.

This event was to take place in Dublin, Ireland, on April 30, 1988. Little known in Quebec, this contest — an event telecast on all the European national networks and watched by over 500 million viewers — had taken on over the years the proportions of an Olympics of song. Aware of the scale of the event, coming along at just the right juncture in Céline's career, René told his protégée the history of the Eurovision Song Contest. He told her that the group ABBA had won the competition with "Waterloo" in 1977, that France Gall had achieved real stardom when she won the contest with "Poupée de cire, poupée de son," and that Julio Iglesias and Nana Mouskouri had also competed.

Céline broke off her tour and travelled to Europe with René to take part in the various rounds of the competition. She was among the finalists, and the Dublin bookies put her among the three top favourites. Place your bets!

An irony of fate brought René back to gambling. He who had always kept his professional career apart from his passion for gambling was confronted by a strange dilemma. In Dublin, a city of gamblers, it was possible to bet on the Eurovision contestants.

Urged on by the organizers, who knew about his passion for gambling, René reluctantly placed a bet of a few hundred pounds.

Céline didn't particularly like the song she was to champion, "Ne partez pas sans moi," and it didn't appeal to René, either. But they had to make the best of it, so Céline put her heart into it and gave it her all. Until the last minute it was very close. In the end she won by a single vote, and René had literally won his bet. It was his lucky day.

The Eurovision contest could change a career, and René knew this. Now he was holding a trump card. It was a real stroke of luck.

Jean Beaulne hadn't had as much luck. When in the 1970s he was managing France Castel, the most promising singer in Quebec at the time, he too had dreamed of bringing off an international coup with his protégée. She had been invited to the Athens festival, at the time the foremost music festival in Europe. Although he had carefully planned the Quebec singer's participation, she let him down, claiming to be ill. In fact France Castel, who today is an accomplished actress with a healthy lifestyle, was dependent at the time on alcohol and drugs as if the success she had enjoyed very early in her career had been too much for her.

History will do doubt record that as a very young girl and throughout her career up to the present, Céline Dion was able to avoid the pitfalls and temptations of show business. When we compare her development to that of rival singers like Mariah Carey and Whitney Houston, we can appreciate the strength of her personal discipline. How could René have failed to admire her from the outset? And how could he not have fallen in love with her?

56

TRUE LOVE

A FTER THE YEARS OF MYSTERY and rumours surrounding the origins of his love relationship with Céline Dion, René Angélil has finally lifted the veil from what was an open secret in the couple's immediate circle and among the media. Everybody in Céline's orbit knew she had been in love with René since 1986, and perhaps even 1985. She had first been attracted to the unhappy, lonely, distraught man he was after the separation from Anne Renée. Her maternal instinct compelled her to draw closer to a man who was suffering, to shelter and protect him and never do him any further harm. At seventeen or eighteen Céline was going through what has been called a "nurse complex," and was attracted by the child in René Angélil — a child who acted grown-up in front of the media. Céline no longer believed in this image he projected. She preferred the man she was beginning to discover, imagine, and desire. But when and how could she tell him that she loved him?

René dates the exact moment they confessed and consummated their love to the precise point we have reached in our story. It was to Céline's official biographer, Georges-Hébert Germain, in 1997, and a few years later to Stéphane Bureau, that he recounted the beginning of his love relationship with his protégée. It happened in a Dublin hotel, when the couple was in Céline's room, still enjoying the euphoria of the Eurovision victory.

"After her physical transformation in 1986 I no longer saw Céline in the same light. I found her physically attractive but … I controlled myself, trying not to think about it. I thought I would damage Céline's career, that I was too old, and that people would never forgive me." Georges-Hébert Germain gives the official version of what happened in his biography of Céline:

> Every evening since the first tour they did together in 1985, he would kiss her on each cheek and wish her good night … And now on this night of fame and triumph, he was about to leave without kissing her. He had already opened the door. He smiled. She came across and clung to him. "You didn't kiss me, René Angélil." She kept her head and her eyes down …
>
> He didn't understand what had happened, even though for some weeks he had been thinking about such a scene and imagining it a hundred times. He leaned towards her and kissed her on the lips and neck, and clutched her in his arms. Then he abruptly relaxed his embrace and fled back to his room. She was speechless for a moment, her heart beating.
>
> It was she who called him back: "If you don't come back, I'll come knocking on your door."

Such is the official version given by the person involved, and the one that will remain forever, if René Angélil has anything to do with it.

It has to be admitted it's a perfect scenario, a real fairy tale in which Céline's triumph coincides with love on an evening of celebration.

So what exactly should we make of it? René was so obsessed with his media image, but also with Céline's image of him, that it is quite likely that is really the way it happened — or nearly so, to within a few months, or years, if we are to believe some reports that no longer matter today.

Since the beginning of their association the relationship between Céline and René has always been equivocal, and it couldn't have been otherwise. The relationship between an agent and "his" singer is like a love relationship in so many ways.

Jean Beaulne gave me a long account of the inevitable and often necessary intimacy that exists between the agent and the artist:

> They work together. They eat together. They travel together. The agent has to protect the artist's money, health, and mood, protect her against the hazards of the job, and above all against bad influences. The tension is enormous, the responsibilities overwhelming, and, in addition, he has to live with the constant fear of losing his artist. In such circumstances it would have been difficult for René and Céline not to fall in love — particularly since René was a genuine hero in Céline's eyes, and that for her part the singer was becoming more and more breathtaking from one performance to the next. They had a great deal of mutual admiration and trust.

It was something René had been very careful to avoid during Céline's adolescent years, but no one can deny that he was possessive and unwilling to share his protégée with anyone. Céline had very few boyfriends. First there had been a boy called Sylvain, in Charlemagne, for whom she had a passing infatuation, and then the hockey player Gilbert Delorme. Céline met him while she was filming her first video, and it was love at first sight. She was dazzled by the athlete's good looks, and he could also be very charming with her.

When René heard about this dalliance he literally exploded. He went into a real fit, very akin to a fit of jealousy. He could never permit another man to interfere with his plans. He could never admit that Céline might fall in love and experience a great passion while he was struggling to build up her career. Neither Delorme nor Paul Lévesque, her first agent, nor her too-daring male fans, were allowed to get too close. It is hardly surprising that Céline didn't have any love affairs before being united with René, for he had created a vacuum around her and knowingly driven off any potential suitors.

There again, the situation was equivocal to say the least. René remembered Alain Charbonneau, who had taken Ginette Reno away from him. Never again did he want to experience that kind of humiliation.

But wasn't he subconsciously playing the part of Pygmalion, planning a complete union with his protégée at the appropriate time? Maybe so, but he'll never admit it, either to us or to himself.

Before giving in and allowing himself to be loved by Céline, René had gone through months of anguish, and this is understandable. By loving her openly he would have ruined his handiwork and squandered his winning hand. But even while he concealed this love, he feared Céline's spontaneity, her confidences, and her giddiness.

"There's nothing worse for an artists' agent, whether René or someone else, than to see his artist fall in love," explains Jean Beaulne. "Then and there, the agent loses all control over his protégée. In some cases it can be catastrophic. The artist becomes less available, distances herself, and a certain bond of trust with the agent is broken. Love often makes people lose their heads, and the artist, who is by definition a particularly sensitive person, reacts much more to the pressures from the person she loves than to her agent's demands as he tries to bring her back into line."

René, who knew his rock classics, had read the sad story of Jerry Lee Lewis, who lost everything when he married a fourteen-year-old girl. That was in 1959, while Elvis Presley was doing his military service. Lewis, who had reached the top of the American hit parade with "Whole Lotta Shakin' Goin' On" and "Great Balls of Fire," was supposed to be Elvis's heir. During an English tour, a journalist learned that the young girl was actually his fourteen-year-old wife. Questioned about this, Lewis didn't deny it, and appeared proudly in public with his young spouse. The next day the news had travelled all around the world, and he performed to empty seats for the rest of his tour. In the United States his records were smashed on the air on most radio stations, and Jerry Lee Lewis would never take Elvis Presley's place. Now getting on in years, he is still looking for work.

Yet Elvis also loved a fourteen-year-old girl he was able to hide away in his grandmother's home in Memphis, not very far from his house. He was never touched by scandal, nor did he ever let the public hear of Priscilla Beaulieu before he married her.

René was neither Presley nor Lewis, nor was Céline fourteen any-more, but he feared rumours and innuendoes and damage to his or Céline's image. As a reader of biographies he also remembered the case of Charlie Chaplin, who married the daughter of playwright Eugene O'Neill, who was only eighteen when they first met. A short while later Chaplin was driven out of the United States during the famous witch hunt of the McCarthy years. The general public doesn't always appreci-ate a big age difference in its idols' love affairs. René was aware of this, and questioned himself for months. He confided in Eddy Marnay, who was still his friend and confidant, and in his children. Céline's mother was no longer expected to accompany the couple during their travels, but as any good mother would, she noticed her daughter's ardent pas-sion, and early on was unable to accept this relationship. She wanted a younger husband for her daughter — a man without children of his own, and one without a past. She viewed René as a businessman, an ambitious producer, the best person to propel her daughter to the top, but certainly not as a lover.

Mme Dion knew, like many mothers in similar circumstances, that her daughter was in love with René. She had had a frank and lively dis-cussion with him during a trip to Paris, and found she was dealing with a deeply disturbed man. Himself a father, René understood Mme Dion's resistance. Parents don't generally like to see their daughter falling for a much older man.

57

THE FIRST
ENGLISH-LANGUAGE ALBUM

L OVE MUST GIVE WINGS, FOR Céline and René took flight towards success in the spring of 1988. They summoned up an incredible amount
of energy, and did so in every department. René negotiated an agreement
with Chrysler, and another with the Simpsons chain. In each case Céline
was to get more than three hundred thousand dollars, and she was said
already to be a millionaire. There was no mention of what René would
get, though a good proportion of his protégée's earnings would go to him.
From now on we can assume there was a fifty-fifty split between the still
secret lovers who each had such a stake in the singer's international career.

In May, René went to New York with Vito Luprano to meet Sony's
artistic director, Richard Zucherman. Céline's success in Dublin had
certainly impressed the people at Sony, but Zucherman was cautious
and avoided rushing into anything. Time would be required to assem-
ble a team around Céline. Time would also be needed to find the right
songs and the best marketing strategy.

René didn't make the mistake of trying to force things. With total
humility he listened to the directives of the Sony boss and went along
with his decisions.

The budget was unlimited, and at Zucherman's discretion. René
adopted a strategic approach. He had learned that in such circum-

stances it was better to distrust one's ego. He never forgot the arrogance he had displayed in this same city of New York fifteen years earlier when negotiating with one of the big names in the recording industry. This youthful error had literally scuttled René Simard's international career. But some observers still wonder about one thing even today. Didn't René surrender his control in the deal with Sony? Did he give up his grip on Céline's career? Did he sacrifice himself to ensure Céline Dion's breakthrough on the international market?

Jean Beaulne can't believe for a moment that the control freak René Angélil has always been could have surrendered even some of his power under the agreement with Sony.

But this is to misunderstand the way the industry functions today.

"René didn't give up anything," Beaulne explains. "Of course he included a provision in the contract giving him the last word on the choice of the songs and style of music most suitable for the artist. It's the agent's role to protect the career of the artist he is working for, in both the short and the long term. Some companies have messed up artists by a poor choice of music. Imagine for instance if Michael Jackson was required to record cha-cha tunes!"

In the meantime, Céline carried on with her Quebec tour, performing in more than 150 shows in the province. Success was assured, and the critics recognized the qualities of a singer who literally lived for the stage.

58

PROFESSOR FOSTER

IN THE FALL, CBS, WHICH had already been taken over by Sony, pro-
posed (but actually insisted on) three directors to bring out Céline's
album. René had thought that David Foster would be in charge, but
Sony decided otherwise, and René had to give in to the demands of the
powerful record company. In addition to Foster, Andy Goldmark and
Christopher Neil were to direct other tracks on the album. Foster began
working with Céline at the end of the year, and worked tirelessly on her
voice for weeks and months. The man who had worked for a long time
with Barbra Streisand softened Céline's voice, gave it even more colour,
got rid of a few somewhat nasal intonations, and improved her vocal
technique. Foster behaved like a particularly demanding professor, and,
strangely, Céline, the most disciplined singer in the world, was delighted. She had found her music teacher, and was making steady progress.
She was working in Los Angeles with her producer, and René took
advantage of this to take a breather, enjoy himself, and, of course, go
gambling in the casinos of Las Vegas.

Love and music were a good combination, and Céline finally
recorded Foster's songs in an atmosphere of great tenderness. Being little known in this corner of the United States, Céline was able to express
her love more openly. René was happy.

Céline also recorded in New York with Andy Goldmark and in London with Christopher Neil. René was chafing at the bit. He pressured Sony to get the album out. He couldn't wait to take the plunge into this American market he had been dreaming about for so long. The songs were good, he was sure of that. He shed tears as he listened to "Where Does my Heart Beat Now." Neil, the composer, was euphoric, and Céline had dazzled everyone. So what were they waiting for? The people at Sony still weren't completely satisfied. They felt that a few songs would have to be added to really grab the public.

René was beside himself. The man who had shown such humility in the Sony offices in New York reverted to type, even threatening to leave and make the record with a competitor, Atlantic Records, which had already shown interest. René was obviously bluffing, but it is worth pointing out that he didn't abandon Céline to the tender mercies of the almighty Sony.

Vito Luprano mollified him and showed him that maybe Sony was right. Actually, David Foster, Céline's teacher, hadn't written his best songs for this album, and this had been noticed in the Sony offices. So in the end Céline went back to the studio to record "Any Other Way" and "If Love is Out of the Question."

The year went by, and the record still hadn't come out. It was finally on April 2, 1990, that the launch of the album *Unison* took place at the Metropolis, Montreal's most popular disco. As was his wont, René had organized a monster event that attracted thousands of fans, who clogged St. Catherine Street. The most with-it radio stations in the city participated in the event, playing tracks from Céline's first English-language album all day long. That evening she sang six songs from the album on the gigantic stage of the disco. René had invited along Paul Burger, the president of Sony, and this time around the English language occupied the first place in Céline's music and in her life.

The album was well received at first, and well publicized in the media, being played on just about all the radio stations. However, it wouldn't be quite accurate to speak of a real rush to buy it in record stores after that. Some critics expressed serious reservations, claiming that the record bore René's stamp, and that some of the songs weren't appropriate for someone Céline's age. They also complained about an unevenness in the recording. Nevertheless, they all agreed about the impressive quality of Céline's voice, which had improved even further. In my opinion the involvement of too many different directors and studios explains the strange inconsistencies on this long-awaited record. But Céline's voice triumphed over it all, and René would use this recording as a visiting card in conquering the international market. Céline was now well known in English Canada, and for now that was the important thing. Indeed, René used Quebec as a springboard to launch each record because this enabled him to attract the attention of Sony's top people in New York and Los Angeles. After all, since his protégée had already sold so many records in her own country she was a pretty safe bet.

The sales of this record petered out just about everywhere, and even in Quebec (at 125,000 copies), but René was already turning to the stage as a way of giving sales a fresh boost. He was now holding another trump card. Céline had become an accomplished stage performer after the *Incognito* tour, and he intended to use her physical presence to sell records. This was a card he hadn't been able to play before.

David Foster is one of the greatest songwriters, composers, and producers of the twenty-first century.

The greatest compliment anyone can pay a musical creator is to tell him he has a good ear. And, in Foster's case, he also has a good eye! David has the gift of being able to recognize the potential of a piece of music and create the visual identity to express the essence of his creation.

A fourteen-time Grammy winner (including Producer of the Year on three occasions), and with forty-one nominations, Foster had come on the Los Angeles musical scene in 1971. He had his first success with his rock group Skylark in 1973. He quickly became established as one of the best keyboardists in the industry. He then became much in demand as a studio musician, working with John Lennon, Diana Ross, George Harrison, Rod Stewart, and Barbra Streisand, among others.

Then he applied himself above all to writing and producing songs. He worked with Hall & Oates and Boz Scaggs. In 1979 he won his first Grammy for the song "After the Love Has Gone," recorded by Earth, Wind & Fire. Then he moved on to producing musical comedy and film soundtracks, among them *Ghostbusters* and *Footloose*. And every style suits him marvellously, whether rock, R & B, pop, soul, country, jazz, or even classical.

He continued his dazzling climb with hits like "Somewhere" (Barbra Streisand) and "We've Got Tonight" (Kenny Rogers). At the end of the 1980s he came out with a fabulous series of radio hits, sung by superstars like Michael Jackson, Paul McCartney, Chicago, Neil Diamond, Alice Cooper, Manhattan

Transfer, Phil Collins, The Pointer Sisters, Aretha Franklin, and many others.

In 1993, Foster was named Top Singles Producer and Top R&B Producer by *Billboard* magazine, and was awarded a Grammy for the soundtrack of the film *The Bodyguard,* with Whitney Houston. Over the next few years he produced songs that won worldwide acclaim, sung by major stars like Céline Dion with "Falling Into You," "Because You Loved Me," and "To Love You More."

Between 1994 and 1997 four of his productions reached the top of the charts, including Céline Dion's "Because You Loved Me" for a record forty-two weeks. In 1994 he became vice-president of Atlantic Records, and the following year created his own label, 143 Records Inc., distributed by Atlantic. In 1997 he became senior vice-president of Warner Music Group, with which he had become associated.

Later, music lovers all over the planet were charmed by this Canadian's latest creations: "It's Your Song" by Garth Brooks, "Let Me Let Go" by Faith Hill, and "Tell Him" sung by Céline Dion and Barbra Streisand. He was awarded a Golden Globe Award in January 1999 for "The Prayer," sung by Andrea Bocelli and Céline Dion. He has also won numerous awards in Canada, including two Geminis and five Junos, and has been a member of the Canadian Hall of Fame since 1997.

He has long been an advocate of children's rights. He established the David Foster Foundation to help the families of children waiting for organ transplants. To date the foundation has raised several million dollars and helped countless children throughout North America. He has also supported the André Agassi Foundation, the Race to Erase MDS, Malibu High School Scholarships, and several cancer foundations.

Born in Victoria, in British Columbia, Canada's most westerly province, Foster now lives in Los Angeles with his wife, Linda Thompson, and their six children. Linda is also his collaborator and frequently co-writes songs with him.

At the age of five he was already considered to be in advance of children of his age in piano. At thirteen he became a student at the University of Washington. At sixteen, he was already on the road with the legendary Chuck Berry. In 1971, he founded his own group, called Skylark. In the years that followed, his remarkable talent would make him one of the greatest musicians and producers in the musical history of the planet. From Quebec, where Céline was born, to Tokyo, Japan, his creations have left their mark on the lives of the thousands of millions who have recognized themselves in one of his magnificent songs!

JEAN BEAULNE

59

CÉLINE THE ACTRESS

IN 1990, CÉLINE ASSERTED HERSELF. She made one of her big dreams come true by agreeing to act in a miniseries on Quebec TV, called *Des fleurs sur la neige* ("Flowers on the Snow"). She was moved when she read the script, originally entitled *Elisa T.*, the real-life story of an unfortunate girl living in poverty and abused by her parents, who finally won through thanks to her strength of character and determination.

René disliked the script and thought Céline had nothing to gain by playing the part of this poor young country girl, badly dressed, bowed down, crushed and unloved. He was afraid above all that people might confuse Elisa T. with Céline Dion from Charlemagne, who was much more robust, better loved, and certainly not living in poverty. He thought the part didn't suit her image — an image he had spent years creating. But Céline saw things otherwise. She had always dreamed of acting, and her recent stay in Los Angeles had revived her old dream. In spite of René's disapproval, she agreed enthusiastically to film the series. It was no use René telling her that such an escapade would do nothing to help her international career, since the miniseries would never be shown outside Quebec, for Céline dug in her heels. She just wanted to learn a new skill, and had no desire to serve her screen-acting apprenticeship in the United States.

For one of the few times in his career René backed down and allow the love of his life to express herself, hoping it wouldn't hurt her too much.

The actor's world is very different from the singer's, as Céline would quickly learn. With her usual discipline she arrived very early on the set, learned her part impeccably, and behaved like a true professional. Jean Lepage, the director, was impressed by the singer's readiness and adaptability, showing more humility than the actors around her. People also noticed Céline's fragility and sensitivity, as she put herself heart and soul into her part.

"I'm not acting," she told the press. "I *am* Elisa, and I'm really suffering and shedding tears as if I was experiencing my character's emotions."

Céline didn't spare herself. She worked twelve hours a day on the set while still pursuing her career as a singer, spoke to journalists, and took part in several promotions, all without complaining. She was too excited by her new experience in acting.

It is easy to imagine René Angélil's reaction when he read the following in the newspapers:

> I *am* Elisa, someone completely different from me. Her whole attitude is different from mine. For example, the way she walks, the way she holds herself. I'm accustomed to walk in a relaxed way and look around a lot to make eye contact with everyone during a performance. But Elisa doesn't like herself, so she shrinks up all the time, and that has to show in her behaviour.
>
> She doesn't wear makeup. She's very skinny, and wants to occupy as little space as possible. I have to think of that all the time, and make people forget about Céline.

These words are completely unlike what was heard from her when her manager was around. We can understand why René wouldn't agree with them, since his mandate consisted precisely in never allowing Céline to be forgotten, and in protecting her image. But she was reading about the Stanislavsky method and enjoying this foray into acting enormously.

Colonel Parker, René's idol, had once gone through a similar situation with his protégé, Elvis Presley. The Colonel was offered a role for

Elvis that was certain to bring him an Oscar. The Colonel read the script and absolutely refused to enter into negotiations. The role in question was that of the Texan male prostitute in the film *The Midnight Cowboy*. The part later went to Jon Voight, who co-starred opposite Dustin Hoffman. Parker also turned down for Elvis the part of the has-been singer in *A Star is Born*, in which he would have played opposite Barbra Streisand. Worse still, he was steadfastly opposed to Elvis taking the leading role in nothing less than *West Side Story*, arguing that playing the part of a young delinquent belonging to a New York street gang would also tarnish his protégé's reputation as nice boy from a good family. Maybe if he had played all these parts Elvis would have won recognition from the movie industry, but Colonel Parker preferred to protect his singer's image. René's mind was on the matter of image, too.

On the evening of July 9, Céline fell asleep at the wheel of her Chrysler Laser as she was driving on the Laurentian Highway. She woke up to realize she was driving on the wrong side of the road. She let go of the steering wheel and closed her eyes. The car zigzagged and spun several times before coming to a halt in the ditch. She was more frightened than hurt.

"My first experience with acting left a deep impression on me," Céline would relate later. "It was the most intense experience I've had for a while. I let myself be caught up in the part, and I loved living my character to the limit of my powers, but it was very trying psychologically and emotionally. I'm sure my car accident was caused by the fatigue and tension I felt when the filming ended."

René has never made any comment about Céline's acting on film. Speaking to the media he completely ignored *Des fleurs sur la neige* — a silence that speaks louder than words. When it was suggested to him Céline should sing the theme song for the four-hour miniseries he refused point blank. He could put up with her making a foray into acting, but no way would he allow her to spoil her image as a healthy, energetic young singer.

Long before he began working with Céline, René Angélil had been an admirer of Colonel Parker, Elvis Presley's manager.

At the time of the Baronets, he was already talking about him as an example to be followed. Influenced by the Colonel's marketing strategies, but also by Brian Epstein, the Beatles' manager, and Johnny Stark, who managed Mireille Mathieu, René applied promotional strategies inspired by these people, though without treading in the footsteps of the Colonel, whose reputation wasn't entirely spotless.

Both of them had the gambling bug, and René often had the opportunity to meet Parker in Las Vegas. They gambled at the same table on several occasions. After they developed a friendship René even visited him in his home.

The real name of the man nicknamed "the Colonel" was Andreas van Kuijk. He first saw the light of day in Breda, Holland, on June 28, 1909. As a child he astonished his brothers and sisters with his different ways of making money, buying and selling all kinds of things. Very young, he even set up a little circus in his yard and asked each young neighbour who wanted to go in to pay a modest sum!

At sixteen, he left the family home, and at seventeen he crossed the ocean by ship, reaching the United States. Lacking identity papers, he was able to join the army, and assumed the name of Tom Parker, an officer he liked. After leaving the army he worked for a travelling circus, advertising it by walking about as a sandwich man leading an elephant. In 1940 he became a dogcatcher in Tampa, Florida. In return he was provided with a free apartment furnished with a desk, some wheels, and gas! He inundated the local newspapers with photos and stories about abandoned animals and started a campaign to help them. For the first time ever the humane society made a profit! Then he opened one of the first animal cemeteries and began to sell tombstones. He also provided a grave maintenance service, decorating the graves with flowers discarded by florists. To increase his earnings even further, he produced a show in which chickens danced on a hotplate. When he wanted them to dance faster, he just turned up the heat.

Turning next to musical promotion and production, he became manager for a certain Eddy Arnold. A tireless worker, he succeeded in putting him at the pinnacle of country music in the early 1950s. Then, joining the William Morris Agency, he managed to obtain a film contract for his protégé. This association came in extremely useful in managing someone named Elvis Presley, who in 1954 began to record for Sam Philip's Sun Records. It was through Oscar Davis, Parker's partner, that he got to know Presley, quickly seeing his tremendous potential. Astounded at the audience's reaction during his performances, he offered to make him known in the length and breadth of the country. But Elvis, who was already being managed by Bob Neal, first wanted him to prove his talents as a manager.

That was when Parker managed to convince the largest company at the time, RCA Victor, to buy out Elvis's contract with Sun Records, and had him sign with Hill and Range, the top music publishing company. The rest is well known. Elvis became the biggest American star and a major post-war icon. After the King's death in 1977, Parker settled in Los Angeles, where he regularly patronized the casinos.

Towards the end of his life his weight had risen to over 130 kilograms. He died of a heart attack on January 21, 1997, at the age of eighty-seven.

JEAN BEAULNE

60

NICKELS

T HE EARLY 1990S SAW THE start of a new period of prosperity for the Dion-Angélil couple. Their fortune wasn't made yet, but things were going well. Céline participated in advertising campaigns for Chrysler and Simpson's that earned her almost a million dollars. The *Incognito* tour finally paid off, record sales were significant, and TV specials and corporate shows also brought in large fees, fattening the wallet of the parsimonious Céline. René was never very long away from the gambling table, but in 1990, he decided to go into the restaurant business. It was the first time Céline and René were investing in anything other than show business.

A lover of good food, the wily Angélil killed two birds with one stone when he bought shares in the Nickels restaurant chain, along with Céline. On the one hand it was a business that promised to be profitable, and on the other it was an investment liable to consummate and tighten the family bonds between the Dion and Sara families.

Paul Sara, René Angélil's maternal cousin, had, like René, been a bank teller in his youth, rising to bank manager before going into the restaurant business. After experiencing some financial difficulties he gave up his shares in the Swiss Chalet restaurant on St. Catherine Street in Montreal, and finally reached an agreement with René involving him financially in the Nickels restaurant venture.

A year later, a second Nickels restaurant was opened in Laval, another suburb of Montreal, with a thousand of Céline's fans in attendance. The restaurant's decor was solidly retro, with posters of Elvis Presley, Marilyn Monroe, James Dean, and other idols of René's younger days. The "nickel" was of course Céline's famous lucky five-cent coin. She personally designed the waitresses' uniforms and her mother sewed the first of them before they became factory made.

Later, a good few members of the Dion family were employed by Nickels. Dominique and Paul Sara were among the shareholders, as were Peter and Lawrence Mammas, who had been in the restaurant business for some time.

René the family man was pleased with this association. The business turned out a real success, and in 1993 there were already nine restaurants in operation. Mrs. Dion, who had already launched her famous little pies, managed the Nickels in Repentigny, Claudette managed another restaurant in the chain, and the whole family ended up doing well. From the outset the Nickels restaurants were associated with Céline Dion and René Angélil, and the singer's fans would come together in one of their idol's restaurants, thinking she was the sole owner. Actually Céline and René never owned more than 20 percent of the shares in the restaurant chain, which benefited from Céline's growing popularity. Nickels was a clean and nostalgic, but joyful, simple, and warm restaurant, in Céline's image. Ultimately about fifty franchises would be opened in Quebec, Ontario, and Florida, and the enterprise continued to flourish.

In 1999, however, the image became irremediably tarnished when the restaurant chain was investigated. In December, a dozen restaurants received a visit from agents of the Quebec Revenue Ministry. Certain restaurants in Greater Montreal were suspected of using "zappers," a software program that allowed certain income to be concealed from tax inspectors. The newspapers latched onto the affair, and René Angélil made it known through a press release that he and Céline had not been shareholders in the Nickels chain since 1997.

In May 2000 the Nickels restaurant chain pleaded guilty to sixty-four infractions of the tax laws. There was a fine of $3 million, while the franchises had to pay the taxes owing, amounting to almost $3.5 million. However, the managing company undertook to reimburse them. With losses of over $4 million, the business was forced to go into bankruptcy protection in December 2000. Paul Sara, René Angélil's cousin, was the president and chief administrative officer of the company, while Lawrence Mammas acted as secretary-treasurer of the firm and of the numbered company 3415724 Canada Inc. The franchise agreements between the company and the different owners were transferred to another company. Strangely, René had never publicized the end of his association with the restaurant chain, and he would never mention Nickels again.

61

THE *UNISON* SHOW AND
RENÉ IN POLITICS

IN 1990, A TRYING YEAR for Céline Dion, she was filming the TV miniseries *Des fleurs sur la neige*, learning English, and preparing for her
first show in that language. The offensive on America had begun, and
now it was René's turn. The album *Unison* hadn't shattered any sales
records, but no matter: he was starting out on a long journey, and would
employ a total strategy to achieve his objectives. His persistence and
almost obsessive stubbornness would attract notice. There could be no
question of going easy on Céline now that she had reached the most
important turning point of her career — and of his, too, of course. It
was during this year that Céline's voice cracked while she was performing in Sherbrooke, obliging her to rest it. We mustn't forget that she had
already lost control of her car after a day on the set. But the mechanism
was primed and couldn't be stopped.

René-Richard Cyr, a young, exceptionally talented director, was
chosen to put on the dynamic, pulsating sort of show that was popular at the time. "Mégot" returned to lead the band. Lacking the
funds to finance the *Unison* show, which was to be presented all over
Canada, René called on Jean-Claude L'Espérance, a Quebec producer who had long been teamed with Guy Latraverse. L'Espérance hesitated, and finally admitted he didn't believe the project could suc-

ceed. He didn't think Céline could cross the language barrier that divides Canada.

René was outraged. At the very moment when Céline was ready to take off to conquer the English-speaking market in Canada and the United States, along came someone to sow seeds of doubt! Without a moment's hesitation René turned to the Montreal producer Donald K. Tarlton, who had produced the great majority of American shows put on in Montreal (including Michael Jackson, the Rolling Stones, Paul McCartney, and Madonna). He wasn't a doubter, and agreed to produce Céline's new tour. René would never again work with Jean-Claude L'Espérance, for he had committed the worst of all sins where Céline was concerned: he had lacked faith in her.

In his long climb to the summit, to the promised land of every performer on the face of the earth, René demanded belief more than anything. "Mégot" was a believer, and so were Sony, Mme Dion and the Dion family, Eddy Marnay, Michel Jasmin, and Michel Drucker. And he wouldn't forget that. But neither would he forget Trans-Canada, Jean-Claude L'Espérance, and all those who had failed to believe.

The long ascent had a difficult beginning, because, like Jean-Claude L'Espérance, not everybody in the artistic milieu and the media believed in Céline.

In October 1990, the press attended some previews and the premiere, held in the Théâtre Saint-Denis. The reviews weren't unanimous. There was a sort of malaise in the air, as if people found it difficult to accept Céline's English-language repertoire, or as if they couldn't accept this sudden metamorphosis of the girl from Charlemagne, Quebec, into a Céline for New York or Toronto. They had accepted the transformation of the sweet little girl into a sexy woman, but they couldn't accept the metamorphosis of the francophone singer into an anglophone performer. I think, in retrospect, that they were afraid they would lose Céline forever.

In September she had appeared on the *Tonight Show*, hosted by Jay Leno, singing "Where Does My Heart Beat Now." At the end of the show Leno was holding the *Unison* album. Some Quebec journalists had accompanied Céline to the NBC studios in New York — René's idea. Céline had been intense and edgy during her performance, but she sang vibrantly in this different country, and spoke a different language.

Things got more complicated at the ADISQ gala — a prestigious annual event that rewards all the artisans of the recording and variety industries in Quebec. It caused quite a sensation when Céline Dion refused the Felix for the best English-speaking performer: "I'm not an anglophone, and the public at least knows very well that I'm still a Quebecoise and a francophone, even if I sing in English. This Felix should be for the performer who most distinguished him or herself internationally," Céline declared, taking everybody by surprise. There was a moment's uneasiness, followed by thunderous applause in the hall.

In the newspapers next day all the talk was about the Céline scandal, with the result that the award winners of the evening were almost forgotten. Most observers recognized Céline's courage, while others, including the singer Ginette Reno, criticized her for her backstage attitude. The prevalent view was that Céline had spoken on the spur of the moment, but in fact this wasn't so. "Why didn't you warn us sooner? Why didn't you withdraw Céline from the category when she was nominated?" asked the gala's organizers. "Since she was insulted publicly, Céline owed it to herself to answer in front of everyone, at the gala itself," replied Angélil when he was questioned after the gala. Either the ADISQ people were dumb and couldn't see the injustice they were doing Céline, or else they were smart and acting maliciously.

The trophy awarded Céline was a poisoned one. "Maybe she'll sing in Spanish some day," her agent continued, "but that won't make her a Spanish artist — no more than the New Kids on the Block, who have sung in French but are still American." René would eventually admit to my colleague Bruno Dostie that he had prepared Céline's response three weeks in advance of the gala, and had weighed his words carefully. The people who gave Céline a hard time had got it all wrong, because it was René's words she uttered in front of 2 million TV viewers — a masterpiece, there can be no doubt about that.

The debate was launched. The media spoke of nothing else but Céline's statement. Even politicians got involved. In Quebec, as soon as it's a matter of the French language there's a general outcry, old wounds are reopened, and the fighting begins. René had put the public in the picture. Without people really being aware of it he had put across a message that said: "Céline is a proud Quebecoise and will never abandon you — even if she does sing in English. And above all, don't drive us out of Quebec! It means a lot to us!"

I read somewhere that René would have made a brilliant politician. I couldn't agree more.

Though he is avowedly a convinced federalist, René has never said anything against Quebec nationalism. Master of his own domain, he has invented a personal form of nationalism in which the Arab, Quebec, Canadian, and American cultures form a harmonious blend. He has spoken English, French, and a little Arabic since birth, and has no problem mixing languages and lifestyles. Even more, he would like to bring together all the North American cultures in his approach to conquering the American market, and the international market along with it.

I remember one short conversation in Quebec in which I discussed with him how Diane Dufresne had distanced herself by moving to Paris, where she remained for a long time.

"I'll never make that mistake," he told me. "It's doesn't matter if Céline travels all over the world and wants to conquer all America, she always comes home again."

Before Céline, all the Quebec artists who tried their luck outside the province seemed to have abandoned Quebec, as if they had gone into exile — Alys Robi, Félix Leclerc, Riopelle, Borduas, Glen Ford (born in Quebec), Aglaé, Suzanne Avon, Geneviève Bujold, Leonard Cohen, Donald Sutherland, and many others.

Living in French in North America is always problematic. We Quebecois are a people of contradictions, and even René, who is of Arab origin, prefers to speak French. He surrounds himself with Quebecois friends, dreams of a career in America, is passionate about hockey, and hires Quebec musicians to accompany Céline in the United States. He eats both fast food and Arab dishes, and puts the Dion family from Charlemagne together with his own family from the west side of Montreal. He likes games of chance, golf, Florida, and hockey in the winter.

René isn't someone who likes confrontation, despite his anger with his peers or lesser people than himself. He operates diplomatically, surrounding himself with the best people after he has wooed them skilfully. From the outset of his career as an artist and manager he has relied on others. Now it was Tommy Motolla he had in his sights. Motolla, the top man at Sony, was particularly tough, and was considered by those in the know as the biggest shark in show business. A career on the international level could often depend on him, and René knew it.

First, he invited the top brass from Sony International to come and see Céline perform at the Théâtre Saint-Denis, and this enabled him to make some allies who would take him right to Motolla. René manoeuvred so skilfully that he was able to communicate with Motolla — which was already quite a feat in the milieu. Even better, Motolla liked René.

Mr. Akio Morita, born in Japan in 1921, was one of the most important creators of Sony. The son of a wealthy man, he was interested in American music. Listening to classical music, he realized that there was money to be made in the electronics field. In 1946, together with a Mr. Ibuka, Morita founded a company called Tokyo Telecommunications Engineering Company.

The company first manufactured replacement parts for record players. Then, gradually, it began to design tape recorders, personal stereos, etc.

In February 1960, Sony became officially established in the United States. Trade was excellent, and the firm grew to gigantic proportions. Morita, its founder, retired at the age of sixty-six, opening the door to a new generation of creative leaders. Towards the end of the 1980s, Norio Ohga pulled off one of the most impressive deals in history when he bought Columbia (Music) and Tri-Star Film Studios for $3.4 billion.

But five years later the company showed an enormous loss of $3.2 billion! So everyone buckled down, with the result that since 1994 Sony has once again been very profitable. Sony Music Entertainment is now divided into four labels: Epic Records Group, Columbia Records Group, Relativity Records Group, and Sony Classical.

Sony now has the top stars of the moment in the world under contract: Carlos Santana, Slayer, Bruce Springsteen, Shakira, Notre Dame Peace, Billy Joel, Las Ketchup, Tori Amos, 3LW, Leonard Cohen, Destiny's Child, and Céline Dion — a remarkable gem among the scores of artists who are honoured to be associated with this vast company.

JEAN BEAULNE

62

A CANADIAN TOUR

IN THE WINTER OF 1991, Céline's English-language tour began in Vancouver and continued through the major Canadian cities. The audiences were small to begin with, for this Quebec singer was still an unknown outside of her home province. Her name even had to be spelled for journalists from the western provinces. But Céline and René worked as if possessed. The victory would be hard won, and they put their all into bringing it off. At this stage, they were investing their health more than anything. But no matter, they could only achieve their common goal. They knew this, and could see the first signs of success.

The first of these was extremely indicative: the song "Where Does My Heart Beat Now" reached charts in *Billboard*, the bible of show business in the United States. The appearances on the *Tonight Show* were bearing fruit. René kept a copy of that issue of *Billboard* and showed it to everyone as if it was a trophy. When Céline reached the fourth spot on this prestigious chart she couldn't be ignored any longer. Now the Americans were buying Céline Dion. Sales of the album were constantly climbing, and approaching a million. English Canada, always on the coattails of the United States, was displaying more and more interest in the young Quebec singer.

But Céline didn't forget Quebec. On June 19 she celebrated the tenth year of her career at the Montreal Forum, before sixteen thousand delirious fans. It was an emotional show during which she talked about herself and sang the top hits of her career.

She had won over English Canada, and now needed only to take the final step to make a real breakthrough on the American market.

63

IT WAS CÉLINE WHO
CHANGED RENÉ

A S THEY FOLLOWED THE DIFFERENT stages of Céline's climb to the top, people close to René Angélil, particularly those who had known him for a long time, noticed a strange phenomenon. He was a changed man. Just as the failures, trials, and incertitude of his younger years had brought out the worst in him, now his successes and the challenges he had risen to brought out the best. By the time he reached this ultimate stage of international conquest, René had changed. He had been constantly evolving, and was already displaying the traits of a great manager, making more and more sound decisions, taking more and more successful initiatives, and having more and more good intuitions.

In the course of our conversations, Jean Beaulne told me he had come to the conclusion that it wasn't so much René who had changed Céline as the reverse. It wasn't that she had taught him his job, or anything he didn't know, but that her attitude, inborn determination, steadfastness in confronting difficulties, and talent had transformed a man who had been going nowhere before he met her. Beaulne explains:

> René offered Céline the image of an ideal man and agent when they began to work together. It was on that basis they pursued their professional relationship. René

had taken himself in hand, and continued to put new challenges to Céline and subject her to enormous pressure. In her place a lot of people would have gone to pieces. Sometimes it was almost inhuman. René's big surprise was to see that she always rose to the challenge, usually better than he could ever have imagined. She continually exceeded his expectations.

In the circumstances, to maintain this image as an ideal manager, he had to set another, greater challenge for himself. He was hoisted with his own petard. It takes time for a manager to really get to know his artist. I'm sure René had no idea, in the beginning, how far Céline could go. And we mustn't forget that many artists succumb to fame and success, or very quickly allow themselves to be intoxicated by them. Most of the artists I know couldn't have held up under such pressure and avoided so many pitfalls. To avoid losing Céline, René surpassed himself because he too wanted to live up to the image he'd given Céline. Of course he had a dream of international fame, but it was a dream he shared with Céline. Actually, it was Céline who encouraged it.

You have to have followed Céline's steps the way I have for so long to recognize her rare stamina and unfailing equilibrium. She has never been associated with any kind of scandal or involved in any sordid affair. She's had no difficulty preserving her perfect image. That's why Sony chose to back her rather than Whitney Houston or Mariah Carey, even if the latter was married to the boss of the company. All Céline's biographers have to agree that she has always been above reproach — distressingly above reproach, for in her case the gossip columnists have to make do with malicious tales and rumours! It is the people around her and the events she is involved in that provide the stories.

So how can we account for the survival in the often less than savoury world of show business of such an untroubled, wholesome image as Céline's?

"It's because of her family's support," says Jean Beaulne. "Céline's strength comes from the large family she has around her, and that allows her to recharge her batteries continually. Since she was a little girl, she has never been left alone. Within the family circle she can recover her equilibrium, regain a firm foothold, and discuss things with her brothers and sisters as well as with her parents, all of whom can speak to her frankly. In a big family there aren't any stars, just normal relationships."

When Céline was a child she was always enveloped in a cocoon. At school she had very few friends and was considered an outsider. Sometimes she was even made fun of, and occasionally they laughed at her aspirations when she said in the schoolyard that she wanted to become a great singer. She never liked school, mostly because of the other kids. She sought a refuge in her family, where there was singing and celebration with music — always with music.

Even today she is still protected by this same cocoon. Of course her brothers and sisters are sometimes demanding, passing on their bills and financial problems to her, but in general Céline owes as much to her family as her family does to her.

And at the same time it was essential for René, in safeguarding Céline's image of him, never to disappoint her family. He succeeded very well in this because from the outset he enjoyed Mme Dion's constant support.

René had always relied on someone else on his path through life. With Céline he learned to count on no one but himself for several years. Céline's docile nature and the faith she placed in him gave him confidence in himself. Her ignorance of the entertainment world and her blind faith in him forced him to discover who he really was and to probe his limits. René had never had so much latitude. He had never had the opportunity to show his full potential. With the Baronets, Ginette Reno, or Guy Cloutier he had never had so much elbow room or such complete control of his and his artist's future. He had always had to compromise with other forces that were not always favourable to him. René Angélil needed to be in control, and Céline allowed him control. She reflected back to him a splendid image — a new, successful image. How could anyone not fall in love with a woman who gives you back your life in such a way?

More than a million copies of the album *Unison* were sold, but mostly in Canada and Japan. In the United States a major coup was still needed. And that major coup seemed to come with the offer for her to sing "Dream to Dream," the theme song of *Fievel Goes West*, a film produced by Steven Spielberg. René was overjoyed. This was just the opportunity he'd been waiting for.

Céline loved the song, and sang it dreaming of everything it signified for her. But then misfortune struck. The song wouldn't be recorded by Céline because of a dispute between Sony and MCA Records. *Fievel Goes West* was to be filmed by Universal Pictures, who had their own record company, MCA. An agreement was still possible between the two companies, but Sony's Motolla refused to "lend" Céline to MCA. Things dragged on. Motolla changed his mind, but too late, and in the end "Dream to Dream" was recorded by Linda Ronstadt. It was a terrible disappointment for René. It seemed as if all his dreams were coming to nothing. He was convinced it was by way of the cinema that Céline would make her entry into the United States. And, besides, a Spielberg movie was a once in a lifetime opportunity. Indeed, he was so shattered that it was Céline who consoled him.

Yet for Céline Dion's career, this misfortune turned out to be the best thing that could have happened.

64

BEAUTY AND THE BEAST

T HE DION-ANGÉLIL COUPLE TRAVELLED a great deal in 1991. In addition to putting on shows in Canada and some in the United States it was also necessary to promote *Unison* in a number of countries, including Japan and England. It was in England that René got a call from Disney Productions with an offer for Céline to record the theme song of an animated movie called *Beauty and the Beast*.

This time around it couldn't be said there was great enthusiasm on Céline's part, and her wariness was understandable. She had been hurt as much as René by her first abortive experience with the cinema. Nevertheless, she did go to the Disney studios and gradually allowed herself to be convinced. The song was very moving, and the film was sure to be a big success.

And that's the way fate intervenes with a master's hand, confounding the calculations of those who strive to tame it. What is more, it defies the laws of logic, using absurd means to achieve its ends. René Angélil, the great strategist, was powerless before it. The Spielberg film in which such hopes had been placed didn't have any success, and neither did the song "Dream to Dream." But in the meantime the gates of the promised land of Hollywood were thrown wide open, and the last step was taken. After years of effort and hard work, of investments at all levels, the dream was coming true — the greatest dream an artist on this continent can have: music and Hollywood.

Beauty and the Beast would be a stunning success and would make Céline Dion a star of American song. The time had come for Céline to make her entry into the United States.

It is impossible to imagine the kind of stress René Angélil was under as Céline took part in the Academy Awards ceremony at the start of the 1990s. When she was asked at the last moment to replace Barbra Streisand, meaning she had to learn a new song in less than twenty-four hours, the tension was enormous, particularly since she was to sing before more than a billion viewers and in the presence of a demanding audience containing among others some of the top brains in Hollywood. As for René, he must have been keeping his fingers crossed, hoping Céline wouldn't have a memory lapse or an uncharacteristic bout of stage fright.

Founded on May 27, 1927, in California, the Academy of Motion Picture Arts and Sciences had thirty-six members, with Douglas Fairbanks as president. The first award ceremony took place in 1929, after talking movies came in. The price of admission was ten dollars at the time, while now it costs one thousand dollars. The winners' names used to be released the previous evening, but starting in 1941 they were announced during the ceremony itself. Broadcast on radio for years, the event was shown on television for the first time in 1953, by NBC. That was the twenty-fifth gala, hosted by Bob Hope. Since 1976 it has been televised by ABC, whose contract will remain in force until 2008. After changing cities several times, the ceremony has been held in Los Angeles since 1969.

As for the Oscar, the famous statuette awarded as a prize, it was designed by Cedric Gibbons, the artistic director for MGM. It represents a knight standing on a roll of film with five spokes. These spokes are a reminder that the event is dedicated to the actors, writers, directors, producers, and technicians. Made of

24-carat gold, the statuette is 34 centimetres high and weighs 3.8 kilograms. Since 1927, 2,365 statuettes have been awarded. In 1927, thirteen categories were honoured, while in 2002 there were twenty-five. Each year fifty to sixty statuettes are made by twelve individuals who devote about twenty hours to finishing them off perfectly. Over the years the Oscar has been refused by only three winners. A seven-metre-tall version of it can be admired in Los Angeles.

Before it was christened "Oscar," the now famous statuette was called by different names: the "Academy statuette," the "golden trophy," the "statue of merit," and "the iron man." Popular history recounts that it got the name "Oscar" from one of the executive directors of the Academy, Margaret Herrick, who thought it resembled her uncle Oscar. The name was adopted officially in 1939. In the 1930s a miniature statuette was awarded winners in the minor categories. It is also said that a ventriloquist was given a statuette with a mouth that opened and shut, while the great producer Walt Disney, when being honoured for his film *Snow White and the Seven Dwarfs,* was given a statuette accompanied by seven miniature copies. One interesting piece of trivia is that the televised ceremony with the largest audience was in 1998, with 55.2 million viewers — that being the year of the movie *Titanic.* As for the longest ceremony, the one in 2002 broke every record, lasting four hours and sixteen minutes on air.

JEAN BEAULNE

65

PLAMONDON AGAIN

IT WOULD BE EASY TO think that Céline had made it. Now she might have had an opportunity to catch her breath, needing only to allow herself to be carried along on the wave of her success and devote herself to her American career. Nothing was further from the truth. She was already rehearsing an album of songs by Luc Plamondon, called *Dion chante Plamondon*. With the famous lyricist she chose eight songs from her repertoire, to which she added four new ones to complete the album. René told Plamondon that the launch and promotion of the record would have to be speeded up, for a second album in English was soon to be launched by Sony. This was to include the song "Beauty and the Beast," which Céline was to sing as a duet with Peabo Bryson.

"René is an impulsive guy who never lets up," explains Jean Beaulne. "He's a perfectionist who does everything to excess, never allows himself a moment's rest, and never allows anyone else a moment's rest either. He's constantly pushing the envelope, as is Céline."

The album *Dion chante Plamondon* was launched at the Metropolis disco as usual in November 1991 and already over fifty thousand copies were on order. A month later, sales of the album had topped the one hundred thousand mark in Quebec. France was still to come. This time the critics were astonished, for the quality of the recording was amazing. The full range of Céline's talent was also revealed, for she had been involved in the production of the album. She had taken several of Plamondon's hits and given them a new complexion, a fresh rhythm, and a particularly original interpretation. For the first time René gave Céline the responsibility for a good part of the record's production in Paris. In 1992, which was beginning to look like a magical year, the Quebec singer learned that she was to sing "Beauty and the Beast" as a duet with Peabo Bryson at the American Music Awards in January, and at the Academy Awards on March 30 — her twenty-fourth birthday. The song had been at the top of the American charts since the beginning of the year, with five hundred thousand copies sold. Céline was already queen of the "Hot 100."

At the Academy Awards, held in the Dorothy Chandler Pavilion, René once again became a starstruck child in a shop of toys out of his reach. He became a groupie, watching all the personalities of the entertainment world participating in the event, which attracts over a billion viewers each year. Unknown to Céline, he had brought the whole Dion family to Hollywood. The Dions had all come from Charlemagne to witness their little sister's coronation. Quebec too was watching, across the American continent, in front of their TV screens. It was the first time a Quebec artist had participated in the Academy Awards.

The fairy tale was complete when the song sung by Céline and Peabo Bryson won the Oscar for Song of the Year.

Taking advantage of the event, Sony launched the album *Céline Dion*, recorded in the top studios in America and putting together songs by the best composers in the business. The next day Céline went on the *Tonight Show* and was welcomed like a major star. In very little time, after being seen by a billion people on TV, she had become a recognized figure in the American musical world.

Without wasting any time, she started out on a demanding tour of the United States, as if she had to take maximum advantage of the situation and compress all her good fortune into a single instant. Not only had Céline's popularity grown, but René's had also, silencing all his detractors. Now people were talking about his creative genius, his strategies, and his inborn instinct for marketing. This was a period of euphoria in René and Céline's life, and their love was growing stronger all the time. Céline admitted to some journalists that she was in love, but never revealed her lover's name.

René was being carried along on the torrent and driving his strength to the limit. Then on April 29 his heart faltered, and his world came to a standstill.

66

A HEART ATTACK IN LOS ANGELES

O N April 29, 1992, Céline and René were staying in a Los Angeles hotel, enjoying the sun and the swimming pool. It was a brief respite before setting off for New York to get on with business there. René had eaten his fill in the hotel restaurant, where the food was excellent. The couple was trying to use this beautiful day to recover from the powerful emotions they had experienced over the previous few days. René went back to his room, feeling tired. Céline became uneasy. He was having difficulty breathing and seemed completely confused. She immediately feared the worst. She had had a premonition that something bad was about to happen. Right away she alerted the hotel staff and asked for a wheelchair. Quickly! Off to the hospital — by taxi, by ambulance, or whatever!

The ambulance took René to Cedars Sinai Medical Center in West Hollywood, five minutes from the hotel. In the hospital Céline raised her voice, not in song but to make herself heard by the staff. There was as much grief as anger in her voice. She demanded immediate attention for René. A young doctor examined Céline's companion and sent him off to intensive care without delay. He didn't say anything, but Céline understood: René was in grave danger. Jean Beaulne recalls:

If he had reached the hospital five minutes later, René was a goner. I know Los Angeles, for I lived there for several years, and I know the hotel where they were staying, and fortunately it's very near Cedars Sinai. They had just enough time to get there.

In addition to undergoing the enormous stress of Céline's success, René ate very badly. I remember once when I went to see Céline perform at the Théâtre Saint-Denis, and when it was over he ordered a meal in the Italian restaurant opposite the theatre. He had ordered one of his favourite dishes, an enormous fettuccine with cream sauce that he gulped down, accompanied by a large Coke. Then he ordered a huge three-layer chocolate cake that he also wolfed down. I told him to be careful, to eat more slowly, and to choose healthy dishes. But he wouldn't listen, and as usual told me to mind my own business. So I told him that if he didn't take care, he'd kill himself. I didn't say it in a mean way. I was worried about him. I've a reputation for always being concerned for other people's health, and it pained me to see him ruining his by eating food so harmful to his organism — what is more, the kind of food I've always known him to eat. René has never really taken any care about his diet, and he gets angry as soon as I bring up the subject. So I usually try to restrain myself, but sometimes I can't stop myself giving him advice.

Jean Beaulne drinks herbal tea with all his meals, even at lunch. He's obsessed with healthy eating, and will go out of his way to fetch spring water from Sainte-Agathe, a hundred kilometres from Montreal, or to pick up organic bread from a specialized bakery. At the age of sixty he still regularly covers tens of kilometres on his bike, and has never had a serious illness.

In hospital, René was told that he had to keep to his room for at least a week. He would do so for several weeks. On René's request, Céline called his mother, whom he wanted to come. He also wanted to see his children, Patrick, Jean-Pierre, and Anne-Marie, the youngest, aged fourteen.

The whirl of show business had come to a complete standstill inside René Angélil's head. Now he was a frail man, fearing death for the first time in his life. He still wasn't sure he would survive this heart attack. He wept, and in a dramatic gesture he asked to make his will. He was even thinking of his inheritance, and listed the names of those who were to look after Céline in case he passed away. Who they were we shall never know.

René went through a battery of tests that took longer because of the Los Angeles riots. He had plenty of time to see his family and old friends, and to reflect on his life. Fame and fortune meant little to him now. He was concerned for his life, and for the quality of that life. He thought of his childhood, his career, the mad career of the past few years, and recognized he had to slow down. More than ever it was brought home to him that his fiftieth birthday had taken place in January. Until then he hadn't had any time to think about it. He hadn't had time to take a breath during a half-century spent pursuing wealth, defying chance, and struggling to become tops in his field. He had achieved this, but now here he was, lying in bed, a crushed man. Jean Beaulne had certainly been right to worry about his pace of life and poor eating habits.

Céline, who undertook more and more tasks on René's behalf, carried a great sense of guilt with her all this while. She considered herself responsible for the breakdown of her lover's health. However, she didn't speak openly about it. Later she would allow a remark pregnant with meaning slip out in a journalist's presence: "If he had died, I'd have told myself I had killed him." And she would have obeyed his last wishes. She would have gone on singing — for him.

René thought his stay in hospital was dragging on for too long. He was worried about Céline's career, for she had a lot of engagements to fulfil, but she was staying there by his side as if no one else existed in the whole world. Seeing that René's condition was improving and that he was gradually getting better, Céline decided to travel to New York and Europe without him. He needed rest and calm, and, for one of the rare times in his life, to be alone. Céline set out on the trip accompanied by her mother.

René didn't insist. He no longer had the strength to be caught up in the whirlwind activity of show business, and submitted completely to his doctor's orders. The lover of splendid premieres and spectacular record launches travelled back to Montreal in the profoundest of silences, completely incognito, on May 18, and shut himself in at home. He went to bed early, followed the diet ordered for him, and exercised. He was closely supervised at the Centre Épic in Montréal, where he went three times a week to use the treadmill or exercise bike. He was unrecognizable. He had lost weight and was living in a disciplined way.

Very few people in Quebec knew the details of the cardio-vascular attack that had nearly carried him off while he was staying in Los Angeles. René did everything possible to screen the information and conceal his true state of health. It would, he felt, have been bad publicity that might harm Céline's career and possibly weaken her leverage in the international show business environment. However, he did confide in one trusted journalist:

> I was lucky, and I thank God for that. With Céline's intervention, taking charge of everything, in control of everything just the way she is on stage, I was able to get to hospital right away. It's thanks to her cool head I'm here today. When we went into emergency she shouted so loud that the doctors reacted right away. I've the best of intentions, but I know that the memory is a faculty very liable to forget. But when I look at Céline and my three children I know I'll never forget. I've a tremendous responsibility to them, and I don't want to be parted from them.

Later, René would call the drama he had lived through a "bit of a setback."

Actually, however, he was all too aware he was living on borrowed time. His hair had turned completely white in a short while, and, during the preceding few years he had often felt his strength abandon him. He had plenty of time to reflect during the first weeks of June, and his thoughts were often negative — a normal reaction in someone recovering from such a trauma. He thought of the years remaining to him. He thought of the young woman he loved, only twenty-four years old and full of energy. Would she grow tired of an older man, and a sick one like him? He mulled over such dark thoughts as summer was awakening from its long slumber.

67

CÉLINE'S INDEPENDENCE

AFTER THE CRISIS IN Los Angeles, René Angélil became a changed man. The relationship between manager and artist changed, too. We might say that Pygmalion had completed his work, for now a new woman was looking down at him from the heights on which she stood. In this mad career, this ascent to the Hollywood summit, the only thing that had mattered was her work. There had been only the world of music and the images that obsessed them. Now human values regained their true importance. After neglecting his physical health and his heart for too long, René looked back at the road he had travelled, and ahead at the life remaining to him.

After coming so far, Céline contemplated her future life. She didn't have much education, but she had learned a lot about life during the preceding years. The shock she had just had on seeing the man she loved in such a weakened state allowed her to realize her own strength. For the first time, she took control of the situation. She had never had so much power. She realized that she had a power given to her by her youth, good health, talent, and now her popularity, and indeed celebrity. She would never abuse her powers, for she was connected to, tied to, and deeply rooted in the man who had made her what she was as an artist, a woman, and a celebrity. She would use only one of her powers: the power of love.

68

SEVILLE

IN JUNE 1992 CÉLINE TRAVELLED to Norway, Sweden, Holland, and Paris with Vito Luprano of Sony to look after the organization of the tour. On June 26, René accompanied her to Seville, in Spain, where she had been invited to participate in the Canada Day festivities as part of the Universal Exhibition in that city.

In the show Céline sang some songs from her new album, a few songs in French, and, of course, an aria from the opera *Carmen*, for the local people. She told them she had a Spanish ancestor, and that she had every intention of learning the language so that she could sing in Spanish.

Pierre Leroux, a journalist I have worked alongside for many years, was impatient with this kind of nonsense and was waiting for the press conference to end so he could winkle out of Céline some more interesting statement he could get his teeth into. A highly cultured individual who spoke French with an accent like a Frenchman's, Leroux loved to unmask, castigate, and set traps for artists he considered over-popular. Knowing his article would appear on Canada Day, he took Céline to one side (away from René, in particular), to broach the subject of Canadian unity. She said:

Of course I'm against separations of all kinds, for I travel a lot. What I see in Germany, or in Switzerland, where there are three cultures that live in harmony even though it is one of the richest countries in the world, gives me hope that people can get along together, and shows me how lucky we are to have two cultures in Canada.

It's true I don't know a lot about politics. ... The only way to keep a country strong and healthy is mutual respect. People are scared, and hope there won't be any separation. I think the idea of separation is dreadful.

Pierre Leroux was content: he had his scoop. The next day an explosive headline appeared on the front page of the *Journal de Montréal*: "SEPARATION WOULD BE DREADFUL." Beneath it was a photo of Céline "coming to the defence of Canada," said the most-read daily in Quebec.

The statement came at a most inopportune moment, for not all the Canadian provinces had accepted Quebec's demands during a premiers' conference at Meech Lake. Almost half the population of Quebec had voted for sovereignty in a referendum, and the failure of this meeting stirred up a wave of Quebec nationalism. A poll now showed that the majority of Quebecois were in favour of Quebec's political independence.

There were expressions of anger towards Céline in the newspapers and on open-line radio shows, while the Dion-Angélil couple, in blissful ignorance of what was going on, completed their visit to Spain. But news travels fast, especially this, which had shocked a good number of Quebecois.

This time René intervened. Never, and not in any circumstances, could he accept that Céline's image be tarnished, least of all in her own country.

On July 11 *Le Journal de Montréal* published an exclusive article entitled "Céline explains." The explanation came from a shaken woman — one who had fallen into a trap and who was hurt by the reaction of some of her compatriots who wanted to throw out her records:

That is the last time in my life I intend to speak about politics. I'll never venture into that field again. My mother scolded me for it. Of course I'm for Quebec and for a better world. I'm a Quebecoise, and proud of

it, and I've always said so … I'm not a spokesperson for
Canada, and we even refused to make a commercial for
Canada's 125th Anniversary. I'm a Quebecoise, and a
proud one, whether Quebec separates or not. … I don't
want people to throw out my records. I love people, and
I need them to return my love.

While people were reading this statement in the newspaper, Céline
was setting out on an American tour that took in about twenty cities, in
the first part of the American star Michael Bolton's show. This was
another of René's strategies, for he wanted to advance step by step with
the American public. But Céline had to return to Quebec. She was
afraid. René insisted: if she didn't go back immediately and appear in
her own country, and above all in her own province, her words in Seville
would be subject to wrong interpretation.

"I can't wait to appear in Quebec," she said diplomatically, "but with
everything that has happened I've the impression I've lost my public.
I'm afraid of how our people will react."

She returned to Quebec on August 14, setting out on a tour that
would take her all the way to Chandler and Gatineau in early September.
It was a daughter returning to the bosom of her family, and the gaffe in
Seville was soon forgotten. If, at this precise moment in her career, she had
neglected Quebec, her statement in Seville would have been seen as dis-
owning her own people. And while this controversy was going on, René
Angélil was able to divert attention from his state of health. Talking about
his health was harmful to his image — and to business, too.

69

LISE PAYETTE

S O WHAT ABOUT THEIR FEELINGS for one another? The question was
inevitable, and reporters never missed a single opportunity during
interviews to glean some information about Céline's love life. When she
felt too pressured by questions on the subject, Céline would invariably
answer, "Yes, there is someone in my life. Yes, I'm in love with someone,
like all women my age, but I can't tell you his name." The questions
became more and more frequent. In 1992 people were more interested
than ever in Céline's amours, and she was beginning to show signs of
considerable tension whenever people raised what was, to say the least, a
sensitive part of her private life.

For years Céline, a very passionate woman, had wanted to reveal her
love for René Angélil to the general public. The two lovers had now been
living as a couple for four years, and it pained Céline to have to keep it
secret. The situation provoked many arguments between the two of
them. René insisted on silencing the woman he loved. No, he wasn't
being domineering, and no, he wasn't abusing his natural authority: he
was just afraid of others, of his image as a husband who was too old,
afraid of the consequences, and above all afraid of having to expose private emotions to public view.

In the fall he accepted an invitation from the researcher of a new program called *Tête à tête*, hosted by someone the critics considered the most gifted talk show host in Quebec, Lise Payette. (A good comparison might be with Barbara Walters, another TV woman who never allows herself to be intimidated by a guest or his or her entourage.) In addition to pioneering the talk show in Quebec, Lise Payette served as a minister in René Lévesque's sovereigntist government before returning to the TV screen.

Encouraged by the host's respect and empathy, Céline unburdened herself as she had never done before.

"Basically, I'll never achieve what I want. My career is great, but there are always 'buts' with my agent, my family, and my fans, and always more advice. All the time. René tells me I whine too much. Every time my family calls it's about money. If it's between a hundred and a thousand dollars I can't say no. Now they have to go through my accountant."

"And what about love?" asks Lise Payette.

"I'm in love, and I'd like to shout it from the rooftops, but I can't tell you his name. It might harm my career."

Céline burst into tears, and Lise Payette handed her a tissue.

"René was there when we recorded the program," remembers the host of the show. "He was in the production room, and I glanced at him while Céline was pouring out her feelings. I noticed he was in tears just like her. He seemed so unhappy I felt sorry for him."

René had a lot of respect for Lise Payette, and there was no question of his attempting to control the program's content. Recorded in September 1992, *Tête à tête* would be broadcast in October of the same year, without any opposition from Céline's manager. However, the program would never be repeated, nor would it be used for any of the documentaries or specials made about Céline Dion.

Céline kept her secret, but the media didn't miss the opportunity to indulge in commentary or speculation about her love life. People talked about Céline's romance in offices and living rooms. People also discussed the age gap. "It's common knowledge that she's in love with René," declared "well-informed" people in entertainment circles — but no one dared to say it publicly. Besides, the two lovers were behaving with the greatest discretion. They never kissed in public, and they never held hands. So to the discipline required by the profession there was added a discipline of the heart, one that would require many sacrifices.

The journalist Agnès Gaudet finally decided to speak the unspeakable, even if it upset the person in question. "Let's be frank. People say Céline has been in love with her manager, René Angélil, for years. Yet there has never been any proof. No one has dared to say anything, and no one has ever been able to make them admit it. Perhaps their age difference is the key to the mystery."

The year 1992, which René called a magical one, despite the "setback" of his heart attack, was nearing its end when Céline learned she was to take part in the gala to celebrate Bill Clinton's investiture as president of the United States. The event was to take place on January 19, 1993, and the top rock musicians and performers were invited, including Michael Jackson, Fleetwood Mac, and even Barbra Streisand.

"Céline is the future," Sony Music declared, with youth in triumph about a U.S. president who was younger than Mick Jagger — a president who played the saxophone and loved jazz and the old-time rockers like Little Richard and Chuck Berry.

René informed Quebec journalists that no fewer than 50 million American homes would see and hear the only Canadian invited to this celebration of youth. Céline's manager attached great importance to numbers. He always had a whirl of numbers spinning inside his head. Ever since he learned to play cards as a small child he had never stopped exercising his memory. He knew a hundred or so phone numbers by heart, remembered the date of every birthday and anniversary, and could reel off statistics, record sales figures, TV audience numbers, and past events, all with disconcerting precision. He often had the last word simply because he knew and remembered better than the other person.

He knew, for example, that there was nothing more prestigious for an artist wanting to have a career in the United States than to carry off a Grammy Award. And, precisely, that the Grammy ceremony was to take place in Los Angeles on February 24, and Céline had been nominated in three categories. In the end she was awarded the first Grammy given to a Quebec artist, in the category Best Pop Performance by a Duo or Group.

This was recognition on a par with winning the Oscar as best leading actor or actress.

"Céline would never again be an unknown in the United States," said René. "Her name will be on a Grammy, like the top musical performers in the United States." And then the whirlwind activity started up again, with all of Canada wanting to pay tribute to "sweet Celeen" at the Junos, which she hosted in English. She carried off four Junos, including the one for Best Female Vocalist of the year for the third year in a row. It was a lot — even too much for some Anglophone journalists, who thought Céline was overexposed.

René was almost flattered. He had never feared overexposure for Céline. He had always claimed that she could become a winner only by becoming known in every quarter and being seen as much as possible. He never feared any backlash or saturation, not in Quebec, and above all not outside the province.

"An artist who wants to have a career outside Quebec and France has to go by way of the Junos. In 1987 Céline's career took a new turn when she sang 'Just Have a Heart' at the Juno ceremony. That's what allowed us to negotiate a big amount with Sony."

70

THE ENGAGEMENT

R UMOURS ABOUT THE ROMANCE BETWEEN Céline and René were rife, and the tension was becoming intolerable. Céline herself had let the cat out of the bag by saying she was in love. Sooner or later the whole thing would erupt, and René was determined to control the eruption. It couldn't just be a matter of casually announcing the love between himself and Céline to the entire world. It had to be something big, but something that wouldn't affect his companion's reputation.

He was thinking mostly of her when he planned an unforgettable, romantic evening in a suite in a major Montreal hotel. Céline had no idea of what her lover had in mind as he ceremoniously prepared a candlelight dinner. Suddenly, he presented her with a little box. She opened it and gazed for a long time at an engagement ring. It was Céline's twenty-fifth birthday, and she could have hoped for no better birthday gift. This ring was the symbol of her triumph, and on this thirtieth day of March 1993, it meant more to her than an Oscar, a Grammy, a Juno, or a Felix — or all the awards put together.

"I've never had an adolescence, and I left a good part of my life behind in planes and VIP lounges, so I don't intend to miss out on love," the singer confided to one of her friends. This ring meant that her love was at last released from its silence. René thought that at twenty-five his companion was old enough to choose the man she would love for the rest of her life.

Next he thought about the second step in publicly acknowledging his love story. Of course the engagement had taken place in the utmost secrecy. But the time had come to announce it to the world, and discretion was no longer appropriate. Nor would it ever be again.

Céline was preparing to record a third English album, and René Angélil the master strategist had no intention of wasting such an opportunity as the public announcement of his love for Céline. For the first time since he began his career as a manager he was going to emerge from the wings, where he had reigned supreme 'til then, and enter the spotlight the way he used to do as a Baronet. He was himself responsible for staging his performance.

He first chose "The Colour of My Love," his favourite among the songs on the recording, as the album's title. He also chose the place — the Metropolis — and the stage on which he would make his entrance. It was the very last scene, the scene of the kiss, when Céline would announce that "The Colour of My Love" was indeed René. Once she had sung half of the fifteen songs on the album, Céline was to bring René up on stage and kiss him on the mouth. The privacy had ended: more than two thousand people had managed to squeeze into the Metropolis, and two TV channels, Musique Plus and Télévision Quatre Saisons, together with the major Montreal radio stations, were broadcasting the event live.

René had excluded the cameras of TVA from the Metropolis. Loyal in his friendships but vengeful against anyone that stood in his way, René Angélil still hadn't forgiven Michel Chamberland, the TVA program director, for having insisted that Céline's appearance on the program *Ad Lib*, hosted by Jean-Pierre Coallier, be exclusive. This had occurred a few years earlier when Céline was launching *Dion chante Plamondon*. The promotion of the album had begun on Radio Canada, on *Studio libre*, and Michel Chamberland had refused to have Céline on the program a few days after she appeared on Radio Canada. René had sworn then that the singer would never take part in any program on TVA as long as Chamberland was still around. So, on that particularly emotional evening of November 8, 1993, the cameras of TVA were not permitted to show the first kiss publicly exchanged between Céline Dion and René Angélil. Love wasn't enough to make him forget an old grudge.

71

PUTTING QUEBEC FIRST

A LL THROUGHOUT CÉLINE DION'S CAREER, René Angélil put
Quebec first. This son of a Syrian immigrant, raised in a different culture from that of the Quebecois, had still always associated
Quebec, especially Montreal, with all the major events surrounding
the rise of the superstar Céline had become. Strangely, his approach
contrasted with that of many Quebec artists, who distanced themselves substantially from Quebec in the hope of having a career elsewhere. His attachment to Quebec could put to shame a fair number of
Quebec nationalists who have often neglected Quebec in their pursuit
of the international market. Diane Dufresne "forgot" her Quebec public for several years when she pursued her career mainly in France.
Geneviève Bujold has rarely appeared in Quebec since filming *Anne of
a Thousand Days* with Richard Burton. Roch Voisine was little seen in
Quebec while enjoying success in France. Daniel Pilon stayed for a
long time in Hollywood and forgot about Quebec when filming with
John Wayne. Jean Leclerc was far from Quebec when he played
Dracula on stage, or acted regularly in American soaps. Very often,
these artists were so committed to having an international career that
they couldn't appear in their country of origin. But this was never true
of Céline, for René insisted on her returning home at regular intervals.

To say that Céline Dion was Quebec's best ambassador over the last decade is no exaggeration — far from it.

All this was because of a Syrian who could well have lived a long time away from Quebec. What is more, he insisted on using Quebec musicians on Céline's American tours. He also regularly invited Quebec journalists to attend his protégée's great triumphs. The launches of Céline's records, in both English and French, took place in Montreal. Céline and René got married in Montreal, and René chose Montreal for her last show of the millennium. When all these events and many others are taken together, one can see a constant concern on René's part to make Quebec part of everything he undertook. He didn't need to create any illusion that Céline had never left Quebec, for indeed she never did. Furthermore, whenever she appears on a talk show with Larry King, Oprah, or David Letterman, she always manages to speak about Quebec in one way or another. She has sung several times in French in the United States, and was able to sell the *D'eux* album in the land of Uncle Sam.

The Quebecois, accustomed to seeing their hockey stars stolen from them by the Americans and their best minds leave the country without any hope of returning, have been surprised by Céline's attachment. They thought that when she reached the pinnacle of her art and won recognition in every country in the world, at least where pop music is played, Céline would no longer need Quebec.

René didn't seem to see things that way.

I asked Jean Beaulne, who knows the American as well as the Quebec market, what he thought about this.

> René's strategy was to keep her in Quebec. We mustn't forget that Quebec means a market of buyers, of consumers. Per capita, more records are sold here than anywhere else. It's an important market for him. It was a base he could build on, because the success of a record in Quebec influences the other markets. It's easy to negotiate abroad when you can say your artist is selling well at home.
>
> What's more, you can't compare the American market to the one in Quebec. Here, you only need to get on

the first page of the *Journal de Montréal* or *La Presse*, organize a promotion with the radio station CKOI and then a big TV appearance, and you have the market in the bag. You only need hit three or four targets to reach everybody, for the media are concentrated. In the United States, it's not so easy — far from it. You have to work for a long, long time and travel a lot to sell your product — first Los Angeles, then New York, then Chicago, and then negotiations with a lot more media that René doesn't know as well. Quebec is a money spinner for him, and he can do what he wants there.

With no further delay the pair of lovers started out on a long promotional campaign that brought them through English Canada and the United States. On the most popular talk shows in the United States Céline talked about the content of her new album, but above all about her romance with René Angélil. After their discovery of Céline, the Americans were now discovering René. In fact they were simply discovering love. Céline sang about love six times on the album, and with real feeling too. She was quite right, for her love album was triple platinum in Canada and a five-time platinum record in the United States two weeks after it came out.

In early 1994 sales of *The Colour of My Love* topped the million mark, and Sony was gearing up for worldwide distribution. Now, after this enormous success, René had his sights set on the world market. She travelled across the United States several times, triumphed all over Canada, and went to Europe and Japan. By the summer of 1994 sales of *The Colour of My Love* were approaching the 5 million mark. René announced that the so eagerly awaited wedding would be celebrated in the following months in the Church of Notre Dame, in Montreal.

72

THE WEDDING

René Angélil took Céline Dion as his wife in the Church of Notre Dame in Montreal on December 17, 1994, on one of those winter days when the bitter cold turns you to a block of ice where you stand. Behind the scenes, it was the manager rather than Céline Dion's future husband who planned a royal marriage surrounded by excess and controversy, as the event assumed surreal theatrical proportions.

René was acting like royalty, annulling his previous marriage the way Caroline of Monaco, separated from Philippe Junot, and the great nobles of the past had done. With Céline he made a retreat to a Carmelite nunnery to pray, the way people did in the Middle Ages. He invited the people to celebrate, but personally chose one of the media, Trustar, to share the privacy of the marriage. He had the power to do so. Throughout the entire event, René always behaved as if he was creating a personal royalty. He gave his marriage a dimension unequalled in a land lacking in kings or queens. While Quebec has never obtained its sovereignty, on that day in December he was crowning the sovereign lord and lady appropriate to it, in a modern context. Quebec was crowning the king and queen of show business, and blessing their love.

The newspapers waxed indignant at his manipulation of the media. Intellectuals denounced the extravagance and commercialization of the event, but the good people dreamed, thronging around the church in spite of the cold, wait for the princes of show business to appear. They looked for Michael Jackson, Madonna, and Jack Nicholson, whose attendance had been announced. But they recognized only familiar faces — the couple's friends. But no matter, it was the event that counted. The dream became a reality, the doors opened, and the limousines arrived one by one. Céline was as dazzling as a madonna on her way to the church, René's bearing was regal, and the court followed. Montreal was proud. American television was there to record this extravagant wedding for the entire world.

After the ceremony, Céline and René would give a press conference to satisfy all the media from Quebec and beyond. Then they would celebrate at the Westin Hotel with their friends and guests, all handpicked, until the early hours. René had thought up a casino with play money and other rooms with a fairy-tale look. It was an otherworldly day, surreal and excessive like the man himself.

In the days that followed people literally fought over the souvenir booklets of the marriage of the year, as if they were the most precious relics. Immediately, sales of a special issue of the magazine *7 Jours/7 Days*, published by Trustar, containing exclusive pictures of the wedding and reception, exceeded four hundred thousand copies. They later printed two hundred thousand copies of a luxury souvenir booklet on glossy paper containing five hundred photos. Any left over were shipped to Japan, which was crying out to get them at any price. In the end, not even employees of Trustar were able to get their hands on the last available copies.

The fairy tale ended, the newlyweds departed, and the bills for the most beautiful marriage in Quebec history were totted up. The cost came to five hundred thousand dollars, but the souvenir booklets would bring in several hundred thousand dollars as a lump payment, plus a certain percentage of the sales. In addition, several sponsors, whose names were announced during the reception, had paid for the furs, the clothes, the limousines, and even the wooden walkway leading into the church.

Jean Beaulne was at the party at the Westin until the small hours of the morning. Recently divorced, and without a serious lady friend, he was accompanied by his daughter Mélanie, aged twenty-one, who would admit a little later that she had never seen anything as extraordinary as this wedding. In the course of the evening, Jean Beaulne would hear the musician David Foster declare to the guests, after performing at the piano: "René is the real godfather of Quebec."

73

COMPULSIVE, TO SAY THE LEAST

THE PERIOD SURROUNDING Céline AND René's marriage was probably the most productive and fertile in the singer's career. This enormous success, hoped for by all the popular performers on the planet, would be enjoyed by a rare few. The dream of breaking into the American market had been realized for René and Céline, but their success was even greater than that. The album *The Colour of My Love* was in first place on the chart of the prestigious *Billboard* magazine. Sales had surpassed 13 million copies, putting Céline among the most popular artists in the world. Now she was on a par with people like Michael Jackson, Barbra Streisand, Mariah Carey, Whitney Houston, and a few others — a select few.

Where music is concerned, America sets the tone for most of the world. Céline's records are played in all the major capitals. Her voice and her name are recognized, and people look for her picture in Paris, Rome, Oslo, Dakar, Istanbul, London, and even in the remotest villages on the face of the planet. Now they needed only to hold the ground gained by her records and cassettes.

What did René do? He continued with the launch of the album *Céline Dion à l'Olympia* in November 1994, and of another album, *Les Premières Années*, at the same time. It is not hard to believe that he wanted to take advantage of the mania Céline had inspired, but that didn't suffice for him. He was working on an album for the French-speaking market. He had already found a songwriter and composer, Jean-Jacques Goldman, widely considered one of the best writing in French, and was negotiating to record the next album in English, the album that would be the biggest success of Céline's career. As a gambler he was compulsive, and as a manager no less so.

"He's like a machine that runs day and night," Jean Beaulne would say. "He doesn't want to stop; he can't stop. In the Baronets days, René would play Monopoly until ten or eleven in the morning. Or he'd go to Laurentian Bowling, open twenty-four hours, and stay there till eleven o'clock or midday. Of course the betting was fast and furious on every game."

He was like a gambler intoxicated by his winnings at the gaming table, who bets again and again, thinking he is carried along on the wings of good fortune — by a good run of luck, as he used to say. Events often proved him right. Céline went from success to success, but he was a driven machine, and the human being in him was suppressed. René had forgotten his heart problems. He had forgotten the successes of the past. He was pushing and heaving to move mountains, and the mountains were become heavier and heavier, more and more immense.

The album *Dion chante Plamondon* (renamed *Des mots qui sonnent* in France) was enormously successful, and Luc Plamondon was looking forward to collaborating on Céline's next album. Goldman expressed the desire to be totally involved in this recording. That meant he wanted to work alone with Céline and use her full range. Once again, René shut the door on Plamondon. The machine wasn't about to stop. He no longer wanted just a major success, he wanted the best.

One of René's undoubted talents is his ability to pick people to work with who can bring about whatever it is he most ardently desires. He knew instinctively that Goldman was a songwriter and composer who could propel Céline to the pinnacle of French song. René now wanted reputation, quality, and great songs. Under Jean-Jacques Goldman's aegis Céline would record the best album of her career. *D'eux* would become nothing less than the most popular album in the history of French song.

It was asking a lot of the young bride, in 1994–1995, to dominate both the American and French markets at the same time. It was perhaps the greatest achievement of her career on the human level.

74

GOLDMAN

JEAN-JACQUES GOLDMAN WAS VERY little known in Quebec before
working with Céline Dion and writing the words and music for two
of her albums, *D'eux* and *S'il suffisait d'aimer*. It was he who took the
initiative and, through Sony, got in touch with René Angélil. Goldman
had been fascinated by Céline's voice ever since he had heard her sing
"D'amour et d'amitié." As a musician, he had noticed a special quality
in this voice, and it had remained in his mind ever since. He had followed the different stages of Céline's career, even reading the articles
and biographies written about her. So, aware of the importance place
René Angélil had in Céline Dion's life, he invited him to meet him in
Paris, the city of his birth.

René didn't know Goldman, and in his turn he read everything
he could find about this songwriter. The result was that each knew a
little about other, but it remained to be seen whether they could
work together and whether Céline would be able to communicate
with him.

At first glance Angélil and Goldman had almost nothing in common
apart from a shared admiration for Céline Dion. But that was enough.

The son of Jewish immigrants from Poland who had fled the
country to settle in France in the 1930s, Jean-Jacques Goldman was

born on October 19, 1951, in the nineteenth *arrondissement* of Paris. From his communist parents he inherited a taste for sharing, solidarity, and equality. He was an idealist, a leftist who avoided all formality, and who fled the bedlam of the city to take refuge in the country. He studied violin, guitar, and organ before joining a church choir in Montrouge. He graduated from high school in 1969, began to study business at the École des hautes études commerciales (EDHEC), but dropped out when he discovered Léo Ferré and the group Zoo — a revelation that led him to form his own group, Tai Phong. They soon had a first hit with "Sister Jane," followed by "Windows" in 1977, and "Last Flight" in 1980. His solo career took off after the group broke up in 1980. He wrote, composed, and sang "Il suffira d'un signe," "Comme toi," "Envole-moi," and "Je te donne" in the 1980s. Later he wrote for other French stars like Johnny Halliday, Patricia Kaas, and Marc Lavoine. And now along came Céline Dion.

Wearing a leather jacket, with his motorbike parked at the door, he met Céline and René in a Paris bistro. There would be many more meetings, and a close bond grew between Céline and Jean-Jacques Goldman.

He would write songs that appealed intimately to Céline. He is probably the songwriter and composer, and also the producer, who best grasped her possibilities and her true personality — and who also held her in the highest esteem.

Working under high pressure day after day in the studios in Céline's company, he continued to discover the Quebec singer's possibilities and her true nature.

"To start with, I tried to give Céline's voice a more modern sound," he recalls. "She sang like the traditional singers of the French-speaking world — Mireille Mathieu or Ginette Reno. Her vocal power needed to be controlled and nuanced, and she had to listen to herself, to let the singer in her come out. And it was even better than I ever imagined."

The *D'eux* album was launched on March 28, 1995. For the first time in her career this album left everyone unanimous about Céline Dion. Quite apart from the sales figures, which shattered all records, *D'eux* put the Quebec singer among the great stars of French song. The record-producing machine stopped when Céline put herself in Jean-Jacques Goldman's hands. Better than anyone else he allowed her to express herself as an artist. They later worked together on the album *S'il suffisait d'aimer* and became fast friends. When Céline feels the need to confide in someone she calls Jean-Jacques Goldman.

René recognized Goldman's excellent work and merit. He too agreed that this was Céline's best album.

75

CÉLINE AMONG RENÉ'S IDOLS

SONY FULLY INTENDED TO PROFIT from Céline's popularity, and brought pressure on her to record a fourth album in English. The sales of the preceding one, *The Colour of My Love*, which surpassed 15 million copies, increased René Angélil's pull with the Sony management. Now he was in a strong position and could impose his choice of artists and producers. He first thought of Phil Spector, a producer who had become famous in the 1960s when he revolutionized rock music.

Spector had contacted him after hearing Céline sing "River Deep, Mountain High" on David Letterman's *Late Show*. He claimed that Céline was having to make do with songs rejected by Whitney Houston and Mariah Carey, and that she had never had the backing of writers and producers capable of allowing her to give complete expression to her talent.

The famed producer had some fantastic ambitions for Céline. He wanted to use her to write a new page in history of music. Spector utterly despised the people at Sony, and most other record producers on the face of the earth. The creator of the famous "wall of sound' in the sixties, this eccentric individual came to be considered a genius when he crammed two drummers, a pianist, guitarists, a brass section, and vocal groups into his tiny New York studio. The Chiffons, the Ronettes, the Righteous Brothers, and Ike and Tina Turner came and went in his studio, trusting in the genius of this producer who at the time was not yet thirty years old. As the years passed and his successes accumulated, Spector developed an intolerable ego. Very few artists were prepared to work with him.

Spector had been in retirement since the early 1980s, and René had been warned of his idiosyncrasies. But he didn't want to miss the opportunity to work with one of the idols of his youth — for we mustn't forget that even the Baronets had been inspired by Spector's sound.

René's first disappointment came when Spector, unable to tolerate his presence while he worked with Céline, asked him to leave. Spector worked in a state of extreme tension, swearing at his musicians and making them re-do again and again any passage he didn't like, and time meant nothing to him. Céline and René couldn't afford such a luxury. Their time before the next video or stage performance was limited. When Spector started working on the fourth song, he kept them waiting in the studio for four or even six hours before coming to them. Céline and René didn't have that kind of time to spare.

The Phil Spector episode soon ended. Spector was frustrated, and threatened to put out a pirated record with the four songs Céline had recorded. René and Sony knew very well that legally he couldn't do this.

In the end, Céline recorded "River Deep, Mountain High" as a souvenir of her experience with Phil Spector. She would never see him or work with him again. René did a good job concealing his anger during this failed experiment, but it should be noted that he has never discussed this episode with the media, as if he wanted to forget even Phil Spector's name.

René maintained good relations with Disney while Céline recorded "Because You Loved Me," the theme song composed by Diane Warren for the film *Up Close and Personal*, which was being filmed before the launch of the album *Falling Into You*. The songs "All by Myself," "Falling Into You," "Seduces Me," "(You Make Me Feel Like) A Natural Woman," and "I Love You" were also on this album, which was eagerly awaited all over the world.

The launch took place on March 11, 1996. No less than 3 million copies of *Falling Into You* were snapped up in the next few weeks.

Diane Warren is considered the most prolific song-writer of today. She is able to write in such a variety of genres and styles that it is hard to believe all her songs are written by the same person.

She grew up in the San Fernando Valley, in California. As a teenager she loved listening to the radio and the Top 40 of the time. She liked her big sister's records, including Buddy Holly's, but was most attracted by performers who wrote their own songs, such as Carole King, Lieber and Stoller, and Burt Bacharach. So she began to compose herself.

In spite of her parents' mixed feelings about her choice of career, she persisted, and in 1983 got her first job as a staff writer with Jack White, Laura Branigan's producer. He asked her to come up with an English version of a French song. Twenty-four hours later Diane came back with "Solitaire," which quickly became Laura's first number one hit. Three years later she wrote "Rhythm of the Night" for DeBarge, which also spent some time at the top of the charts. To present, she has written more than eighty songs that have reached the Top 10.

Diane has written for legends such as Elton John, Tina Turner, Barbra Streisand, Aretha Franklin, Roberta Flack, and Roy Orbison. More recently she composed successes for 'N Sync, Gloria Estefan, Britney Spears, Christina Aguilera, Reba McEntire, Whitney Houston, Enrique Iglesias, Aerosmith, Ricky Martin, Faith Hill, LeAnn Rimes, and Céline Dion!

The song "If You Asked Me" was recorded by Céline, but also by Patti Labelle, the rhythm and blues diva. Her song "Don't Turn Around" was recorded by eight different artists! "I Don't Wanna Miss a Thing," performed by

Aerosmith for the film *Armageddon,* was nominated for an Oscar. Diane's songs have been featured in more than sixty films. She had a major international success with "Can't Fight the Moonlight," sung by LeAnn Rimes in the film *Coyote Ugly.* Warren is able to write songs almost to order. She is not intimidated by anything, whether a ballad, a rock hymn, or an up-tempo song. As of this writing, her songs have been nominated for three Golden Globes, five Oscars, and eight Grammies.

Having had such fabulous financial success, she supports numerous charities. She is a Buddy for Life at AIDS Project Los Angeles and an honorary member of PETA. Diane founded the David S. Warren Weekly Entertainment Series in her father's honour. She also takes an interest in a scheme to distribute musical material to more than a thousand schools throughout the U.S.

Diane has been named ASCAP's Songwriter of the Year on six occasions, and *Billboard*'s Songwriter of the Year four times. Realsongs, her publishing company, is one of the top five in the industry and is the most successful company managed by a woman in the music industry. Warren now has a star on the Hollywood Walk of Fame.

JEAN BEAULNE

76

ON THE SUMMIT

RENÉ ANGÉLIL SUDDENLY BEGAN TO have qualms. Like Céline, he was overcome with a terrible vertigo. Having predicted for years that his protégée would soon achieve glory, he suddenly saw all his wildest dreams come true one after another, in a rush. He no longer had to market Céline Dion, for the whole universe confirmed that people had already bought her. René likes numbers, and suddenly the numbers were becoming astonishing.

In July 1996, at the opening ceremony for the Atlanta Olympics, Céline sang "The Power of the Dream," composed by David Foster, a performance watched by 1.5 billion television viewers. The sales of *Falling Into You* were climbing steeply, and Sony took the opportunity to renew its contract with the man who managed the world's most popular singer. The amount agreed to has been estimated at $100 million U.S. René no longer had any need to plan promotions. He was already planning a two-year tour all over the world, and speculation was rampant among American journalists about the earnings on such a venture. Some spoke of receipts of $1 billion for the tour. In less than a year sales of *Falling Into You* surpassed 20 million and Céline had joined the very select club of performers who had sold over 50 million albums during their career. She was only twenty-eight years old, and had been discovered by the entire world.

This success, which should have had him jumping with joy, caused René some distress. Of course the Dion-Angélil couple was often carried away by euphoria, and tears flowed copiously after some triumphant performances — but what a burden to carry! Can anyone possibly imagine what it means to have everything to lose and nothing to gain? Already a hundred or so international distinctions and 50 million records sold in the world! There is so little room at the top in show business in this world, and it's such a vulnerable position. All you can do is protect, safeguard, and maintain your position.

René knew the history of the entertainment world. He knew everyone experiences a decline after reaching the summit: Frank Sinatra, Elvis Presley, the Beatles ... so many of them had fallen. So his attitude changed radically in 1996. Now Céline Dion's manager went on the defensive. He had nothing, or very little, more to prove, but he suddenly felt afraid of losing — a fear that would increase with the years. A worrier by temperament, he had to live with the burden of knowing all his dreams had come true. But René and Céline forgot all this in the heat of the action. The tour, beginning in Australia in March 1996, would bring them to all the major cities in the world. Now the sky was the limit.

77

OF LOVE AND BIOGRAPHIES

RENÉ FELT THAT CÉLINE HAD found her niche: love — love in all its power, but wrapped in romanticism and abandonment, a love that brought dreams and kept the fairy tale alive. Of course Sony supported this approach, for love is a money-maker everywhere in the world. Céline was inspiring the dreams of lovers — and of bankers — all the over world. By the end of 1996 she was one of the ten richest women in show business. Of course she shared her fortune with René, who was thinking of investing in a new chain of Italian restaurants. He already owned a golf club, had been associated with the Nickels restaurant chain, and was still trying to break the bank at the casino. It was in the Caesar's Palace casino that he felt most comfortable. Strangely, he didn't invest as much as he might have done in the commercial world. People consider him a businessman, though his career is much more like an artist's — an artist who was encouraging Céline Dion to speak of love in early 1997, when she was beginning to record the album *Let's Talk About Love*.

It was René who had the idea of pairing the singer with a number of artists of his own generation in making this recording. And so it was that Barbra Streisand, Carole King, the Bee Gees, and even the greatest tenor of his age, Luciano Pavarotti, agreed to sing duets with the most popular singer of the moment.

Throughout this period René Angélil had to cope with a new phenomenon: the incursions of authors into Céline's and his private lives. Now that the singer had reached the pinnacle of her art it was only to be expected that her life and career would become the subject of biographies, authorized or not. Such is the lot in this world of every celebrity who fascinates and intrigues people all over the world. Strangely, Céline had escaped the attention of biographers until now. Only one book had been written about her, in 1983, when Marc Chatel's *La Naissance d'une étoile* was published by Quebecor. Since then René Angélil hadn't authorized any further biographies.

"Céline is still too young for a biography. Later on, we'll see," he said. In 1997 no less than six writers from France, Italy, Canada, and the United States announced they would publish a biography of Céline Dion within the year.

First Ian Halperin, an English-speaking journalist, castigated the couple in his *Céline Dion, Behind the Fairy Tale* (published only in English), as if he had some kind of a score to settle with Céline and René.

Françoise Dolbecq, a French journalist who wrote for the magazine *Elle*, wrote a biography that appeared in France and Quebec.

Barry Grills, who had already written biographies of Anne Murray and Alanis Morissette, did it again with *Falling Into You: The Story of Céline Dion.*

Francesco Fabiano and Claudia Rossi published a collection of texts collected from all over the world and translated into Italian in a biography entitled *Céline Dion, tutti i testi con traduzione a fronte.*

Georges-Hébert Germain wrote the only authorized biography, called simply *Céline.*

Finally, there was an unauthorized biography by Jean Beaunoyer, co-author of this book, called *Céline Dion, une femme au destin exceptionnel,* published by Québec-Amérique in November 1997.

Even before these books came out, Céline, with René at her side, declared in a press conference that "writing a biography without having met the person the book is about is plain stupid!" And René agreed, of course. But, given the examples of Elvis Presley or the members of the Beatles, each able to point to more than twenty-five unauthorized biographies, it should have come as no surprise to

René and Céline that people wanted to write about them now that they were famous.

Before these books appeared in bookstores, newspapers very discreetly mentioned the non-publication of a biography of Céline Dion written by Nathalie Jean. This young journalist and writer, aged twenty-five, had already published *La Vraie Histoire d'Émilie Bordeleau* before launching out on her volume about Céline Dion. René Angélil decided this biography wasn't "in accord with Céline's image" and, to prevent the book from being published, paid the derisory sum of ten thousand dollars to this young woman, who had devoted a year, in good faith and with respect, to writing a biography of the singer. There was nothing in the book attacking either Céline's or René's reputation — quite the opposite, in fact, for it was an admiring biography that related Céline's success. This fragile, vulnerable young woman finally accepted Angélil's cheque, to which was added the sum of seven thousand dollars, paid by the publisher Libre Expression. Intimidated by Céline's manager and discouraged by the publisher, who told her there would be little demand for her book, Nathalie Jean gave in, but would come to regret her decision. She would later learn that a French publisher had already made an offer for her book and that in Quebec the anticipated sales were much better than she had been led to believe. She told her story to the French magazine *Voici* a short time after agreeing to the settlement. What is more, she was pregnant with twins at the time, and the traumatic experience she went through almost caused her to lose her babies.

It was Nathalie Jean's story that motivated me to write this unauthorized biography of Céline Dion for the publishing house Québec-Amérique.

The editor-in-chief of this publisher, Jacques Fortin, had seen Nathalie Jean in his office and she had asked him for advice. That was how I was able to obtain all the information about this matter and make contact with the young woman, whom I thought was subject to deep depressions.

So, equipped with all this information, I set out to write Céline Dion's biography. I was taking over from Nathalie Jean. Of course she hadn't written her book in the hope of winning a major literary prize, as she was quite ready to admit. But she was the first to have the idea of writing a biography of Céline Dion at the pinnacle of her career, and what is more, she had a perfect right to do so.

Not only was that right taken from her in return for very little money, but the agreement prepared by René Angélil stipulated that she could not write anything else about Céline until the year 2000. It was in the name of freedom of expression that I undertook to write Céline Dion's biography, and there was no question — absolutely none — of it being an authorized one! In Quebec, however, no one, as far as I knew, had until then written an entertainer's biography without his or her collaboration. In the mind of the general public, unauthorized biographies had a bad reputation. They were seen as aiming to shock and satisfy an appetite for sensational revelations and lacking in credibility. I had to change all that and undertake a serious work based on authentic documents, the accounts of known witnesses, and historical research. Furthermore, I asked for, and obtained, a team of researchers to assist me, taking my cue from the approach used in television.

I began work in state of feverish enthusiasm. I had carte blanche and an almost unlimited budget to work with, and the undertaking began to look like a military operation. It was strategically important that at all costs no one should become aware of the existence of this biography. All my communications with the publisher were carried on using a code name so that no one could be aware of the project, not even inside the publisher, apart from a few authorized individuals.

Researchers also had to be found, and were recruited from among young or former journalists, preferably unemployed. I had also requested the participation of a lawyer.

Not neglecting a single detail, we required each applicant for the position of researcher to sign an undertaking of confidentiality before would we reveal the exact nature of their work to them. No names were to be mentioned on any document.

We had a lot of very well qualified applicants — indeed overqualified in some cases. It promised to be an exciting venture. But very soon we changed our tune. To my great surprise, most of the candidates withdrew when they learned what the book's subject was to be. They feared René Angélil. They feared reprisals. They were afraid to be associated with such a risky, unauthorized undertaking.

Some accepted, but then very quickly backed out. In the end there remained only a young lawyer who had given up practising law and a young student whose mission it was to observe the Dion family. The operation was a dangerous one, because we were prepared to go where our research took us and tell the truth about the Dion-Angélil clan, whatever the consequences might be. At the time rumours were circulating about Céline and René's secret life. Apart from their public statements, promotions, and a few rare in-depth interviews, very little was known about the couple's real story.

We searched through all the publications, met dozens of people, and checked out even the most far-fetched rumours. From the outset it wasn't a matter of dragging up scandal, but of relating the true story of the Dion-Angélil couple and establishing the facts, while avoiding the seductions and manipulations of Céline's entourage.

How many discussions were held with the little team of researchers and the management of the publishing house! We remade the world, and René and Céline's, over many evenings. Gradually we developed an attachment to these people, after tracking them for so long. None of the rumours had any foundation. Céline seemed to me, despite all the fame surrounding her, someone who had absolutely no skeletons in her closet. No, she didn't take drugs, nor did she have any kind of perversion. Her life was respectable and stainless, without any inconsistencies, like an Olympic athlete's. It is impossible to appear on stage for nearly twenty years and live in a constant state of jet lag without being in total, healthy command of your resources. She had fallen in love with a man older than herself. She devoted her life and her career to him. Did he deserve all this? That was the real question.

In the course of our research, I became fascinated by two men. The first was Adhémar, Céline's father, who had always avoided the media, the extravagance, the travel, and anything a bit too glamorous. He was an upright, direct, straightforward human being, like Céline. René, quite the opposite of Céline and Adhémar, is someone full of contradictions, difficult to pin down, calculating, and strange, but emotional, fascinating, and puzzling, with a history behind him — quite a history, one people do their best to tell, but one that isn't simple.

As you trace the course of his existence, you find he has left very few tracks behind, often leaving a cloud of mystery instead. Céline's story is to some extent, even to a great extent, his, too. To begin with, he isn't particularly likeable, and I don't think he particularly wants to be. I undertook my research with the trauma he had caused Nathalie Jean at the back of my mind and, quite frankly, I imagined the worst. Was he a tyrant, a dangerous manipulator, a real godfather who caused everyone around him to shake in their boots? At the time some actions of his — the lawsuits, the disputes he seemed to enjoy — gave the impression he was someone who would stop at nothing to achieve his goals.

An atmosphere of paranoia developed in the publisher's office as our work was carried on in the utmost secrecy. We had to prevent the Angélil clan from hearing of the existence of this unauthorized biography just when he himself was planning to publish an official biography expected to beat every sales record in Quebec. The engine was already turning over. We had to avoid any misstatement that might be considered defamatory, and any unfounded or unproved statement. Three lawyers constantly read over what was written so that nothing could slip by. The worst disaster would have been a court injunction preventing or delaying the book's publication, so we had to proceed with the utmost caution.

One of the researchers took his zeal as far as seducing a young person from the Dion-Angélil clan in order to obtain information. I had the impression I was living in a bad spy novel. Actually, it was more like an absurd comedy that didn't produce any great results. The researcher quickly disappeared from the scene, no doubt leaving a bit of a broken heart behind.

To get close to Céline's world I spent about ten days living in Charlemagne, eating poutine, hamburgers with onion rings, and cheese curds — all so I could get close to Céline's childhood world. Believe it or not, I enjoyed the experience and wrote my best pages in the peaceful atmosphere of the small village. We had to work quickly, for the competition was already announcing an upcoming book launch. The young lawyer literally lived in the courthouse, collecting as many documents as possible: marriages, divorces, bankruptcies, and lawsuits, the whole shebang — a colossal task, always carried out anonymously.

For my part, I didn't breathe a word about the project to my newspaper colleagues at *La Presse* and focused all my attention on the theatre, thus avoiding any contact with Céline and René's circle. My publisher's strategy was to take people by surprise. And so, on Monday, November 10, 1997, the press was invited to the launch of an unauthorized biography of Céline Dion, scheduled to take place at eleven o'clock that morning. Sick with nerves before going to the press conference, I mislaid the brief speech I'd prepared for the occasion. To my great surprise all the media were there, and in the end, before a battery of cameras, I improvised a little disquisition that came straight from the heart. A friend had said to me that morning: "Don't think about it, just let it come out." And that's what I did.

I learned that René read my book in Los Angeles, the day after it appeared. He didn't react much, saying just that I was a nobody, a "poor guy," even though I worked for a major Montreal newspaper. I thought to myself with a little smile that a father paying to put his three daughters through university is a poor guy indeed! Subsequently I've often been asked if René Angélil carried out any reprisals, made any threats, or pressured me in any way. Absolutely not: he's much too decent a person to do anything like that. I had got to know him through my research, so it came as no surprise to me. He's someone who has a sense of values, and was able to recognize that the biography was respectful, and neither untruthful nor defamatory. Céline emerged from it with increased stature, given that the book was written by an independent person in no way connected with his organization. René was shown respect in it, too, even if as a journalist I felt uneasy at the control he continued to exert over the media. Actually, in a press conference, more than anything else I blamed journalists for failing to do their job. When Céline called us (i.e. myself and others) "plain stupid" for writing her biography without consulting her, no one questioned what she said. I was never given any right of reply — a basic principle in our profession.

During the promotional tour that always follows the publication of a book, the researchers from a TV program called *J.E.* invited me to relate to the cameras how I had gone about writing this unauthorized biography. I agreed, not knowing that Georges-Hébert Germain, the author of Céline's official biography, which had came out a few days after mine, would also be a guest on the show. We had both fallen into a trap! It was very much to our respective editors' advantage to stir up a war between us, and people were expecting a real cockfight between the two authors, on live television. It was also in the interest of the program's producers to put on a good show for their audience. The publishers and producers were certainly disappointed when they saw that neither Germain nor I had fallen into the trap. We were basically two journalists who had already worked for the same newspaper, who respected one another, and who had no desire to be manipulated by book merchants. That day the "battle of the Célines" was launched, with piles of Georges-Hébert's books to one side and mine to the other. It was the authorized biography vs. the unauthorized one! People in the street were interviewed on TV and asked which biography they'd pick. The reply was often that they'd probably end up buying both. And that was exactly the right thing to do.

Georges-Hébert and I agreed not to read one another's books. According to our readers, on the other hand, we had two different approaches, two different styles, and our biographies complemented one another. Georges-Hébert is a charming individual who doesn't seek confrontation. He is also a talented writer, the author of many successful biographies, who has related the life stories of hockey player Guy Lafleur, Christopher Columbus, Monica la Mitraille, and, of course, Céline Dion, several times.

Strangely, during this "battle of the Célines," which also involved other biographies, it was Georges-Hébert who received the most criticism, even though he was the author of the official biography. People accused him of working under the direction and supervision of René Angélil, and above all of being the partner of Céline's publicity agent, Francine Chaloult. Georges-Hébert has always defended himself, saying he had been able to write about his thoughts and experiences while spending time in Céline's company, and that René had allowed him a completely free hand.

When some time had passed I finally did read his book and it inspired me to write this biography of René. I think Georges-Hébert is telling the truth, and that René didn't need to intervene, since Georges-Hébert censured himself to avoid hurting the people in Céline's entourage he loves. He has never claimed to have distanced himself from the Dion-Angélil clan in order to write a critical book.

But that was what I had set out to do — not to defame or to settle accounts, but to write a critical work, put together with detachment. And, God knows, detachment is inevitable when all doors are closed to you and you have no access to the couple. I have often envied Georges-Hébert the close contacts he had for a whole year with Céline, René the story-teller, and their entourage before writing his first book about the rise of the greatest Quebec singer we have ever had.

Considering the limited access I had to my subject, I've often felt flattered that my biography was compared to his, and very thrilled when *Time* magazine rated my biography the best published up to that point. It was a satisfying victory of David over Goliath.

By Goliath, I mean of course the machine René put into action to ensure a wide distribution of the book, in collaboration and association with a daily newspaper, *Le Journal de Montréal*, and with a spectacular publicity campaign.

But in controlling the book's publication and marketing René was taking on a market he wasn't familiar with. Very quickly he found out that the world of publishing is different from the recording and entertainment world. It's a strange world, dominated by intellectuals and businessmen who try to get along together, though their interests are often opposed. It is a more complex world than René imagined, with its whims, contracts, and authors' rights, all differing from one country to another. René admitted publicly that publishing wasn't his field, and so he entrusted to French publisher Robert Laffont the publication of another book by Georges-Hébert Germain called *Céline Dion, ma vie, mon rêve*, which was very successful in France.

78

TITANIC

I N 1997 CÉLINE CARRIED OFF two Grammy awards — this time no
great surprise — one for Pop Album of the Year, and the other of
course for Album of the Year, for *Falling Into You*. It was at this time
René realized one of his great dreams by becoming the owner of the Le
Mirage golf club.

René Angélil is someone who negotiates incessantly with Lady
Luck. He has the reflexes of a seasoned gambler, of course. He assembled major stars around Céline to record *Let's Talk About Love*. The
album showed every sign of being highly acclaimed, and the newspapers were already talking about the friendship, and even bond,
between Céline and Barbra Streisand. Other articles spoke of the
recording sessions with the Bee Gees, a group that had already had its
best hits but was still a legend of pop music. There was also mention
of the great master of classical singing, Luciano Pavarotti, who sang
along with Céline. All the required elements seemed to be in place to
record a memorable album.

Yet the story of one song was to leave its mark on this record — a
simple song that Céline was to sing on her own. And this is where we
can see the importance of the luck factor in René Angélil's life. It was
obviously Céline Dion who contributed the talent and emotion

required to sing what would become a classic of American song, "My Heart Will Go On."

But it was thanks to René's luck that it happened. The story dates back to 1991, when Céline was to sing the theme song for the Steven Spielberg movie *Fievel Goes West*. James Horner, who had written the song, strongly suggested to Spielberg that Céline Dion should sing it. Spielberg had preferred Linda Ronstadt. The Quebec singer had then fallen back on the main song of the film *Beauty and the Beast*, and, in an irony of fate, she won an Oscar for it.

It was this Oscar that had opened the door to America for her — an incredible stroke of luck. *Beauty and the Beast* became a hit, as did its theme song, while Spielberg's film was a failure. But surely no one could hope for such a stroke of luck to happen a second time. Yet happen it did.

The same James Horner who had suggested Céline's name to Spielberg now came on the scene again, this time suggesting a song he had composed for director James Cameron, who was making *Titanic*. Cameron told him he wouldn't include a pop song in his movie.

But Horner didn't give up, going to Las Vegas to meet Céline and René and letting them hear "My Heart Will Go On." Both were impressed by the intensity and emotion conveyed by Horner's song. He openly admitted to René that the director Cameron was against his idea.

René thought Cameron would never change his mind, unless … Céline recorded the song and submitted the final product to him. He decided to cover the costs of the recording, which was done in New York, and to support Horner's efforts. So René would produce a demo, something that quite bowled Horner over, for he hadn't expected anything of the sort —that a star like Céline would agree to make a demo.

"Marlon Brando auditioned for the part in *The Godfather*," René Angélil replied.

At the recording session, Céline, contrary to her custom, swallowed two cups of coffee. She was tense and feverish, and sang Horner's song with her heart and soul and a bundle of nerves. Only one take was needed.

A month later James Cameron heard "My Heart Will Go On" for the first time and completely fell for Céline. He agreed to use the song in his movie.

But it still wasn't in the bag. Success was far from assured, for Cameron was flagging under the burden of filming *Titanic*. It was the most expensive film in the history of cinema, and its launch had already been delayed by six months. Journalists joked about a movie fated to sink — like the *Titanic* itself. The vibes were negative, and the worst seemed imminent. René and Céline had seen the rushes and wept like babies. They at least believed in Cameron's enormous undertaking.

René had pushed his luck yet again. It wasn't a pure, easy stroke of luck, one that happened by magic. It came from having faith in spite of everybody, when the film had been practically damned by the press.

The end of the story is well known. *Titanic* became a historic box-office success, winning the Oscar for Best Film of the Year, and Céline won an Oscar, by herself this time, for "My Heart Will Go On." Composer James Horner was rewarded for his persistence by earning almost $20 million in rights to the song in the first year after it came out. "My Heart Will Go On" set an audience record in the U.S., with more than 500 million hearing the song on the radio.

79

ALICE SARA PASSES AWAY

R ENÉ ANGÉLIL LOST HIS BEST friend on May 25, 1997. His mother, Alice Angélil, née Sara, passed away in the Montreal Heart Institute at the age of eighty-two. This good-humoured, lively, intelligent woman was the beacon of the Angélil family. It was she who established a line of communication between René and his father, who were rarely on the same wavelength. It was she who ran the household and who watched over her two sons like a mother hen. She particularly kept an eye on René, the elder of the two, who wasn't very serious and was often irresponsible in his youth. She spoiled him, even with the limited financial means available to her. On several occasions she paid René's gambling debts at a time when he was scraping the bottom. She lectured him, of course, but this generous, optimistic woman always supported him. A seamstress who worked from home, like Céline Dion's mother, Alice Sara always understood and accepted René's career, even if she had hoped for a while he would follow in his brother André's footsteps and go into business.

Alice was René's confidante, and she spent three weeks at his side in Los Angeles when he had his serious heart attack in 1992. René was afraid he would never recover from it and wanted to have his mother at his bedside.

The youngest of a family of four children, Alice Sara, born on May 4, 1915, was called by her pet name, Tété, meaning "grandmother" in Arabic. Céline and the Sara and Angélil families were around René at his mother's funeral service, which took place in Saint-Sauveur church a few days after her death. Concealing his grief behind dark glasses, Alice Sara's grown-up son said goodbye to the real woman of his life on that spring day. Jean Beaulne remembers:

> Mme Angélil watched over René like a mother hen all her life. She paid much more attention to him than to his brother, André, who was much more sensible and better behaved. André and René shared a bedroom as children. André was a retiring, unassuming guy who now owns a video club in Laval.
>
> Mme Angélil was gifted with great intelligence, and there was no doubt about her support for the Baronets. She always had an encouraging word for each of us, understood the challenge we wanted to meet, accepted our lack of experience and respected our enthusiasm and energy. She never allowed any of her concerns about René's future to show. She was a woman for whom I had great admiration, and of whom I still have a positive memory today — the memory of a courageous human being, whose greatest reward, after so many years of worry, was to see René succeed. Fortunately she lived long enough to enjoy the success of someone she had helped create, in her own way.

80

1998: HOW TO PARTY

IN 1998 PEOPLE WERE BECOMING accustomed to Céline Dion's success, as trophies and honours literally rained down on her. After the Academy Awards, which crowned *Titanic* with eleven awards, including one to Céline for her performance of "My Heart Will Go On," René had no intention of being outdone. He wanted to take advantage of Céline's birthday — she would turn thirty on March 30, a lucky year, it seems — to create a sensation with a spectacular present. Céline's companion loved to create a sensation on her birthdays, and this time he outdid himself.

In total secrecy he hatched a plan involving the purchase of the famous *Titanic* necklace, the Blue Diamond, two days before it was due to be auctioned. He had retained the services of an anonymous buyer, who acquired the precious stone for $2.2 million — an amount that was far from ruining René. *Forbes* magazine estimated Céline's fortune in 1997 at $200 million, and her annual income at $85 million. Imagine what it would amount to today!

"It's a marvel, a work of art, it reminds you of Versailles," exclaimed Céline on opening her best birthday present ever.

Céline recorded the album *S'il suffisait d'aimer* during that year, and, once again, the critics were full of praise for Goldman and Céline. While Céline was being feted all over the world, Quebec was celebrating her success. The governments of Quebec and Canada both wanted to be part of the festivities, and, within an interval of less than twenty-four hours, decided to award Céline the Order of Quebec and the Order of Canada. Not wishing to provoke a political incident, the Quebec singer accepted the honours with as much pleasure in Quebec City as in Ottawa. After the episode in Seville she never again wanted to get involved in political debate. And we hardly need say that René was on his guard and certainly wouldn't have allowed Céline to be trapped by journalists' questions.

"This is a free country," Céline declared in the presence of the premier of Quebec, who had presented her with the decoration, "and today's occasion has nothing to do with politics. If I'm being granted this honour, it is by the people, and whether it is through the government of Quebec, Canada, or France it makes no difference."

Céline had learned her lesson well — from René Angélil.

At the end of the summer Céline Dion started on the most important tour of her career — the ultimate tour, which would take her into the year 2000. For the purpose of this tour, equalling anything the Rolling Stones, U2, or Pink Floyd had undertaken, Céline would have a Gulfstream jet available, hired by René. This machine was to transport the 105 members of her team, along with Céline herself. The tour began with a sold-out house in Boston, and would continue through fourteen countries in the Americas, Europe, Asia, and Australia.

Numerous articles recounting the Dion-Angélil couple's fairy tale appeared in newspapers and magazines, invariably accompanied by photos of the dream houses owned by Céline and René — one in Jupiter, Florida, valued at $30 million, and another near Montreal, on Île Gagnon, valued at $15 million. One unfortunate cost of their celebrity was that a helicopter company took advantage of their presence to lay on sight-seeing flights, so that from morning to night the clatter of rotor blades resounded over their home, which, as one can easily imagine, was extremely disagreeable.

Dream images: a life that seemed woven from gold and silver, with love thrown in, and the children Céline hoped for. At the age of thirty, Céline Dion had reached the pinnacle. At the age of fifty-seven, early in 1999, René Angélil had also reached the top of his craft and knew the world of show business well enough to evaluate the risks of so much success — as if it all had suddenly come to seem just too good, too perfect.

THEY'RE OVERDOING IT,
BUT WHO CAN BLAME THEM?

When René first took over Céline's career he had high ambitions for his protégée, without being really convinced she would turn into a superstar. But as he got to know the young girl better he realized that this young singer had what it takes to be an international star. The first step in his strategy was to make her a star in Quebec — an obvious choice!

But events moved so fast that they allowed René to plan out an international career for her. Of course there were disappointments along the way, but these setbacks became assets for Céline's career. When they were turned down for the theme song for a Steven Spielberg movie because of a disagreement between two record companies, Disney came along almost right away to offer the theme song for *Beauty and the Beast*.

Céline's extraordinary performance next brought her another prestigious contract, this time for the song "Because You Loved Me" in the movie *Up Close and Personal*. Further recognition followed when she was chosen to appear at the Olympic Games in Atlanta, a performance watched by 1.5 billion television viewers. And then there was "My Heart Will Go On," the theme song for *Titanic*. Who could have thought this film would become the biggest production in the history of cinema, setting all-time sales records with a budget of $200 million? So it was this song and the prior events that allowed Céline to rise to the rank of a superstar. The song set a world record for the largest radio audience, having been heard by 105,577,700 listeners during the week of January 27. The previous record had been held by Donna Lewis, for "I Love You Always Forever," with 101 million listeners in May 1996. Two weeks later "My Heart Will Go On" broke its own record with 117 million listeners, becoming known all over the world and bringing her contract offers from all parts of the planet.

But there's always the other side of the coin, and life as a superstar isn't always a bed of roses. Prisoners of the system, René and Céline can never, day or night, escape the attentions of the paparazzi, intrusions by the media, the company of bodyguards and the risk of blackmail, extortion, kidnapping, etc. Let us recall that Elvis Presley performed wearing a bullet-proof vest because some lunatic accused him of seducing his wife. That evening there were several hundred police in the auditorium, for he had been warned he'd be killed during the show. A performer's life isn't easy!

JEAN BEAULNE

81

CANCER

WHILE ACCOMPANYING CÉLINE DION TO Dallas as part of her world tour, René was discovered to have a worrisome lump on his neck. Céline was giving him a gentle massage and noticed the abnormal swelling. The next day he went to a Dallas hospital, where Dr. Robert Teckler diagnosed a cancer of the throat: a carcinoma with metastatic squamous cells on the right side of his neck. René had fainted on an escalator in a golf club in the U.S. — already a sign of great fatigue. This time, however, he couldn't ignore or conceal his condition. It came as a great shock for everyone around him. Some journalists predicted the worst, and people were already speculating about Céline's future. What would become of her without René, the hand guiding her career? As was usual for him, he provided very little information about his state of health or his real intentions.

So, in the utmost secrecy, he began a series of thirty-seven radiotherapy and chemotherapy treatments. The media announced the news but were unable to obtain further details about the exact nature of his illness. It was known to be a form of throat cancer, and the names of the doctors treating him were sometimes cited, but it was impossible to communicate with any of them. Céline cancelled several performances scheduled to take place in Europe and America. It was a desperate woman who went to her residence in Jupiter, Florida, to look after her husband.

"René has decided to fight, for my sake and his family's," announced Céline.

"René was physically very strong," explains Jean Beaulne. "Often I saw him stay up all night, play a round of golf the next morning, and eat anything at all at irregular hours. No one else could have stood it. His physical stamina and immune system are extraordinary, but the time comes when any mechanism, however tough, can't take it any more. Bad eating and stress poison an organism if it never takes time out to recharge its batteries. That's when cancer can so easily develop."

The media were full of René's struggle for survival. A wave of affection and sympathy washed over René Angélil and Céline Dion. She cancelled a number of shows in the summer of 1999, but couldn't allow herself to give up what would probably be the most impressive performance of her career. René had to stay in Florida to continue his treatment, but he persuaded Céline to go to the Stade de France. Fate can be capricious, and sometimes cruel. René, who had attended almost all Céline's shows, missed the most important of all — a show that set a new attendance record, for she became the first artist to fill the Stade de France, with its capacity of ninety thousand. The idol of the French, Johnny Halliday, and the Rolling Stones had performed there for a single evening.

To communicate from Jupiter with Céline during the show, René asked for a miniature earphone to be fitted in the singer's ear. This even allowed them to talk between songs.

An important event took place during that final year of the millennium: Sony announced that Céline Dion had sold 100 million albums, putting her among the greats of contemporary music. The company organized a party to mark the event.

After that achievement and the greatest show of Céline Dion's career, René, confined to his room for some time, was questioning himself. He was still fighting the vicious illness that had attacked him and was going through a difficult time. There was no end to the treatments in sight, and the road to remission was a long one. He was thinking of the future, his family, and the child he would possibly never be able to have with Céline. He knew only too well that chemotherapy can affect a man's fertility.

It was only months later, in November 1999, that people found out that René had had some of his sperm frozen in March, after learning he had cancer. It was on Larry King's show on CNN that Céline announced the news to the entire world, pointing out that having some sperm frozen isn't such bad idea, for chemotherapy and radiotherapy can kill not only bad things but good ones, too. Confiding especially in Larry King, Céline announced in the same breath that she would renew her marriage vows with her husband at five o'clock on the evening of January 5, 2000, at Caesar's Palace in Las Vegas. She added that 238 members of her family would be invited to Nevada to celebrate this special event, which coincided with the fifth anniversary of their marriage. It was obvious that Céline was particularly overwrought at that moment, as if she wanted to move mountains, to believe that everything was possible, and that René would win through.

82

RENÉ UNBURDENS HIMSELF

AT THE END OF 1999, René consented to open up in a way he had never done before, before the cameras of Radio Canada, on the program *Le Point*. The host, Stéphane Bureau, went to interview René Angélil at his Jupiter, Florida, residence, hoping to discover what kind of person he really was, and René didn't resist. It was a warm and at times even moving interview.

At the end of the millennium, coinciding with Céline's temporary break from performing, René made some strange revelations:

> I know it all has to come to an end some day. Someone else will come along, and Céline's popularity will decline, it's only normal, but I'm not afraid. …
>
> I'm not looking past 2000. Céline is taking a break from the stage, and I don't know how long it will last. It might be for five years or ten. Maybe she'll act in a movie, two years from now. I've no plans for after 2000. I miss my family, my children, and my friends. When show business gives up on you, all you have left is your family. The life we're

living is an artificial one. We've often said we were going to stop. This time it's for real. We have to stop.

And, in conclusion: "There's a price to be paid for reaching the top. Absolutely."

It was a tired, frail man who was speaking, and he ended the interview with a sob in his voice. René weeps very easily — out of joy, sorrow, or fatigue.

Did he shed so many tears back in the Baronets days? "No! Absolutely not," answers Jean Beaulne.

> He lives under constant pressure. As it's put so well by the words of a song Luc Plamondon wrote for the rock opera *Starmania*, his business sense has destroyed his sense of humour. When you live as intensely as he does, the mind works at full stretch, so that your ability to laugh is replaced by perpetual anxiety. It's difficult to imagine what he has to put up with. In addition to overseeing the entire organization of Céline's career, he has to make the right decisions, please a lot of people, and never panic when other people lose their cool. A manager's responsibility is overwhelming, and sometimes René has to let off steam.

In addition, René was a sick man, handicapped by numerous cardiac problems and suffering from cancer. Strangely, he tried to make people forget his state of health. He mentioned it very rarely, as if afraid people would pity him or stress his aging too much, or that it might harm Céline's image, and their image as a couple.

Céline remarked, around the same time: "We work so hard that we've neglected ourselves, René and I. I know him as a producer and manager, but I don't know him as a person, because we haven't had the time. And I want to know him, because he won't always be there. I miss him."

Not only did René Angélil control the world of information, particularly in Quebec, he also extended this practice to the arts of the stage and recording. An unparalleled manufacturer of images, a fascinating storyteller, an artist at marketing, and a creator of events with a strong promotional content, René Angélil has always been able to outwit the real sources of information. With time he succeeded in outmanoeuvring and even silencing ones that weren't led up the garden path.

Charming some and threatening others, Angélil exercised this control all through his career without too many obstacles being put in his way in the journalistic sphere. Far from relaxing this control, he even tightened it as the years went by, particularly following the repeated successes of his protégée, Céline Dion. Some people would say he was a master at his job. Others might well feel uneasy about certain journalistic practices in Quebec.

If we restrict ourselves to isolated cases, René Angélil's conduct, however questionable, seems not to have had any really significant consequences. It is the cumulative effect of the manager's actions on the media that becomes a problem and allows us to assess the true stature of René Angélil's personality.

He was able to outwit the press very skilfully in 1966 when, on December 11, he married Denyse Duquette in total secrecy. Yet he was a member of the Baronets, who were at the peak of their popularity at the time. To avoid the news leaking out he carefully avoided informing the two other members of the group about his marriage celebrations. Some time later, Jean Beaulne also tied the knot, and it made the front page of the newspaper *Échos-Vedettes*.

In 1974, when he launched out on a career as an artists' manager, René Angélil thought up what would turn out to be one of his best publicity coups when he told journalists that René Simard, the Quebec Joselito, was selling more records in Quebec than the Beatles and Elvis Presley together. Even the *Wall Street Journal* in New York took the bait and gave it prominence. It wasn't entirely false, since Simard had indeed sold thousands of recordings in a few weeks. But actually, overall, the young singer was not at all in the same league as the two giants of rock music.

After he claimed to have discovered Céline Dion he totally obliterated the presence, name, and even shadow of Paul Lévesque, Céline's first manager. His name is mentioned nowhere in the first biography written about the singer (*La Naissance d'une étoile*, published by Quebecor in 1983), in newspaper articles, or in radio and television interviews. Yet Lévesque and Angélil fought over Céline's contract for five years, even taking it to court. All's fair in love and war, they say, but did anyone dare to investigate what was going on? Did anyone dare to print it? And how can we explain this silence?

Later, the fairy tale began to take shape. Angélil let people think that he had mortgaged his house to launch the young Céline's international career. But the official documents and various other pieces of evidence confirm that René Angélil was insolvent at the time, and that his house was already heavily mortgaged. Nevertheless, the press has perpetuated the legend. For several years, Céline and René were obviously a couple in love — a fact that didn't escape a fair number of journalists covering the entertainment field. Even though Céline was an adult, not one journalist mentioned the love story, which would have been front-page news.

In 1991, the program *Bleu poudre* was all the rage on Quebec television. This comedy program made young people in Quebec laugh at its absurd characters, and its irreverent comments often ridiculed the most prominent personalities of the day. Céline Dion wasn't spared. The Raymond Beaudoin character, played by Pierre Brassard, took advantage of a press conference to ask Céline, "You English with America, you English with Johnny Carson ... Do you French with René Angélil?" The imperturbable René went calmly over to the camera and said, eyes blazing, "Guys, you're not going to show that!"

Actually, the scene never was shown on TV! A short while later the program made fun of Pierre Elliott Trudeau, who physically assaulted the Raymond Beaudoin character — but in that case not even a former prime minister of Canada was able to prevent the brawl from being shown on air!

In 1992, René Angélil's control of the press failed him when Céline stated, on Canada Day, July 1, that the separation of Quebec from the rest of the country would be "dreadful." He repaired this monumental gaffe by having the singer explain herself in an exclusive interview granted not to the journalist who had set the trap for Céline but to Suzanne Gauthier, a journalist closer to the singer, and more "human," as we say in the trade.

In 1993, René rejected every request from the TV network TVA, which was trying to obtain the rights to cover the launch of the album *The Colour of My Love* in the Metropolis Disco. For two years he had been boycotting this Quebec TV station for insisting on an exclusive interview with Céline — something that didn't fit in with René's plans.

In 1994, René Angélil sued the paper *Photo-Police* for the sum of $20 million — a Canadian record. It had insinuated in an article that he had had sexual relations with Céline when she was only fifteen. The suit was justified, but why was this the only paper he went after when the article had taken its inspiration from revelations in the *Globe,* an American publication?

In 1995, René continued in a fairy-tale vein when he helped a lady of seventy-six who had lost her way in La Guardia airport in New York. All flights were grounded by a snowstorm. Céline and René became the old lady's guardian angels, offering her their limousine, a hotel suite, and meals at their table. The next day, Mme Jeanette Caron was featured on the front pages of every newspaper in Montreal. The press had been summoned to Dorval airport. "It was a fairy tale both for us and for her," Céline declared. "We've become friends. I hope we'll see one another again." Guess who had called from New York to alert the journalists!

René outdid himself a few days before his wedding to Céline in Montreal, by selling the media rights to the event to the highest bidder. For the sum of $200,000 Trustar obtained exclusive rights to the photos taken in the church and at the reception, and certainly a percentage of the sales that has never been divulged on top of that. Some newspaper owners, particularly the large Montreal company Quebecor, reacted by asking for an injunction. In the end this request was turned down, and Trustar brought out a number of publications on the ceremony in different formats and at different prices, bringing it huge profits.

Very often Céline Dion's manager communicated personally with the management of specialist journals or even daily newspapers to ensure the best possible image of his protégée was presented. He could even question the heading given an article and obtain information about the placement of a photograph in the text. He didn't hesitate to complain about the photo that appeared on the front page of a Montreal daily, *La Presse*, showing a completely natural Céline leaping with joy after making a good stroke in a golf game.

In 1996 he went even further, exerting strong pressure on Nathalie Jean, a young writer in her mid-twenties, to prevent her from publishing a biography of Céline Dion. He gave her a cheque for ten thousand dollars, to which the publishing house Libre Expression added the sum of seven thousand dollars. In return, the intimidated young woman had to undertake not to write, translate, or publish anything about Céline Dion's life or career until July 31, 2000. Bruised by this affair, she abandoned the world of publishing.

Following his lengthy boycott of the TVA network, René went beyond a mere reconciliation, becoming involved in production and a partner of Julie Snyder, who produced her own talk show for TVA. This explains how Julie was able to obtain exclusive reports on the progress of Céline's career, in addition to presenting specials featuring the singer. As a co-producer of Point J Inc. René could legitimately act as an adviser for Julie's programs, and we can assume he had a say in the choice of guests. It was total, subtle control over one member of the media. Could Michael Jackson or his manager have co-produced the *Tonight Show* on NBC?

In November 1998, the French weekly *Voici* was on the receiving end of René's wrath for publishing an article speaking of Céline Dion's "unfulfilled desire for a child." The claim was for twenty-seven thousand dollars. In February 2000 the *National Inquirer* printed a headline saying that Céline Dion was pregnant with twins. The suit was for $20 million U.S. The couple's lawyer in the case was Marty Singer, whom we met before in the sexual abuse case brought against René Angélil. In the end, he obtained a formal apology from the tabloid.

The announcement of the birth of René-Charles, Céline's and René's son, travelled around the world. The media had long been awaiting the baby's arrival, and had been preparing a front page to do justice to the event. In Canada the birth appeared on the front page of all the newspapers and magazines and was also a news item in the U.S., France, and numerous European countries. In Quebec the front page of the magazine *7 Jours* would feature the headline "My son already has a twin," referring to the fact that the baby had been conceived *in vitro:* René became aware of the headline and called the publisher, demanding the headline be changed. The paper complied by withdrawing the two hundred thousand copies already printed and making up a new front with the headline *"Céline a cœur ouvert"* ("Céline unburdens herself") — a change that cost it one hundred thousand dollars. Over the next few days there was a lively discussion about the control exerted by René Angélil over the media. Magazine publishers met and argued, *7 Jours* defended itself, and the freedom of the specialized press was seriously harmed. No matter, René still had the last word.

In 2000, René sued the paper *Allô Vedettes* and the journalist Michel Girouard for $50 million. The reason given was that it harmed his reputation. The columnist had picked up a piece of gossip published in the American paper *Star,* which claimed that the couple had spent five thousand dollars a day to have exclusive use of a hotel swimming pool so that they could swim in the nude. Angélil withdrew the case after the events of September 11, 2001, in New York. Shaken by this terrorist act that took the lives of thousands of people, he wanted to make peace. We shouldn't forget that all the peoples from the Middle East suffered from the fallout from September 11, and that a lot of Americans were calling for revenge. Fortunately, Céline would sing in New York at the site of the attack, standing next to the American flag.

In 2002, not in the least impressed by the discussions about freedom of information and the reactions provoked by his suit against the magazine *7 Jours,* Angélil went after CKMF, a Montreal radio station that had parodied one of Céline's hits, "I'm Alive." He had a formal demand sent to the news manager Luc Tremblay, requiring him to immediately remove the parody from the airwaves and no longer allow one of the station's hosts to imitate him.

On the grounds that the copyright laws were not clear, the station manager withdrew the parody. Furthermore, he was reluctant to incur considerable legal fees by standing up to Angélil. However, imitations of Angélil would continue, for there is no law to prevent it. Angélil took advantage of this opportunity to demand that the station no longer play any of Céline's songs, using the pretext that he didn't want to be associated with what he considered programming in poor taste.

JEAN BEAUNOYER

83

LAS VEGAS

I T IS HARDLY SURPRISING THAT from his early days René Angélil was attracted to Las Vegas. This Nevada city resembled him in its excesses, its ambitions, its nightlife, and its uninterrupted activity. Like Las Vegas itself, René wanted never to stop, to defy time and transcend human limitations. Las Vegas reinvented the world in its own way, and so did René. The city sprang up out of an arid soil, on which it erected castles, just as René sprang up out of the Quebec winter to install his princess Céline and his lavish houses. Las Vegas is big: it thinks big and lives big, exactly like René.

With its 33 million visitors annually, the entertainment capital of the world has grown spectacularly. Its population has doubled during the past ten years, now totalling more than a million inhabitants. But it is the visitors who really matter: in 1988 they earned $8 billion dollars for the State of Nevada. That was the year when a sixty-six-year-old gambler took the progressive Megabuck Jackpot of $27 million at the Palace Station Hotel Casino. Nothing is impossible in Las Vegas: making a fortune, getting married in a drive-through without getting out of your car, or a forty-five minute divorce, and the stars of show business are seen everywhere.

Las Vegas has changed a lot over the years. It was in 1931 that the State of Nevada legalized gambling, at a time when puritan America was still undergoing prohibition. The law was already flexible where gaming, prostitution, and divorce were concerned, hence its nickname of "Sin City." In 1946 the modern Las Vegas came into being when the American gangster Benjamin "Bugsy" Siegel built the Flamingo Hotel. Controlled by the underworld and immortalized by Hollywood, the city became the symbol of American glamour. Siegel, who had both class and ambition, ruined himself in this enterprise and was killed six months after the Flamingo opened. Warren Beatty would play the part of Siegel with considerable historical verisimilitude on film in a production that faithfully reproduced the extravagant, flamboyant atmosphere of Las Vegas of the 1940s and 1950s.

In the 1960s, eager to redeem its reputation, the city declared war on the mafia. In an incident that was reported in all the American newspapers, the Department of Gaming Control prevented Frank Sinatra, suspected of having ties to organized crime, from acquiring the ownership of a casino. The Hilton hotel chain and the eccentric millionaire Howard Hughes arrived in Nevada around the same time and imposed a new moral code. In 1970, the near-monopoly Las Vegas enjoyed in the realm of gambling was dealt a blow when gambling for money was authorized in Atlantic City, New Jersey. A few years later a federal law allowed Amerindian reservations to establish casinos.

Las Vegas decided to diversify its sources of income. In 1984 the city managed to convince Citibank, the leading financial establishment in the country, to establish one of its first data-processing centres in the city. The legislation was changed to allow banks headquartered in other American states to establish branches there. Las Vegas turned to technology, and major firms set up house in this very lucrative town. Labour was plentiful, and employees worked on flexible schedules, since the city never sleeps, and there are no taxes. Then, in the 1980s, the entire philosophy of gambling changed. Gambling became "gaming." In 1989, at the opening of the three-thousand-room Mirage Hotel, Steve Wynn, the developer behind this gigantic establishment, expressed this new philosophy of gambling: Las Vegas had to offer a full range of entertainment, not just for adults but for children, too. Hotels should provide amusements and services, including wedding chapels, to encourage visitors to stay as long as possible.

During the following decade, hotels with as many as four thousand rooms would be built. The major tourist sites in the world are reproduced in the major centres of Las Vegas — the 174-metre-high Eiffel Tower at the Paris-Las Vegas, a two-thirds-size Arc de Triomphe, and the Paris City Hall — everything is there. You have the impression you are travelling while standing still, with sights from Rome, New York, and other capital cities all around you. In less than ten years, fifty thousand hotel rooms were constructed in Las Vegas, and a whole world was refashioned.

Caesar's Palace, René Angélil's second home, opened in August 1966 under the ownership of Jay Sarno. It was a luxurious replica of ancient Rome, with as many as 1,508 rooms and, it is said, the best casino. Sarno liked to say he had built the hotel with the objective of treating every guest like a Caesar, a policy René has never contradicted.

Las Vegas has been cleaned up and given a reassuring facade. Prostitution is carried on discreetly in basements and out of the sight of children, or else in sumptuous hotels on the outskirts of town. The poverty of its less-favoured citizens has been concealed from visitors' view. An illusion of wealth, present or future, is everywhere. Prices are often moderate, with the hotels offering many attractive packages, but the objective is still the same: to encourage the visitor to spend money. If accommodation, food, and drink are offered free, there's a good reason for it. The gambler settles in, eating and drinking what the hotel provides, and stays on, with his judgement impaired.

"High rollers," or big spenders, get special attention. They are given free gifts proportionate to the sums of money they are liable to lose. Alcohol (naturally), royal suites, and limousines are put at their disposal. The sky is the limit for the VIP treatment reserved for the gambling elite.

René Angélil has been a major beneficiary of this treatment. He has been offered his own permanent suite in Caesar's Palace, in addition to many other benefits — indeed all the benefits imaginable, including a helicopter. The large casinos employ "junket reps," high-class touts that are an essential aspect of a big gamblers' stay. Their job is to spot such people and secure their patronage. They are paid a commission, receiving a percentage of the sums gambled. In short, their role is to court and spoil the high rollers.

Knowing René's passion for gambling, the Montreal Casino made an agreement with the Mirage, a golf club he owns. The big gamblers invited to the Montreal Casino can be allowed later checkout times at the Mirage — courtesy of the casino, of course.

"Angélil is considered a high roller," says Deke Castleman, an expert on the gambling industry, who is bringing out a book in the United States dealing with the phenomenon of high-stakes gamblers and the "hosts" who look after them.

Castleman also edits the magazine *Las Vegas Advisor*. "According to my informants," he says, "René Angélil usually stakes between fifty and one hundred thousand dollars. So he's a big-time gambler, and his favourite casino, Caesar's Palace, does well out of him. Céline, like all the artists who appear at Caesar's Palace, is allowed tens of thousands of dollars in free chips. The fact that her husband risks them at the gaming table instead of cashing them in is a rare bonus for the casino."

It's only a short step from "taking good care of" to psychological manipulation, and the casinos, which have enormous financial resources, don't hesitate to hire graduates of Harvard or other top universities to influence their elite clientele. Psychologists, psychiatrists, and other experts on human behaviour are specially employed to develop psychological offensives aimed at encouraging the wealthy to gamble, and, above all, at retaining their patronage. Fortunes have been lost in this way. No matter: Viva Las Vegas!

84

RENÉ'S IDOLS

DURING HIS YOUTH, RENÉ IDENTIFIED with the popular singers of
the time, first Frank Sinatra, and then, with the birth of rock and
roll, Elvis Presley, Buddy Holly, and Little Richard. Later, in his Baronets
days, he became more interested in the people directing the careers of
pop music stars. When the Baronets met the Beatles at the time they
came to perform in Montreal in 1963, René displayed the most interest
in Brian Epstein. After shaking hands with the four Beatles he wanted to
meet their manager, the person responsible for their success. I don't
think that in the confusion of the event René was able to meet Epstein
and talk to him, but his fascination with him endured.

He was also interested in the activities of the famous Colonel Tom
Parker, who directed Elvis Presley's career. Always aiming for the top in
everything he did, Angélil took his inspiration from Parker and Epstein,
the two most famous managers in the history of popular music, who
had shaped the two greatest musical phenomena of our time, Elvis
Presley and the Beatles.

René once mentioned during a press conference that Colonel Parker
wasn't precisely his idol as a human being, but that he liked his marketing strategies. Still, he preferred Brian Epstein's, and this is understandable. He met Parker on two occasions, and I think he was disappointed

with the behaviour of the aging man. During their first meeting, Parker had told him he should never compare Céline Dion to Barbra Streisand, that she should remain herself and make her name as herself. On their second meeting, in the Colonel's home, Parker confided in him that he thought Céline was as talented as Barbra Streisand. Then aged over eighty, he must have forgotten.

If René doesn't claim to belong to the Parker school, once we have obtained some unedifying information about the kind of person Parker really was it has to be admitted that he resembles him in several ways. First of all, the Colonel was an inveterate gambler, like René. As a manager he devoted himself to a single artist, like him. He also had a strong constitution, dominated his entourage, and was a past master in the art of marketing. He was particularly greedy in negotiating his slice of the pie with producers. But the comparisons don't stand up for very long when we look at Colonel Parker's somewhat controversial career.

Born Andreas Cornelis Van Kuijk in June 1909 in Holland, he left the country in mysterious circumstances as a young man and immigrated to the U.S. Some claim he arrived in the United States illegally, without a passport. He initially took an interest in the circus world, which he adored, and then in country music, where he became the manager for Eddy Arnold, a very popular country singer in the 1950s. Arnold fired him, for reasons still unknown. But then Parker hit the jackpot when he met Elvis during one of his early shows, in the Memphis area.

Under the contract he convinced the young star to sign he was entitled 25 percent of the fees, but later, in 1967, he would demand 50 percent. Afraid to leave the country while the great cities of the world were crying out for Elvis, Parker isolated him in his famous Graceland estate during the best years of his life. Parker would never admit that he was the one who couldn't travel abroad because of the celebrated matter of his passport and of his rather nebulous past. Some claim he was able to prolong Elvis's career and string it out for twenty years — but at what cost! He ruined his acting career by having him film thirty or so dud movies, when at the same time he was being offered interesting parts. He was never able to find original songs for him after the early hits. Why was this? Simply because he demanded a share of the rights of the writers who wrote for Elvis. Little by little the songwriters and composers looked for greener pastures. Of course the Colonel was able to organize a real carnival around the King's shows in Las Vegas, but even there he often failed to obtain for Elvis the kind of fees he deserved. Gambler that he was, Parker had special arrangements with certain gaming houses and benefited from personal advantages.

But the worst gaffe Parker made in his career was to sell Elvis's complete catalogue for $5 million, at the end of his career. The Colonel died in 1997, without much attention being paid.

So it's understandable that René didn't claim in any way to be Tom Parker's cultural heir.

On the other hand, the evolution of Brian Epstein's career is more interesting.

Born in Liverpool on September 19, 1934, the young Brian was a poor student who was expelled from Liverpool College at the age of sixteen and decided to work in his father's business. His parents were relieved, for the lad had good business sense. He was interested in furniture, in the theatre, and, finally, in music. The family business sold records, and among the records played most frequently Brian took particular notice of "My Bonnie," by a certain group called Beatles — complete unknowns! So he went to the Cavern Club to meet the four young members of the group, and offered to take charge of their career.

He asked for 25 percent of what they earned. It was a bigger percentage than was customary, but in exchange he promised to spare no effort on their behalf. To begin with, he knocked on the door of many record companies, who all refused to record the Beatles' music. He persevered, however, until finally EMI, whose artistic director was George Martin, accepted Epstein's proposal.

Subsequently, Epstein had the good instinct to get rid of Pete Best, the group's drummer, and replace him with Ringo Starr. With his James Dean looks and flamboyant style, Best was too prominent and wasn't liked by John, Paul, and George. Brian thought the chemistry would be better with Ringo.

Before going any further with the new Beatles, Epstein laid down his conditions, obliging his protégés to submit to certain rules: no more sandwiches and beer; the leather jackets would be replaced by neat, attractive suits; they were to avoid cursing and foul language; they were no longer to sing pub songs like "She'll Be Coming Round the Mountain."

From the outset Epstein was careful about the Beatles' image, and succeeded in transforming four working-class lads into well-dressed gentlemen. Liverpool was chock full of groups at the time, but none had the Beatles' class, and that is what made the difference from early on. Epstein knew that a bunch of louts singing in leather jackets would never go over on TV. He was able to impose changes on the Beatles that were considerable for the time.

Epstein did even more. He was the emotional safety net for a group of intense personalities. He worked ceaselessly to maintain the bond between the four musicians. Through his company NEMS he not only steered the Beatles' professional careers, but also their personal lives. This company looked after all the famous four's domestic and material concerns. Epstein left nothing to chance, keeping the group united and relatively content. He even personally bought ten thousand copies of "Love Me Do" to ensure the Beatles reached the hit parade.

When Epstein died of an overdose in August 1967, John Lennon couldn't help saying he thought it spelt the end of the Beatles.

85

A NEW DAY BEGINS

RENÉ ANGÉLIL HAD CLOSED THE books on the eve of 2000. He had no plans after that date, as if he wanted to stop the world — or, rather, his world — from turning. Céline Dion had had a dizzying rise during the past ten years, and now the husband and manager of the most popular singer in the world suddenly seemed to be stunned by the whole thing. Highly subject to impulses, particularly on the level of his personal life, and impatient like most people born under Capricorn, René Angélil wanted as badly as Céline to start a family, to enjoy their luxurious residence in Jupiter, Florida, and to get back to a more normal existence, if such a thing was still possible. He knew that Céline wanted a child more than anything in the world, more than the fame and fortune she had already won. The couple had not set any deadline for this disengagement from the world of show business. There had been talk in the Dion-Angélil couple's entourage for a couple of years, but the pair themselves became evasive about it, as if this increased their pleasure.

Céline gave birth to a son, René-Charles, on January 25, 2001, in circumstances that are well known, and the couple was finally able to experience the family life they dreamed of. But you cannot keep too far away from the world of show business when it has brought you the some of the most powerful emotions life has to offer. And, God knows,

Céline Dion and René Angélil have lived through the most intense experiences of show business, bringing both laughter and tears.

It was in the theatre in the Hotel Bellagio in Las Vegas that Céline Dion's two sabbatical years came to an end. One evening Céline and René were attending a performance of the show *O*, produced by the Cirque du Soleil and directed by Franco Dragone. It was then that the artist, who for some time had been living cosily in the Jupiter residence, came alive. She was equally captivated by the acrobats, the décor, the music, and the poetic atmosphere of the show. When it ended she turned to René and said, "That's what I want to do!"

René understood immediately, and lost no time in taking Céline into the wings to meet the artisans of this fabulous show. The Dion-Angélil couple had discovered a challenge they wanted to meet, an artistic peak that the manager and his artist still had not scaled. They wanted to experience the magic of the Cirque du Soleil — a circus run by Quebecois who, like them, had lived the impossible dream. They too had reached the top. They too had crossed borders and weren't at all intimidated by the American giant. It was a meeting of two icons of Quebec culture who were attracted to one another.

Céline was experiencing an enchantment that reminded her of her childhood. In those days she was a solitary dreamer, but now she had another dreamer to share her dreams with. René is one of the few managers gifted with an artist's sensitivity. He is able to appreciate the genius that becomes apparent on stage, and he knows how to spot authentic creativity. In Canada, France, and the United States he has always been associated with the best composers, songwriters, producers, and directors. It is not just out of friendship he has worked with David Foster, Phil Spector, Jean-Jacques Goldman, Luc Plamondon, Eddy Marnay, James Horner, Barbra Streisand, and so many other remarkable creators. On this occasion, he recognized who was the soul of the show *O*, the person who had given it its inspiration, its colour, and its poetry. René singled out Franco Dragone and worked to create connections between the Belgian director and Céline's team.

Dragone was going through an extremely important stage in his life at that time. He had broken off his relationship with the Cirque du Soleil and wanted henceforth to control his own life and work. To do so, he had created his own production company in La Louvière, the town where he had grown up in Belgium. Even though he was born in Italy, Dragone had spent most of his life in Belgium. It had become his country, one he adored, and he invited Céline and René to come there to continue their discussions about the possibility of doing a show with him as director. As was usual for him, René was able to win over Dragone, just as he had been able to convince the people from Sony Music, David Foster, Luc Plamondon, and so many others to work with him. He came along at the right moment, for Dragone was looking for a new challenge. Judging by what Dragone confided to the press, it seems René's charm offensive succeeded:

> From our first meetings I felt as if I'd known Céline and René for ever. It's the first time I've worked with songs as my raw material, and I struck it lucky, first of all because Céline is the greatest singing star of them all, an extraordinary talent, but also because she is extraordinarily receptive and remarkably adaptable. I understand why Jean-Jacques Goldman wonders how he can ever work with anyone else. I love this completely new challenge for me, because you must always be adaptable in dealing with your raw material, which is the song, and care not to rush anything in order to discover what each of the songs is able to evoke and create images that make people feel.

Céline and René respected Dragone's need to work at home in the charming but modest little town of La Louvière, and agreed to live there in 2002 while the show (which did not yet have a title) was being developed and rehearsed. No fewer than two thousand people from several countries would come to audition for a part in this spectacular adventure. About seventy were hired for the show, which was to combine music, dance, and acrobatics.

While this was happening, René Angélil, who never leaves anything to chance, was preparing Céline Dion's comeback, and, ever faithful to his old habits, was taking care of her image. After the terrorist attacks on the World Trade Center on September 11, he associated Céline Dion, a Canadian artist, with America's enormous grief. The singer took part in a special telethon in New York on September 21, 2001, singing "God bless America." Seven days later she took part in "Quebec-New-York," a special show intended to help the families of the victims of the attack, and sang a song suitable for the occasion, "L'amour existe encore" ("Love still exists").

And in the same vein, Céline launched an album called *A New Day Has Come* on March 25, 2002. This recording was obviously inspired by the events of September 11, and was a reminder that a new day would dawn and that there was still love in the world.

86

RENÉ'S NIGHTMARE

L IFE WAS SWEET FOR RENÉ Angélil in early March of 2002, as he
paved the way for Céline's return to the stage after an absence of
two years. On a personal level he had everything he could wish for. He
had beaten his cancer and was surrounded by the love of a rested, fulfilled Céline, who was living entirely for her son, René-Charles. His little family was a comfort to him and helped him forget he had celebrated his sixtieth birthday in January.

During Céline's two sabbatical years René had slowed down his
activity, though for the first time since his association with Céline Dion
began in 1982 he had broken his own rule by taking on an artist other
than his life's companion. This was the young singer Garou, whom René
had discovered during a performance of the musical *Notre-Dame de
Paris*. The celebrated manager had immediately seen all Garou's potential for performing on stage and for recording. Garou didn't hesitate for
a moment to entrust his career to one of the greatest managers in the
world. Very quickly he became a star in France and was getting ready to
develop a career in the United States. René would take care of that.

Everything was going well until the day he learned that Yun
Kyeong Sung Kwon, a Korean woman living in California, had laid a
charge of sexual assault against him. The event was supposed to have

taken place two years previously, according to Mrs. Kwon. The charge was laid — certainly not by chance — at the very moment when Céline was setting out on a promotional tour for the launch of her new album, *A New Day Has Come*.

It is easy to imagine the atmosphere in which the media tour took place, as the newspapers in North America — especially Canada — and Europe gave prominence to Mrs. Kwon's accusations against René. Céline had never seemed particularly disturbed by this matter, but inevitably the Korean woman's accusations came up during the interviews. Céline has always supported her husband, and she kept on reassuring the public, but in this sort of thing a lingering doubt always remains, and reputations suffer. I think most people understood and sympathized with René Angélil for the humiliation he was suffering. More and more, doubts were dispelled in people's minds as it came out that the accuser in question was a compulsive gambler who had written bad cheques to Las Vegas hotels that had loaned her, in total, the sum of $900,000. But this information was not provided by René or Céline, who had been ordered by the court to keep silent. For months the Dion-Angélil couple made no comment, preferring to talk about the new album and show. The Kwon-Angélil case remained nebulous.

It was only after a six-month investigation conducted by the Las Vegas police that the facts surrounding what turned out to be a real attempt at extortion became known. It was at the end of January 2003 that the Las Vegas police finally stated that the accusations of sexual assault made before the criminal court by Yun Kyeong Sung Kwon had been dropped and that the case was closed. So ended one of the worst nightmares ever experienced by René Angélil, who was superbly represented by his lawyer, David Chesnoff. Chesnoff declared: "Mr. Angélil never committed sexual assault. The police provided the proof. Mrs. Kwon was unable to produce any evidence, and no charge will be laid against our client. There is nothing worse than being falsely accused of something you didn't do. It's unjust."

It was learned at the same time that Mrs. Kwon had not only received $2 million from René under a confidential settlement, but that after she had lost the $2 million gambling she had made a second demand, this time for $13.5 million.

It was too much, and René had had no alternative but to resist the greed of the compulsive gambler, aided and abetted by her husband. After being obliged to remain silent while the judicial proceedings were in progress, in May 2003 René explained himself to a journalist from the *Las Vegas Sun* who asked him why he had agreed to pay the sum of $2 million to the woman:

> It was to avoid putting any pressure on my wife, who at the time was having fertilization treatments in order to have a child, and because personally I was quite weakened by my cancer treatment. I said to myself that we didn't need that. Let her have the money. She wants money? Well, then, let's give her some. But the fact that I paid $2 million to be done with the matter doesn't prove anything. Some people must even have believed that the allegations were true, since a payment was made. But if those people had been in my place and in the same circumstances, what would they have done? For my own part, I've no regrets about paying the $2 million.

A few months later it was Céline's turn to talk about what she had gone through personally during this trying time. In an interview with Quebec newscaster Julie Snyder she confided, "I've always supported René in this matter, and I was particularly worried about his health. He was so shaken by the affair that I thought he was going to have a heart attack. He was pale and edgy, and I've never seen him looking so frail."

It is worth noting that in the most trying moments of René Angélil's life we always find a stronger, calmer Céline Dion, always perfectly in control of the situation. Jean Beaulne, who knows Céline's passion for her husband very well, often tells me, "She's a one-man woman. She'll never abandon him, whatever happens."

Yun Kyeong Sung Kwon is at the moment behind bars in the Clark County Detention Center. Completely broke, Mrs. Kwon is accused of extortion, in addition to being sued by two Las Vegas casinos that still want to get back the $900,000 they loaned her. There has also been talk of deporting her to Korea.

Relieved, and cleared of all suspicion in this sorry affair, René set about preparing Céline Dion's great return to the stage. He had lost weight, and his behaviour had changed over the preceding months. Jean Beaulne, who had remained in contact with him, noticed an attitude bordering on paranoia. René is afraid of extortion, and understandably so. He fears dishonesty and any kind of violence to which he or Céline might fall victim. He prefers to stay home as much as possible, and is surrounded by increased security when he does go out. For despite everything, the gambler in him still hasn't given up. It is a passion of his that still has a hold over him, but he is obviously more cautious now. Céline Dion is not the only one who needs protection in Las Vegas, for René Angélil is a target for swindlers as well.

87

LIFE IN LAS VEGAS

B UT WHY DID RENÉ CHOOSE Las Vegas, a city that is certainly not without dangers for himself and his family? Why Las Vegas, when he could have chosen any of the great stages in the world?

First of all, to avoid imposing too many boring trips on the couple's child, René-Charles, whom Céline treasures more than anything in the world. It was out of the question for her to be separated from René-Charles too often, for it would have put the quality of his family life at risk.

Besides, René had always felt at home in Las Vegas, in the world of casinos and shows. And then, at the age of sixty-one, after using up all his strength fighting a malignant cancer, René no longer had the energy to go on living out of suitcases.

In the end he settled with his little family in a more modest house than their others, with just three bedrooms, on the same floor, in the smart suburb of Lake Las Vegas. This town, situated thirty kilometres from the strip, is surrounded by mountains, and Céline loves the views and the presence of the neighbourhood families, who remind her of her childhood. However, there is no guarantee that the Dion-Angélil family will live for long in this suburb of Las Vegas, since Céline announced on February 20 that the couple had purchased a twelve-thousand-square-metre lot for $3 million in Jupiter, Florida.

"We want to build a house where our family can live when we return to Florida," Céline confirmed to the press, a few weeks before the opening night of her new show.

It was in the completely new Coliseum, built at a cost of almost $100 million, that Céline presented the world premiere of her brand new show, finally named *A New Day*, on March 25, 2003. People had been waiting for this occasion for months, and in the meantime René Angélil had organized an extremely efficient publicity campaign, inviting journalists from Belgium to attend rehearsals, launching a new album by Céline, *One Heart*, and arranging package tours in collaboration with agencies in Quebec, English Canada, and abroad.

René had negotiated an agreement with Park Place Entertainment, the owners of Caesar's Palace, which houses the Coliseum, giving Céline $100 million for presenting two hundred shows a year, five evenings a week for forty weeks, for three years. But these were her base earnings, for the singer was also to get a percentage, which has been estimated at 50 percent, of the profit on the sale of tickets for the performances. René also reached a marketing partnership agreement with Chrysler, reported to be for $14 million. Nor should we forget the profits produced by the sale of spin-off products. Articles signed by Céline Dion, including perfumes, toiletries, fine lingerie, and even baby's bibs, are sold in the Céline Dion boutique situated close to the Coliseum in Caesar's Palace.

The Coliseum, a magnificent theatre with forty-one hundred seats that Céline wanted to be as warm and intimate as possible, was designed and constructed by the Quebec firm, Sceno Plus. And the company's designers did the impossible by creating a hall with a half-moon shape, making this most attractive performing space a very intimate one.

Céline was scheduled to receive a star on the Hollywood Walk of Fame to coincide with the beginning *A New Day*, and René had imagined great celebrations around the show's first night: a jet-set party after the show's premiere performance, fireworks at Caesar's Palace, and a whole series of spectacular events to celebrate Céline's return.

But his plans didn't work out the way he hoped. The American giant, under the leadership of President Bush, suddenly decided to rid Iraq and the free world of Saddam Hussein, claiming that he was hiding weapons of mass destruction — weapons dangerous to all of mankind and in particular to the United States, the terrorists' favourite target.

President Bush, in his determination to combat the evil represented by Saddam Hussein, called on other nations to assist with his crusade by launching a merciless attack against the Iraqi dictator's army. England immediately joined in, followed by some other European countries, but France and Canada refused to be part of the coalition, considering it was up to the United Nations to decide whether an attack on Iraq was justified.

The U.S. government, and a good proportion of the American people, did not understand and could not accept the Canadian and French reactions when their president was asking them for support. Very soon French products were being boycotted in several American cities, including Las Vegas. It became impossible, for instance, to obtain Perrier bottled water in the hotels and restaurants on the strip. "French fries" were renamed "Freedom fries." Canada's popularity, and of course the popularity of Canadian artists, suffered a drop while the war was going on.

It could not have been a worse moment to launch Céline Dion's new show. This is how René Angélil recounts it:

> When we met, all the members of the show's team, a week before the opening performance, we told ourselves that "the show must go on" anyway. It has to be said that this time the marketing half worked. We already had special appearances on Oprah Winfrey's TV show, the *Tonight Show* on NBC, an interview with Larry King on CNN, and we'd started out with an extraordinary blitz and a spectacular plan, but ...

But Céline was Canadian, René was of Arab origin and culture, and a French song had been included in the show: "Je t'aime encore," by Jean-Jacques Goldman. This song was withdrawn from the show while the war in Iraq was going on, and Céline didn't even dare talk to her parents in French when they came to see their daughter's show. The presentation of Céline's star on the Walk of Fame was postponed.

When a journalist asked her if it was difficult for a Canadian to appear in the United States when Canadian Prime Minister Jean

Chrétien was not supporting American foreign policy, Céline gave a diplomatic reply in which her husband's hand can be seen: "I really don't want to get into politics here. But I can say it's been very difficult for us to say 'it's show time.' I support the troops. And as a mother, just to think that some kids have already lost their fathers, it breaks my heart."

It wasn't a good atmosphere in which to celebrate in the United States in March 2003. People watched the bombing of Iraqi cities on TV and wondered how this war would end, hoping that there would not be too many victims on either side.

Céline's show was dazzling, but it still hadn't struck the spark that had been expected. René counted on time, and sent out more and more invitations. He couldn't lose. Céline's show was a winner, and time would prove him right. Gradually, *A New Day* reached cruising speed. There was a full house every night, and now the general public was lining up at the box office. Céline sang, she danced, and she also … flew. Franco Dragone, the director, who had installed a fascinating stage environment and an innovative technology for the show, was defying the laws of gravity. The musicians, the dancers, and even the musical instruments rose from the ground, and Céline too explored this different space. The effect was spectacular.

A few months after the opening night, Céline could no longer fly. The harness she used to keep her suspended in the air was making her sick. The doctors she consulted were afraid it would get worse and advised her not to continue an activity that was too demanding for someone of her physical strength.

The critics in the American media, usually full of praise for Céline, or at least favourable to her, weren't unanimous this time. Among Céline's detractors the prominent American magazine *Vanity Fair* published a vicious article about her, about the show, and about the city of Las Vegas. Journalist A.A. Gill, the article's author, claimed that "for all her gym-tuned, dance-coached stagecraft" Céline Dion still managed to look like "the fat kid who won Weight-Watcher of the Year," and that her stage presence was a "weird hybrid of Pinocchio and Buffy the Vampire Slayer."

Céline would react to criticism of this kind by saying that "often they've sent people who like heavy rock to review my show, so naturally they're not going to like a romantic show in which ballads are sung."

I myself have seen this show as part of a series of articles on Las Vegas, and it was the best thing I've seen in this city (which can be difficult to take if you don't particularly like gambling). The co-author of this book, Jean Beaulne, was less bowled over by the show, pointing out that Dragone's direction didn't give Céline enough prominence, and that she was not visible enough on the giant screen. According to him, the people who came to see the singer found it difficult to pick her out among all the performers on stage.

The show was criticized, adored, and lambasted, but still it was daring and innovative, displayed impressive artistic craftsmanship, and was popular with the visitors, who filled every seat each evening. I myself had to wait for a week before I could get a ticket.

Other stars, and not insignificant ones, appear on the stage of the Coliseum when Céline takes a few days or weeks of rest as the contract allows. Mariah Carey, Gloria Estefan, Jerry Seinfeld, and Elton John have put shows on there, or are scheduled to do so. Elton John will get $50 million for seventy-five shows over a three-year period.

Céline, as indefatigable as ever, is never idle when she takes one of these breaks. During the spring and summer of 2003, together with Jean-Jacques Goldman and his musicians, she prepared to record an album aimed at the French market. In addition, she stopped all her activity in Las Vegas to take part in a show presented as a tribute to Eddy Marnay, who had passed away a short while previously. This show, put on at the Maison de la culture in Gatineau, near Ottawa, the Canadian capital, was called *Simplement Marnay*. The Odyssey theatre has just eight hundred seats and could not afford to invite Celine to perform. René Angélil reassured the show's producers: "When they approached me, the organizers said they couldn't afford to pay for an artist like Céline to appear. My reply was that it was really we who should pay to make sure everything was done well. We wanted to be sure Céline could sing the songs she'd selected in a way Eddy would have been proud of. We'd cover any costs incurred by the musicians, the back-up singers, in addition to their hotel bills."

It was Eddy Marnay who had composed Céline's early songs. In addition, he was probably René Angélil's best friend. René didn't forget this, nor did Céline.

The launch of the French album *Une fille et 4 types* took place on October 13 in Europe and on the next day in Quebec. "I think this recording is the best Céline has ever done: I compare it to *D'eux*," asserts René, as enthusiastic as ever — as if everything was starting over again, almost as if it was Céline Dion's very first record. It's the same enthusiasm: always the best recording made so far, always the same need to convince, to seduce, to sell, and to believe in the impossible star. He'll never stop. I know that now. Jean Beaulne has known it for a long time.

88

THE FUTURE

THE YEAR 2003 TURNED OUT to be a difficult one for René Angélil and Céline Dion. In addition to the Iraq war, which cast a shadow over the celebrations for the show *A New Day*, and the death of friend and songwriter Eddy Marnay, Chrysler ended its association with Céline Dion at the end of November. The $14-million, three-year contract had to be cancelled because sales of its Pacifica model were not living up to Chrysler's expectations. The public targeted by Chrysler was a relatively young one, while the statistics showed that the Quebec singer appealed to a public with an average age of over forty. Never mind the quality or the attractiveness of the product, Céline's reputation was damaged. Up to this point, all commercial or artistic associations with Céline had been profitable and crowned with success. This was the first failure for the Dion-Angélil couple on a strictly commercial level, and René was concerned about the bad publicity connected with the ending of a contract with one of the big three automakers. It was doubly sad for the couple, for Céline had been associated with Chrysler once before, at the beginning of her career, in the late eighties.

Then, on the last day of November, the month of the dead, the news came of the death of Céline's father, Adhémar. But "the show must go on," and after hearing the news, Céline, with a heavy heart, decided to go through with her show that evening. But, along with René, who had lost his mother in 1997, she attended the funeral, which took place in Charlemagne, Quebec, the town where she grew up.

On January 6, 2004, Céline finally received her star on the Walk of Fame. "My dad was my number one fan, and he still is," she announced to her fans at the ceremony, his death still very much on her mind.

So what does the future look like for Céline Dion and René Angélil?

It's not difficult to suppose that the producers of *A New Day* will try to renew her contract after the initial period of three years. People predict immense success for her, with performances of exceptional quality.

And then how could they forget the stage, the applause, the music, and the voice thrilling the entire audience on a magical evening? René has only ever lived for show business, all through his professional life. Who can claim to know what the future holds for him? No one can! But what we do know is that after overcoming ill health, defeating the designs of an extortionist, and bringing in full houses at the Coliseum in spite of the war and a few critics, the Dion-Angélil couple has proven that they can overcome the most serious obstacles, get back on their feet again, and keep on dreaming — and keep on helping others to dream, as well.